Releasing the Image

Releasing the Image

FROM LITERATURE TO NEW MEDIA

EDITED BY

Jacques Khalip and Robert Mitchell

STANFORD UNIVERSITY PRESS

STANFORD, CALIFORNIA

Stanford University Press
Stanford, California

This book has been published with the assistance of the Faculty Development Fund and the Office of the Vice President for Research at Brown University.

Printed in the United States of America on acid-free, archival-quality paper

Library of Congress Cataloging-in-Publication Data

Releasing the image : from literature to new media / edited by Jacques Khalip and Robert Mitchell.
    pages   cm
Includes bibliographical references and index.
ISBN 978-0-8047-6137-6 (cloth : alk. paper)
ISBN 978-0-8047-6138-3 (pbk : alk. paper)
    1. Image (Philosophy)   2. Phenomenology.   3. Philosophy, Modern.   I. Khalip, Jacques, 1975– editor of compilation.   II. Mitchell, Robert (Robert Edward), 1969– editor of compilation.
B105.I47R45   2011
121'.68—dc22

2010050536

Contents

Acknowledgments

The strength of an edited volume depends largely upon the sum of its parts, so we take pleasure in thanking our authors for their contributions, as well as for their patience and sustained interest in our project. In addition, warm thanks to our superb editor at Stanford, Emily-Jane Cohen, for welcoming the book and steering it along many critical straits, and to Sarah Crane Newman, Tim Roberts, and Cynthia Lindlof for handling our numerous editorial, production, and copyediting concerns. Several people provided great help and intervened at important times: David L. Clark, Kevin McLaughlin, Amanda Minervini, Suzanne Nacar, Inga Pollmann, Michael Powers, Thangam Ravindranathan, Deb Reisinger, Jenny Rhee, Jimmy Richardson, and Pierre Saint-Amand. Finally, we would like to recognize the Office of the Dean of the Faculty and the Office of the Vice-President for Research at Brown University for their generous material assistance.

Contributors

GIORGIO AGAMBEN, an Italian philosopher and radical political theorist, is Professor of Philosophy at the University of Venice. Stanford University Press has published eight of his previous books: *Homo Sacer* (1998), *Potentialities* (1999), *The Man Without Content* (1999), *The End of the Poem* (1999), *The Open* (2004), *The Time That Remains* (2005), *"What Is an Apparatus?" and Other Essays* (2009), and *Nudities* (2010).

CESARE CASARINO is Professor of Cultural Studies and Comparative Literature at the University of Minnesota. He is the author of *Modernity at Sea: Melville, Marx, Conrad in Crisis* (2002), co-author (with Antonio Negri) of *In Praise of the Common: A Conversation on Philosophy and Politics* (2008), and co-editor (with Saree Makdisi and Rebecca Karl) of *Marxism Beyond Marxism* (1996), as well as author of numerous essays on literature, cinema, and philosophy.

PETER GEIMER is Professor of Art History at the University of Bielefeld, Germany. His recent publications include *Theorien der Fotografie* (2009) and *Bilder aus Versehen. Eine Geschichte fotografischer Erscheinungen* (2010).

MARK B. N. HANSEN is Professor in the Literature Program at Duke University. He is author of *Embodying Technesis: Technology Beyond Writing* (2000), *New Philosophy for New Media* (2004), and *Bodies in Code* (2006), as well as numerous essays on cultural theory, contemporary literature, and media. He has co-edited three volumes: *The Cambridge Companion to Merleau-Ponty* (with Taylor Carman, 2004), *Emergence and Embodiment: New Essays on Second Order Systems Theory* (with Bruce Clarke, 2009), and *Critical Terms for Media Studies* (with W. J. T. Mitchell, 2010). He is currently writing a study of the technicity of time-consciousness that explores the transduction of time and media in relation to the computational and neuroscientific revolutions.

JACQUES KHALIP is Associate Professor of English and of Modern Culture and Media at Brown University. He is the author of *Anonymous Life: Romanticism and Dispossession* (2009).

JEAN-LUC MARION is Professor of Philosophy at the Sorbonne and Andrew Thomas Greeley and Grace McNichols Greeley Professor of Catholic Studies and Professor of the Philosophy of Religions and Theology in the Divinity School, the Committee on Social Thought, and the Department of Philosophy at the University of Chicago. In 1992, he was awarded the Grand Prix de Philosophie from the Académie Française. He is the author of many books, including *God Without Being* (1991), *Cartesian Questions* (1999), *Being Given* (2002), *The Crossing of the Visible* (2004), *In Excess: Studies in Saturated Phenomena* (2004), *The Erotic Phenomenon* (2006), *On the Ego and on God* (2008), *The Visible and the Revealed* (2008), and *Descartes's Grey Ontology* (2010).

KEVIN MCLAUGHLIN is Nicholas Brown Professor of Oratory and Belles Lettres and Professor of English, Comparative Literature, and German Studies at Brown University. He is the author of *Writing in Parts: Imitation and Exchange in Nineteenth-Century Literature* (1995) and *Paperwork: Fiction and Mass Mediacy in the Paper Age* (2005); he is co-translator of Walter Benjamin's *Arcades Project* (1999). His current project is entitled *Poetry After Kant: Poetic Force in Hölderlin, Baudelaire, and Arnold*.

ROBERT MITCHELL is Associate Professor of English at Duke University. He is author of *Sympathy and the State in the Romantic Era: Systems, State Finance, and the Shadows of Futurity* (2007) and *Bioart and the Vitality of Media* (2010); and co-author, with Catherine Waldby, of *Tissue Economies: Blood, Organs and Cell Lines in Late Capitalism* (2006). He is also co-author, with Helen Burgess and Phillip Thurtle, of the DVD-ROM *Biofutures: Owning Body Parts and Information* (2008); and co-editor, with Phillip Thurtle, of *Semiotic Flesh: Information and the Human Body* (2002) and *Data Made Flesh* (2003). With Phillip Thurtle, he co-edits the book series In Vivo: Cultural Mediations of Biomedical Science (University of Washington Press).

TIMOTHY MURRAY is Director of the Society for the Humanities, Professor of Comparative Literature and English, and Curator of the Rose Goldsen Archive of New Media Art at Cornell University. He is Founding Curator of the Rose Goldsen Archive of New Media Art in the Cornell Library and Co-Curator of CTHEORY Multimedia. He is currently working on a book, *Immaterial Archives: Curatorial Instabilities @ New Media Art*, which is a sequel to *Digital Baroque: New Media Art and Cinematic Folds* (2008). His previous books include *Like a Film: Ideological Fantasy on Screen, Camera, and Canvas* (1993); *Drama Trauma: Specters of Race and Sexuality in Performance, Video, and Art* (1997); *Zonas de Contacto* (1999); and the edited volume, *Mimesis, Masochism & Mime: The Politics of Theatricality in Contemporary French Thought* (1997).

FOREST PYLE is Associate Professor of English Literature at the University of Oregon. He is the author of *The Ideology of Imagination: Subject and Society in the Discourse of Romanticism* (1995) and a forthcoming book entitled *"From Which One Turns Away": A Radical Aestheticism in the Romantic Tradition*.

VIVIAN SOBCHACK is Professor Emerita in the Department of Film, Television, and Digital Media and former Associate Dean at the UCLA School of Theater, Film and Television. She was the first woman elected president of the Society for Cinema and Media Studies and served many years on the Board of Directors of the American Film Institute. Her essays have appeared in journals such as *Film Quarterly, Film Comment, Quarterly Review of Film and Video, camera obscura*, and the *Journal of Visual Culture*. Her books include *An Introduction to Film* (1980); *The Address of the Eye: A Phenomenology of Film Experience* (1992); *Screening Space: The American Science Fiction Film* (1997); and *Carnal Thoughts: Embodiment and Moving Image Culture* (2004). She has also edited two anthologies: *The Persistence of History: Cinema, Television and the Modern Event* (1996) and *Meta-Morphing: Visual Transformation and the Culture of Quick Change* (2000).

BERNARD STIEGLER heads the Department of Cultural Development at the Centre Pompidou in Paris and is co-founder of the political group Ars Industrialis. Stanford University Press has published his *Technics and Time, 1: The Fall of Epimetheus* (1998); *Acting Out* (2008); *Technics and Time, 2: Disorientation* (2009); and *Taking Care of Youth and the Generations* (2010).

KENNETH SURIN is Professor in the Literature Program at Duke University. He is the editor of *Christ, Ethics, and Tragedy* (1989) and author of *Theology and the Problem of Evil* (1986), *The Turnings of Darkness and Light: Essays in Philosophical and Systematic Theology* (1989), and *Freedom Not Yet: Liberation and the Next World Order* (2009).

Release—(Non-)Origination—Concepts

ROBERT MITCHELL AND JACQUES KHALIP

> Thou Shall Not Create Unto Thyself Any Graven Image, although you know the task is to fill the empty page. From the bottom of your heart, pray to be released from image.
>
> —Derek Jarman, *Blue*[1]

In Derek Jarman's *Blue* (1993), a seventy-six-minute 35-mm film devoid of any visual image beyond a deep blue color projected onto a screen, the release prayed for by Jarman accomplishes nothing less than an alteration of the senses: in the context of this film, "to see" does not mean yielding to an index of a thing or an event that is understood as located in a cinematic beyond; rather, it means reorganizing our assumptions about perception and images.[2] As a film, that is, *Blue* releases us from certain assumptions *about* images—for example, from a narrative theory of the cinematic visual image and a selectional process of cinematic spectatorship. As a consequence, though, and by that same token, *Blue* renders the image otherwise by linking the blue color on the screen with the film's sound track, which includes music, recordings (or simulations) of environmental city sounds, and Jarman's reflections on his films and his own mortality (Jarman was to die of AIDS-related complications just a few months after finishing *Blue* and was already partly blind when he began what was to be his last film). By linking the indexicality of its aural register—the sense, that is, that we are listening to traces and recordings of voices and events that existed before and outside the film—to its refusal of representation in its visual register, *Blue* engenders a new sense of the image, one that is not intended to represent something else, but instead binds seeing and hearing together in a different way, and as such requires the development of new forms of listening and seeing. In a film that gives nothing to see but blueness, the image materializes as a temporally complex entity that nears the blindness intrinsic to perception itself, and "seeing" becomes an encounter with an opacity that is specific to sight. The apparent visual poverty of Jarman's film—a poverty that we might take as emblematic of a more widespread strategy in twentieth-century avant-garde film and visual works of art—is thus an attempt to pose two related questions: what *is* an image? And—perhaps more important—what *can* an image be?

These two questions have increasingly emerged as quite central in the last several decades, as it has become a commonplace to insist that "images" played a central role in twentieth-century culture and promise to play an even more powerful role in twenty-first century life and thought. And if one also believes, as Kaja Silverman has insisted, that visuality is our most significant and primary form of ethical engagement with the world, then the continued refinement of image-producing technologies such as photography and cinema, and their dissemination through multiple arenas of life, ranging from leisure activities to war and surveillance technologies, seems to justify claims that modern society is obsessed with and inscribed by spectacles and images.[3]

Yet Jarman's film reminds us that our current obsession with images is often implicitly understood in terms of an ocularcentrism that is purported to define selves, networks of forces, ethical relationships, and their media within visual economies that conceptually indenture "life" to the image.[4] Whether such arguments perform critical analyses of the hegemonic coercion of the society of the spectacle or aim to generate a redemptive "ethics of appearance," their undercurrent regards the image as the visual key to an understanding of all forms of relationality with the world and with others. The recent rise to prominence of technologies of digitalization has offered possibilities of understanding the image beyond this premise of ocularcentrism, for digital images emphasize the extent to which the indexicality of photographic or cinematic images—the sense of an ontological link between a representation and the "real" objects or actions that it represents—can be produced through manipulation of algorithms. Yet insofar as analyses of the specificity of the digital image are often parsed through a forensic lens that stresses the deception and trompe l'oeil that digitalization makes possible, these attempts to complicate indexicality and representation often end up reaffirming the premise of ocularcentrism rather than expanding the concept of the image.

As a consequence, and despite its apparent ubiquity, "the image" as a category of analysis remains remarkably resistant to theoretical understanding. While cultural critics, new media scholars, and sociologists have cataloged different kinds of images, described the various roles they play in culture, and noted the technological specificity of the media to which images appear to be linked, it is nevertheless often far from clear *what* precisely counts as an image in these studies, and how, or whether, one ought to distinguish images from related terms such as pictures and icons. And even with the multitude of recent attempts to grasp the specificity of the "digital image," it generally remains unclear how this new world of digital high-tech virtual images relates to earlier modes of non-visual imagery (e.g., the images of poetry and literature).[5] In order to stake out the specificity of the digital image, in other words, non-digital images are positioned as "simply" representations to which foundation the digital image then adds a supplement or excess.[6] In this sense, the apparent fate of the image through various contemporary technologies seems to reflect a level of undecidability regarding its dissemination and structure.

Yet as Jacques Rancière has noted in *The Future of the Image*, to speak of a culture of images is to say nothing about what the image, as the center of such a culture, might be. In his own analysis, the very futurity of the concept does not depend upon making any essentializing claims; rather, his point is to foreground an understanding of the various representational regimes that have evoked the "image" as an epistemological, aesthetic, and ethical node of elaboration:

> "Image" therefore refers to two different things. There is the simple relationship that produces the likeness of an original: not necessarily its faithful copy, but simply what suffices to stand for it. And there is the interplay of operations that produces what we call art: or precisely an alteration of resemblance.[7]

For Rancière, "image" stands for ever-shifting processes of inscription and articulation: the "sayable and the visible" refer to connections between sight and writing that mutually inform one another. The production of the image implies not that all images are artificially made, but rather that our capacities for image-making and image-receiving are underwritten by a technicity that relationally unbinds the phenomenological and cognitive subject (13).

By drawing together contributions from the most important contemporary critical theorists, *Releasing the Image: From Literature to New Media* addresses this need to rethink the unbound potentiality of the image. The collective effort of this volume is not oriented toward the illumination of a singular "essence" of all images, but rather toward an examination of the ways in which our epistemological, aesthetic, ethical, and disciplinary concerns might be refocused by considering the image as released from the logic of representationalism, and, in turn, how this release allows us to engage the topics of embodiment, agency, history, and technology differently. The essays included here take up this task by engaging a diversity of objects that range from Cézanne's painting to new media technologies; historical periods that extend from the Romantic era to the present; and theoretical reference points that run from the work of Walter Benjamin and Maurice Merleau-Ponty to Gilles Deleuze and Henry Darger and Bill Viola. Despite this thematic, historical, and theoretical diversity, the authors included in this volume are guided by a common approach: they understand images as something other than simply representations, simulations, or copies of other things, and interpret them as aesthetic modes of manifestation that can be understood only with reference to both that which becomes visible in the image and that which is simultaneously rendered invisible.

For reasons that we discuss at greater length later, this approach to images owes much to phenomenology, which—through the work of Edmund Husserl, Martin Heidegger, Maurice Merleau-Ponty, and others—has developed tools for the investigation of both the representational and non-representational dimensions of the image. What results is a common conceptualizing of the image as that which contains the unseen in what is visible, the historical in what appears transitory, and the ethical in what seems neutral. This economy between appearance and disappearance, moreover, inscribes the image with a power that in some way resembles Marie-José Mondzain's theorization of the relationship between the invisible (image) and the visible (icon) that structures the ways in which our lives are defined within a certain culture of the image.[8] Yet while Mondzain's argument remains to some extent dependent on a premise of visuality, we concentrate on the phenomenological feature of this economy, which specifically rethinks ocular appeals to the image by taking the *imperceptible* within all forms of sensory perception to be fundamental to the image's materialization as something that is separable from indexicality.

Thus what is central to this approach is the notion that the image has indeed been released from representational and visual purposes. Relinquished or freed from a dependency on subjectivity, the image's aesthetic existence is produced in the absence of any consequential relationship to the spectator and generates a referentiality that is not so much enclosed or autonomous as it is internally complex, immaterial, and profoundly self-generative. It enacts a virtualization of experience that is not collapsed into the facticity of events themselves. Giorgio Agamben has noted that photography often records an excess beyond what it depicts, a gesture that releases the substance of the photograph from its everydayness, and imbues it with a revelatory potential. In this way, the image is eschatologically released in the sense that every moment (rather than the end of *all* moments) is now invested with a singularity to be grasped as readily as it disappears: "The photograph is always more than an image: it is the site of a gap, a sublime breach between the sensible and the intelligible, between copy and reality, between a memory and a hope."[9]

While intense contemporary interest in "new media" images serves, in a sense, as the point of departure for *Releasing the Image*, this volume also cultivates the belief that the question of the image must be approached through a more extended historical narrative. The question of where to begin such a historical narrative is of course vexed, for as Gottfried Boehm notes, "the image-question is almost as old as European-Mediterranean culture itself."[10] Our volume, however, is guided by the proposition that a recognizably modern approach to the image begins in the late eighteenth and early nineteenth centuries. This is perhaps not an entirely surprising proposition, and it certainly echoes those critical narratives that locate in this same period the emergence of various projects and practices of coercion that seek to control the subject through an economy of visualization (and indeed, the apparent ocularcentrism of the Enlightenment is often taken as a sign of what Theodor Adorno and Max Horkheimer famously diagnosed as the period's totalitarian desire for mastery).[11] However, we suggest that the emergence in the eighteenth century of aesthetics as a discrete subject of philosophical reflection provoked a more complicated lineage of thought about images, one that emphasized both the sheer *avisuality* of the image and the extent to which images contribute to the subject's dispersal. As we will note in the following discussion, later phenomenological and post-phenomenological approaches to the image have their roots in this alternative archive, one that produces "the image" as an interactive and sensual concept at the limits of sight and thought.

I. Aesthetics and the Romantic Image

The mid-eighteenth-century emergence of the term "aesthetics"—understood, in Alexander Gottlieb Baumgarten's inaugural definition, as a "science of perception"—signaled an important shift in the way in which philosophers understood the role of images in both perception and the production of knowledge. Within classical, medieval, and Renaissance theories of knowledge, images were described as playing a mediating function within the mind: produced by the faculty of imagination, images linked sense perception with the faculty of reason.[12] The basic elements of this account were retained by many eighteenth-century philosophers: in Britain, for example, David Hume famously argued that ideas were simply "the faint images" of sensory impressions that were then employed "in thinking and reasoning," while in Germany, Christian Wolff contended that both "sensations and imaginings are like images [Bildern], such as paintings and statues, in that each is a representation [Vorstellung] of composite entities: and for this reason representations of corporeal things are called images [Bilder]."[13] From this perspective, mental images were understood as simply representations of the external world, and though they served the useful function of distancing the subject from the chaotic flux of pure sensation, they nevertheless also limited thought; as David Wellbery notes, for many Enlightenment thinkers, a "pure intellect" would "achiev[e] its representations entirely without sense images," but because the "intellect of man is mixed," humans had always to make do with "some degree of sense imagery."[14]

While Baumgarten's "science of perception" was developed upon the basis of this same set of Enlightenment assumptions about the relationship between images, representation, and thought, it nevertheless also pointed toward another way of approaching the link between images and thought.[15] Rather than simply positing "mental images" in order to explain the operations of the mind, Baumgarten's philosophical aesthetics highlighted the need for more nuanced accounts of the differences in the way in which different kinds of external images—for example, painted images as distinct from the "images" of poetry—presented themselves to sensation, perception, and consciousness. Gotthold Ephraim Lessing's discussion of the differences between forms of art was exemplary of this new interest in distinguishing between different kinds of images. According to Lessing, time-based arts, such as poetry, differed fundamentally from space-based "image-arts" (*bildenden Künste*) such as painting or sculpture, and this distinction was in large part a function of how each form of art mediated the givenness of reality.[16] Lessing argued that painters and sculptors were limited to representing *one* moment, and thus had to choose that moment that would give "free rein to the imagination"—that is, a moment in which the "more we see, the more we [are] able to imagine."[17] As a consequence, Lessing contended, the painter or sculptor should not represent the climax of an emotion—for example, the actual scream that is the result of a painful action—for this would give the imagination no affordance beyond that which was represented. The poet, by contrast, did not need to "compress his picture [*Gemälde*] into a single moment," but could instead describe actions extended over time (24), for the "succession of time is the province of the poet just as space is that of the painter" (91). Space-based image-arts and time-based poetry, in other words, produced phenomenally different kinds of images: a painting provided a spectator with an image that was to be taken in all at once, while poetry created a series of images that rose up before the reader or auditor.[18]

As Wellbery has noted, Lessing was fundamentally committed to an idealist understanding of the image: for Lessing, poetry was a "higher" art than painting precisely because it more fully freed a subject from the materiality of a medium than did painting.[19] However, what we wish to stress here is Lessing's emphasis on images as something "given" to perception that nevertheless provoked a sense of what was not present or given, but there only virtually (*virtute*).[20] Lessing's approach to the tradition of *ut pictura poesis*, in other words, foregrounded a problem with the fundamental evidence of the image itself: does the image in fact push material perception beyond itself? And if so, does this not suggest that the image is never merely an adequation to reality, but rather a force that solicits an actualization of something virtual? As Wolfgang Ernst has surmised, the possibility that Lessing never saw the Laocoön sculpture also indicates a crucial methodological change in theoretical knowledge: by moving away from empirical description of the thing itself and toward processes of archival research that come to define their own internal logics of operational thought, Lessing can be read as evoking forms of contemplation that seek to transform an "omission" of data into a "strategy of complexity," and that in turn confirm the virtuality of the image as a more significant point of debate over the ostensible given-ness of its material form.[21]

Immanuel Kant's approach to aesthetics in his *Critique of Judgment* (1790) presented a more fully Romantic version of the link between men-tal and external images. On the one hand, Kant too remained committed to a relatively traditional understanding of mental images, arguing in his *Critique of Pure Reason* (1781, 1787) that imagination served to create an image from the manifold of sensation.[22] On the other hand, Kant's *Cri-tique of Judgment* pursued a more phenomenological approach to the im-age, focusing on the ways in which art enabled experiences that revealed the virtual dimensions of the material object. The experience of beauty, for example, was for Kant dependent upon a *sense* of purposiveness that was not actually "given" in the object itself—that is, it depended upon a sense that could not be tied to a determinate (or determinable) quality of the object. The importance of the image, moreover, resurfaced even in what might seem to be its extreme negation, namely, Kant's valorization of the biblical commandment against making graven images (*Bildnisse*). Kant presented this commandment as an instance of the imagination's creative state of restraint:

> The fear that, if we divest this representation of everything that can com-mend it to the senses, it will thereupon be attended only with a cold and lifeless approbation and not with any moving force or emotion, is wholly unwarranted . . . For when nothing any longer meets the eye of sense, and the unmistakable and ineffaceable idea of morality is left in possession of the field, there would be need rather of tempering the ardour of an unbounded imagination to prevent it rising to enthusiasm.[23]

Kant's explicit argument was that the imagination's force is specifically managed by a moderation of sense that in turn enables a sobering moral-ity to gain ground. Yet even here, Kant's apparent dulling of the imagina-tion's "unbounded" capacities suggests that what is at stake is a return to the givenness of *neutralized* representation. Or, to put this another way, Kant valorized a phenomenality that was accepted in terms of those aspects of images that are discovered "*when* nothing any longer meets the eye of sense"—an avisuality endorsed by the ethical shape of Kant's definition of imaginative labor.[24]

A similar emphasis on the excessive potential of the image is evident in the work of G. W. F. Hegel, who presented images as means by which consciousness was able to distance itself from the immediacy of the external world. Recollection, for example, relied upon "images" (*Bilder*) that allowed the subject to free the content of sensible intuition from any particular time or place: I can recall an image of someone even when that person is dead because the image allows an element of the external world to be "liberated from its original immediacy and abstract singleness amongst other things, and received into the universality of the ego."[25] Following the example of his Enlightenment predecessors, Hegel equated images (*Bilder*) with "mental pictures" (*Vorstellungen*) and argued that insofar as both referred their reality to something else (namely, that of which they were the image or picture), they prevented a full grasp of that experience of groundlessness that was, in his estimation, essential to thinking.[26] Critics of philosophy, Hegel famously contended in the *Logic*, were often those who "longed for mental pictures [*Vorstellungen*]" in place of thought; who felt the need "to have before them as a mental picture that which is in the mind as a thought or notion [*Gedanke und Begriff*]."[27]

Yet even as Hegel seemed to present images as simply a limited psychological means that was in the end overcome, his emphasis on both an Ur-subject (*Geist*) and the importance for the image of the experience of temporality helped to establish a path of post-Kantian explorations of the image's disengagement from psychological concerns, as well as its capacity to disrupt normative subject-object relations. For example, in a passage from *The Phenomenology of Spirit* in which Hegel remarked on the relationship between husband and wife as "one in which one consciousness immediately recognizes itself in another," he added the following:

> Because this self-recognition is a natural and not an ethical one, it is only a representation, an image of Spirit, not actually Spirit itself [*ist es nur die* Vorstellung *und das* Bild *des Geistes, nicht der wirkliche Geist selbst*]. A representation or image, however, has its actual existence in something other than itself. This relationship therefore has its actual existence not in itself but in the child—an "other," whose coming into existence is the relationship, and is also that in which the relationship itself gradually passes away; and this alternation of successive generations has its enduring basis in the nation.[28]

Although "image" here appears all too quickly, Hegel's usage is significant. The heteronormative married couple figures for a "natural"—that is, essential—recognition that inadequately figures Spirit because it does not require the kind of dialectical process of purposive reconfiguration that ethical life compels. In this sense, the image of the married couple as a complete unit is "other than itself" because it is singularly non-interpretative: its recognition cannot be brought into an awareness that speculatively lies "outside" the couple's self-referentiality. It is only brought to generative thought through the figure of the child who both confirms the ethics of the couple as well as introduces the futurity of "successive generations" as it is witness to the couple's death.[29] Hegel's figuration of the married couple as an image rather than the actuality of Spirit depends upon the child to underwrite the couple's life, but it is not hard to read in this passage a saturating fear that the couple is only *Bild*—an astonishing negativity that threatens to reduce husband/wife to an imagistic emptiness that precludes dialectical thought and social fulfillment. To think of the couple as only image is to consider them as childless, non-generative, and utterly negated.

II. Images of Modernity

The Romantic philosophical engagements with the image that we have outlined previously were all developed within cultural contexts dominated by print culture, and more specifically, a print culture in which the mechanical reproduction of text and visual images was often understood as a "means" for transmitting thoughts from one individual to another.[30] Friedrich Kittler has emphasized that this dominance of print in the Romantic era encouraged psychological and hermeneutic interpretations of images: that is, images, whether painted on a canvas or described within a book of poetry, were frequently understood as having their origin within the imagination of one individual and their telos in their virtual reconstitution within the imagination of other individuals.[31] As we have noted, authors such as Lessing, Kant, and Hegel also pointed beyond such psychological and hermeneutic understandings of images, theorizing the latter as vexing junctures of presence and absence, productive crossings of death and life, and as fundamentally bound up with what would later be called "time-consciousness." However, further exploration of these a-representational dimensions of the image was significantly facilitated by the emergence in the mid- and late nineteenth century of both inscription media technologies, such as photography, cinema, and phonography, and instruments designed to facilitate experimental psychophysical research, such as mnemometers, kymographs, and tachyscopes.[32] Both sets of technologies challenged the premise that images either simply represented otherwise self-sufficient thoughts or served solely as means for resuscitating an original spirit or intention. Insofar as they employed the active mediation of "automatic" chemical and mechanical inscription and storage processes, media technologies such as photography produced images that seemed in some sense to produce themselves. If such self-production seemed to enable representational indexicality—that is, a fidelity to the source of representation—that exceeded that of earlier media, it by the same token emphasized the extent to which these new images necessarily operated beyond the thoughts and intentions of authors, at least as the latter had been traditionally conceived (a paradox that Peter Geimer explores in greater detail in his contribution to this volume).[33] Moreover, the specific way in which film produced the appearance of motion—projection of a series of still images at speeds sufficient to ensure that retinal retention produced the illusion of motion—complicated the question of the location of the image: were "images" located in the celluloid strip that passed through the projector, on the screen that the spectator viewed, or within the brain of the spectator? Laboratory devices such as mnemometers and tachyscopes, for their part, made apparent the variety of mental processes that occurred below the threshold of conscious attention and perception, suggesting that if indeed consciousness depended upon "mental images," many of these latter remained forever unconscious and outside any central coordinating cognitive location or process.[34]

This matrix of new media and experimental technologies encouraged two quite different attempts to rethink the nature of images. Experimental and philosophical psychologists such as Francis Galton, Wilhelm Wundt, William James, and E. B. Titchner responded to this challenge by simply multiplying kinds of mental images, distinguishing between visual mental images, auditory mental images, motor mental images, and so on. Of more importance to this volume, however, were three responses that each attempted a much more fundamental rethinking of the image: Henri Bergson's process philosophy; Edmund Husserl's development of the philosophical method of phenomenology; and Walter Benjamin's reflections on the relationships among technology, images, and history.

We can understand both Bergson's process philosophy and Husserlian phenomenology as two different strategies for banishing the "psychologism" of the concept of mental images from philosophy.[35] Rather than distinguishing between external and mental images and then further subdividing the latter into different kinds, Bergson proposed to treat all things—that is, each entity in the world of matter—as an "image" or aggregate of images. "It is a mistake to reduce matter to the perception we have of it," Bergson wrote in *Matter and Memory* (1896), but it is "a mistake also to make of it a thing able to produce in us perceptions, but in itself of another nature than they"; as a consequence, we should treat matter—including that collection of matter that makes up a human being—as "an aggregate of 'images.'"[36] However, images differed, Bergson contended, with respect to their capacity to introduce "delays" between action and reaction: a rock-image, for example, is acted upon, and reacts to other, images immediately, while the human brain-image is able to introduce a delay between being acted upon and reacting (30). Bergson argued that this theory of the image overcame the weaknesses of both realism and idealism. Though he acknowledged that his philosophy was in fact dualistic insofar as it posited "the reality of spirit and the reality of matter," his concept of the image was intended "to lessen greatly, if not overcome, the theoretical difficulties which have always beset dualism." Bergson contended that his approach was simply an explication of the commonsense understanding of both matter and the image. It seems more accurate to say, though, that his identification of matter and image introduces to both a vertiginous movement that has served as a resource for several key twentieth-century rethinkings of more limited senses of the image, including Gilles Deleuze's theory of cinematic images and Mark Hansen's "new philosophy for new media."[37]

Emerging at the same time as Bergson's new theory of the image, Edmund Husserl's phenomenological method also sought to rid philosophy of the representational concept of images. Husserl's new science of phenomena was explicitly designed to do away with the "psychologism" of accounts of consciousness and perception that purported to explain these latter via the postulate of mental images; instead, Husserl argued, philosophy ought to analyze how the phenomena of perception and consciousness actually present themselves.[38] We "must not substitute the consciousness of a sign or an image for a perception," argued Husserl, but we should instead focus rigorously on what is "given" to consciousness.[39] The concept of mental images, Husserl suggested, was in fact simply a set of assumptions, or prejudgments, about the nature of consciousness, and it consequently prevented real analyses of its structures of consciousness. To make progress as a science, phenomenology had to root out any hidden residues of commitment to the premises of mental images (and thus, Jean-Paul Sartre later claimed that even Husserl occasionally had fallen under the spell of seeking to explain aspects of consciousness by means of mental images).[40]

Yet the phenomenological suspicion of the concept of mental images produced, as an unexpected consequence, a method capable of extraordinarily nuanced analyses of the ways in which external images—for example, paintings, icons, and other forms of art—presented themselves to consciousness and perception. Maurice Merleau-Ponty's "embodied" phenomenology, for example, began with Husserlian premises but developed into a method especially attuned to the perceptual nuances of external images, and Merleau-Ponty's discussions of painting (and, to a lesser extent, film) have remained central for subsequent analyses of the relationship between media, images, and an embodied subject.[41] Particularly important about Merleau-Ponty's approach to phenomenology was his interest in what Husserl had described as the "natural"—that is, pre-phenomenological—attitude, that way of being-in-the-world in which things are both "given" to us but we are at the same time "given to" things. From this perspective, the images of painting and film (as well as other media) have an especial significance, for they produce something akin to, though not precisely the same as, the "phenomenological reduction," or *epoché*, that is central to phenomenology. Focusing on the case of Cézanne, for example, Merleau-Ponty contended that

> [w]e live in the midst of man-made objects, among tools, in houses, streets, cities, and most of the time we see them only through the human actions which put them to use. We become used to thinking that all of this exists necessarily and unshakeably. Cézanne's painting suspends these habits of thought and reveals the base of inhuman nature upon which man has installed himself.[42]

The specific objects that Cézanne painted—the representational dimension of the painting—should not be subordinated to the presentational dimension of his images for which phenomenology was able to provide a language: that is, the capacity of these images to reveal the dynamics of emergence and disappearance and presence and absence that define and enable our perception of the world.

A more Heideggerian version of phenomenology also served as a vector, especially in France, for drawing new concepts from Hegel's approach to the image.[43] In his essay "The Two Versions of the Imaginary," for example, Maurice Blanchot considered the way in which the cadaver and image become the same, in a sense, precisely because the "image needs the neutrality and the fading of the world; it wants everything to return to the indifferent deep where nothing is affirmed; it tends toward the intimacy of what still subsists in the void":

The image does not, at first glance, resemble the corpse, but the cadaver's strangeness is perhaps also that of the image. What we call mortal remains escapes common categories. Something is there before us which is not really the living person, nor is it any reality at all. It is neither the same as the person who was alive, nor is it another person, nor is it anything else. What is there, with the absolute calm of something that has found its place, does not, however, succeed in being convincingly here.[44]

For Blanchot, the image and the corpse are conceptually simultaneous because he understands the imaginary as a profound negation of normative relationality: the corpse *is* the image in that "the mourned deceased begins to resemble himself . . . 'Himself' designates the impersonal being, distant and inaccessible, which resemblance, that it might be someone's, draws toward the day" (257). The image-corpse resembles the anonymous oneness of itself, its unspecifiable mortality. It is irreducible to personhood: "And if the cadaver is so similar, it is because it is, at a certain moment, similarity par excellence: altogether similarity, and also nothing more" (258). The image-corpse is likeness without an object. Nor is it self-referential, because it cannot imagine anything (like a "self") to which it would bear resemblance and in turn suggest a relationship with some kind of original identity. "But what is it like? Nothing" (258). The image here is the dark non-relational relationality of an imaginary that refuses the Hegelian dialectical structure of ethical life, and pursues an *unmaking* of humanism:

> *Man is unmade according to his image.* The image has nothing to do with signification or meaningfulness as they are implied by the world's existence, by effort that aims at truth, by law and the light of day . . . it tends to withdraw the object from understanding by maintaining it in the immobility of a resemblance which has nothing to resemble. (260)[45]

For Blanchot, the image is an acceptance that there is an utter nothingness of the given that is also, in its own way, "given."

Where both Bergsonian and phenomenological approaches to the image engaged questions of technology and historical change only tangentially, the latter two concerns were central to Walter Benjamin's early twentieth-century reflections on the image. Benjamin's writings were less systematic than Bergson's or Husserl's, and his influences were wide and varied, encompassing Romantic-era philosophy and poetry, Marxist dialectical materialism, and the Jewish mystical tradition.[46] Benjamin's reflections on images were, moreover, much more explicitly "tactical" than either Bergson's or Husserl's philosophical approaches, for they were intended to serve as concrete analyses of both the status of "old" media (e.g., lyric print poetry) within a rapidly modernizing world and the perils and potentials of new media technologies for the future. Though Benjamin used the term "image" in a variety of different ways—he wrote, for example, about "thought images" (*Denkbilder*), "image space" (*Bildraum*), and "world images" (*Weltbilder*), and distinguished between "images" and "copies" (*Bild* and *Abbilder*)—it has been Benjamin's "dialectical image" that has attracted the most attention from later commentators.[47] This concept of the image—first publicly attributed to Benjamin by Theodor Adorno rather than announced by Benjamin himself, as Kevin McLaughlin notes in his essay for this volume—represented an explicit attempt to transform the image into a way of thinking history. Benjamin, like Adorno, understood "history" through the lens of Marxist materialist dialectics, for which class conflict, and the related categories of alienation and ideology, were the keys to understanding social change. Yet Benjamin's understanding of history nevertheless remained, much to Adorno's frustration, both unorthodox and idiosyncratic, and his theory of the dialectical image brings an arguably incongruous redemptive dimension to Marxist theories of history. As Miriam Hansen notes, for example, Benjamin's dialectical image has to be distinguished from "hermeneutical images (in which past and present mutually illuminate each other as a continuum)," for dialectical images are, by contrast, "images 'in which the past and the now flash into a constellation'" (199). Rather than serve as an illustration or representation of a past event, the dialectical image is more akin to a medium that brings the past, present, and future into new relationships.

III. Toward the New Image

Though we have positioned Bergson's process-philosophy, phenomenology, and Benjaminian historiography as responses to the late nineteenth- and early twentieth-century emergence of new media inscription technologies, these approaches are nevertheless not all of a piece. For much of the twentieth century, in fact, these three discourses on the image have been understood as methodologically opposed to—or at best, as bearing an uneasy relationship with—one another. Benjamin was himself critical of Bergson, and many fellow travelers, such as Adorno, as well as subsequent Frankfurt School–inspired commentators, have generally understood both Bergsonism and phenomenology as at best apolitical, and at worse tending toward an authoritarian politics.[48] Phenomenology especially has been taken to task by historical materialists for its attempt to articulate "universal" aspects of experience—that is, experiences explicitly not tied or grounded in particular kinds of bodies or experiences—for this universalist aspiration of phenomenology did not seem to make room for, or at least did not encourage, an analysis of historically determined experience, whether images or anything else; as Vivian Sobchack notes, " the 'lived body' of existential and semiotic phenomenology has been explicitly articulated as 'every body' and 'any body' (even as it has implicitly assumed a male, heterosexual, and white body)."[49] Nor have the relationships between supporters of Bergsonism and phenomenology necessarily been kind to one another, and it has often seemed that there was an either/or choice to be made: one could either follow Gilles Deleuze's appropriation of a Bergsonian ontology that by that same token seemed to be post-phenomenological, or one could retain a more traditional phenomenological emphasis on consciousness or perception (or, in the case of Heideggerian phenomenology, an emphasis on Being at the expense of more local ontological investigations). These approaches, in short, seemed to map out three apparently disjunctive understandings of the image: where Bergson's approach to the image focuses attention on temporal relations of automaticity and delay between things (both human and inhuman), phenomenological understandings of the image emphasized the dynamics of emergence and givenness upon which embodied perception depends, while Benjamin's dialectical image prioritizes questions of technology and history.

What is striking about the authors and essays in this volume, however, is a collective sense that these past antagonisms have become largely irrelevant, as the emergence of both new media technologies and new psychological experimental devices has made it possible to forge new constellations between these different approaches. As Mark Hansen notes in *New Philosophy for New Media*, for example, the ease with which digital images can be translated from one medium to another emphasizes the importance of linking phenomenological observations to a Bergsonian ontology, while at the same time, as his essay for this collection establishes, new techniques of neurological imagining may make it possible to reinscribe "mental images" within a phenomenological project. For example, the possibility of an embodied phenomenology able to attend to gender was emphasized by Judith Butler and Vivian Sobchack in the early 1990s, and though Butler's approach tended to lead away from images and toward "performative acts," Sobchack's emphasized the extent to which a linkage between gender and media technology allowed for feminist reconfigurations of the phenomenological method.[50] Giorgio Agamben's essay, moreover, points to an important resonance between the phenomenological *epoché* and Benjamin's emphasis on the "arrest" produced by the dialectical image, while both Cesare Casarino and Kenneth Surin locate similar moments of arrest in Deleuzian post-phenomenology. And Bernard Stiegler's essay emphasizes that, in an era of ever-increasing new media images, any combination of phenomenology, post-phenomenology, and a digital Bergsonism must also explicitly engage that sense of history that Benjamin's work brought to the fore. These essays thus collectively map out new constellations between elements of these early twentieth-century approaches, which themselves drew upon Romantic approaches to the image for the formation of their own constellations.

IN ORDER to help articulate the reconstellation at work in our own moment, our volume is divided into three thematic parts. We begin with a part entitled "Origination and Auto-Origination of the Image," and the three essays in this section each explore what we might describe as the question of the "whence" of the image: how and when do images manifest themselves, and how can one describe the coming-into-manifestation of the image? Rather than assume that images are made by humans, each of these essays focuses on *acheiropoiesis*, or the "self-generation" of the image, emphasizing those images that seem to be produced outside human agency. Peter Geimer's "'Self-Generated' Images" stresses the importance of the concept of self-origination for an understanding of the photographic image, and, by extension, for our understanding of the history of photography. Outlining a history of "self-generated" images—images understood as having been produced by God or by natural processes such as lightning strikes—Geimer notes that this history highlights the paradoxical dependence of the history of photography on assumptions about authorial intentionality, and he stresses the importance of understanding the image beyond the schema of human agency and intentionality.

Where Geimer's account of self-origination focuses on divine and natural inscription technologies, Jean-Luc Marion's "Cézanne's Certitude" stresses the *acheiropoiesis* of images that seem to be produced by the human hand. As its title suggests, Marion's essay is a response to Merleau-Ponty's seminal phenomenological essay, "Cézanne's Doubt," and it constitutes a continuation of Marion's long-standing effort to understand the image in phenomenological terms.[51] While Merleau-Ponty's essay concentrated on the ways in which the authorial relationality between artist and external world enabled a painting that released the appearance of objects in the world and mediated the dynamic between subject and object, Marion emphasizes that Cézanne's pictorial technique sought to make "things," rather than "objects," appear, and his essay explores the implications of this distinction for a philosophy that understands the image as something that "always appears as an *acheiropoieta*, not made by human hands." Marion argues that for Cézanne, things have an essential "curvature" to which the eye submits, and it is by understanding this curvature that we can understand how an image can come to manifest passively the things of the world. However, Marion notes that this approach to painting also brings with it a difficulty, for "it lacks the possibility in general of painting a face": that is, "the face remains an undecidable aporia for Cézanne," since it "cannot and must not be envisaged starting from itself, because it is intentionally (or rather counter-intentionally) determined within itself by another face, which has the power and right to deface it." Marion's essay thus implicitly poses the broader question of whether *acheiropoiesis* is itself intrinsically opposed to faciality (a question with significant implications for any possible intersection between Marion's and Deleuze's accounts of images).

Giorgio Agamben's "Nymphs," the final essay of this first part, links the question of auto-origination to a Benjaminian understanding of the dialectical image by means of the figure of the nymph. Beginning his essay with a reflection on Bill Viola's *The Passions*, a digital video art project that has been the subject of significant work in new media studies, Agamben emphasizes the extent to which Viola's work "charges" nearly static images with time. However, rather than take this question of temporal charging for granted, Agamben uses Viola's piece as an occasion to ask how an image can "charge itself with time," which itself leads to the broader question of how "time and images might be related."[52] Agamben's answer draws on a series of reference concepts and texts, from the *phantasmata* in Domenico da Piacenza's fifteenth-century *Dela arte di ballare et danzare* (*On the Art of Dancing*) to Aby Warburg's early twentieth-century *Mnemosyne Atlas* to Henry Darger's much more recent *The Vivian Girls*, and then back to the figure of the nymph in Paracelsus's work. Agamben suggests that each of these authors understood the image in terms of the "nymph," for, he suggests, "the nymph is the image of the image." To understand images in terms of the nymph, Agamben contends, is to appreciate them as historical sedimentations: that is, as the "remnant, the trace of what men who preceded us have wished and desired, feared and repressed." This understanding of the image, Agamben concludes, charges us with the task of developing methods that will allow us to "free images from their spectral destiny."

The four essays in the second part of the volume, "The New Media of Images (Video, Sound, Digital)," turn from the "whence" of the image to the "how" of the image, focusing especially on the importance of new media for a philosophy of the image. As we noted previously, the rapid expansion and dissemination since the 1960s of various forms of visual new media, such as computers, digital video, and cell phone screens, has encouraged widespread interest in what W. J. T. Mitchell has described as "the lives and loves of images."[53] While these lives and loves of images often have been treated as primarily visual in nature, the four essays in this section all complicate this premise by considering new media in relationship to mental images (Hansen), sound (Sobchack and Murray), and the "life-image" (Casarino).

Mark Hansen's "From Fixed to Fluid: Material-Mental Images Between Neural Synchronization and Computational Mediation" reminds us that the rise of new media technologies has also been paralleled by a reemergence of the concept of mental images in cognitive psychology, and, more recently, cognitive neuroscience. These two developments are in fact obliquely related to one another, for as Stephen Michael Kosslyn notes, cognitive psychologists' interest in mental images was originally directly inspired by computer research. Guided by the premise that "the language of information processing could be applied as easily to brains as to electronic machines," cognitive psychologists revived the concept of mental images as a means for understanding how the brain "processed" information.[54] However, as Hansen notes, one unfortunate consequence of this more recent understanding of mental images as media of neurological information processing has been a loss of the phenomenological dimensions of the image. Expanding on work he began in *New Philosophy for New Media*, and pursuing a mode of "naturalized phenomenology," Hansen forges more explicit modes of connection between cognitive psychological/neurological understandings of images, on the one hand, and phenomenological understandings of images, on the other.[55] Focusing on recent artworks that take their inspiration from cognitive scientific experiments, Hansen argues that while some of these works too easily reduce our understanding of the image to something psychological or physiological (and thus continue to think of the image as either an internal or external production), others explicitly explore the "microtemporal pattern of cognitive activity," and he reads recent video art as the formal medium through which the image's dynamism is fully exploited.

Vivian Sobchack's "When the Ear Dreams: Dolby Digital and the Imagination of Sound" explores the ways in which *sound* can generate the cinematic visual image. Drawing on Gaston Bachelard's early twentieth-century phenomenological investigation of the poetic image, as well as Don Ihde's and Sean Cubitt's more recent phenomenologies of sound, Sobchack focuses on the short, thirty-second trailers that Dolby Digital produced between 1997 and 2003 for use in movie theaters (and later, DVDs), primarily as a means of promoting its product. As Sobchack notes, "the Dolby trailers are purposefully oneiric—'dream devices' that constitute both an intimate and immense poetic space in which one can wonder at, as Bachelard puts it, 'hearing oneself seeing . . . hear[ing] ourselves listen.'" Though Sobchack agrees with Michel Chion that the rise of digital sound systems does mean in part a loss of the collective experience of sound in the movie theater, she stresses that this new form of sound also enables an "intimately immense" experience of space—and, perhaps even more important, time. Sobchack ends by drawing on Philip Brophy's distinction between the "cinematic apparatus" and the "animatic apparatus" to argue that understanding "the image as an event of sound and the advent of sound as an occurrence of image" helps us to see that these Dolby Digital trailers—and, more generally, many other uses of digital sound in contemporary cinema—"emerge not from the cinematic apparatus but from the animatic apparatus."

Like Hansen, Timothy Murray focuses on recent installation art in "Imaging Sound in New Media Art: Asia Acoustics, Distributed," and like Sobchack, he is interested in the ways in which articulations of the auditory help us to experience and theorize the image. Taking a 2007 installation at Tokyo's InterCommunication Center (ICC), *Life: fluid, invisible, audible*, as a brief archive that foregrounds the acoustic image, Murray explores how an Asian aesthetic and philosophical tradition that runs against Western claims of image-making also coalesces with what Deleuze refers to as "nomadic" versions of sound production. In the art forms in *Life*, sound is treated as environmental, noisy, and disruptive of the subject's supposed ocularcentric transcendence over space, and as such compels us to "dwell on the folding of image into sound, as the aural horizon of intensity itself."

We close the second part of the volume with Cesare Casarino's "Three

Theses on the Life-Image (Deleuze, Cinema, Bio-politics)," which returns to the question of animation that emerged in Sobchack's essay. However, Casarino focuses on a specific video work as a means of drawing on Deleuze's Bergson-inspired work on the "movement-image" and "time-image" of cinema to propose yet another kind of image, the "life-image." Casarino argues that the life-image is a necessary concept that reveals the twentieth century's mounting equivalence of bio-politics with capitalism, an equivalence that makes possible the notion that "for the first time in history *all* those potentials that make up labor-power are in principle exploitable and directly productive." The "zone of indistinction between bio-politics and production" is symptomatic of an era where life and labor-power are separated from one another: life is fetishized while labor-power is hopelessly abused in the belief that "life" might yet be redeemed if production is properly managed. Extending his earlier work on the spectacularization of AIDS, Casarino finds in the spectacle of AIDS a powerful context in which the life-image is at once subject to control and becomes a powerful point of resistance.[56] In a close reading of Peter Friedman and Tom Joslin's *Silverlake Life: The View from Here*, Casarino discovers an evocation of the life-image in terms that are irreducible to the logic of bio-political spectacularization that the film registers, but distances itself from otherwise.

The essays in the final part of the book, "Past and Future Itineraries of the Image-Concept," seek to articulate both the itineraries that have made possible the conjecture of new media and released image explored in this book, and the future paths along which this work can continue to develop. At stake in this section is the question of the *concept* of the image—what has this concept been and what can it be, and, more generally, what does it mean to generate a concept of the image? In "On Producing the Concept of the Image-Concept," Kenneth Surin notes that the concept of the image is itself a paradox, for one of the great divisions in reflection on culture in the Western tradition has been that between the *image* (understood as tied to the domain of experience) and the *concept* (understood as emerging in the realm of understanding or reason). Surin begins by outlining the history of this dichotomy from Plato to contemporary Anglo-American philosophy (in the latter the image continues to be identified with the particular and the concept with the universal), but he focuses primarily on the significance of Gilles Deleuze's notion of the *concept-image* as a significant attempt to cut the Gordian knot of this dichotomy.

Forest Pyle emphasizes continuities between Romantic and Modernist understandings of the image in "The Romantic Image of the Intentional Structure." Pyle focuses on two central problems that link the Romantic poetic image with its Modernist (as well as Postmodernist) heirs: the problem of the mode of origination of the poetic image (which occupies many of the essays in the first part of our volume) and the problem of the dimension of visuality of the poetic image (with which many of the essays in the second part are concerned). Pyle links the role of the image in two Romantic-era poems—Samuel Taylor Coleridge's "Kubla Khan" and Percy Bysshe Shelley's *The Triumph of Life*—with Walter Benjamin's Modernist theory of the image, as articulated in his theses "On the Concept of History," outlining a constellation that begins in Coleridge, jumps forward to Benjamin, and then eventuates in Shelley's theory of history.

Kevin McLaughlin's "Ur-ability: Force and Image from Kant to Benjamin" in a sense continues the work begun in Pyle's essay by emphasizing the Romantic origins of Benjamin's concept of the dialectical image. McLaughlin argues that Benjamin's understanding of the image was grounded in his study of the Romantic-era poet Friedrich Hölderlin, and that Hölderlin's work on the image was itself indebted to what Immanuel Kant called "aesthetic judgment" in his *Critique of Judgment* (1790). Of especial importance here is Kant's analysis of the way in which the dynamical sublime could result in judgments that "call up [a] greater power that virtualizes moving forces while also giving us courage." McLaughlin contends that this Kantian/Hölderlinian understanding of the image became a central aspect of Benjamin's understanding of the dialectical image, and thus, by illuminating the Romantic origins of Benjamin's concept, we are in a better position to understand why he attributed *power* to the dialectical image. More specifically, it allows us to understand that "the search for what Benjamin calls a time that is 'not temporal but image-like' (*bildlich*) turns at once away from and toward Kant, specifically, away from the first and toward the third of Kant's *Critiques*—away from 'time' and toward 'force.'"

We conclude the third part, and our volume as a whole, with Bernard Stiegler's "The Tongue of the Eye: What 'Art History' Means." Stiegler moves farther afield from the specific domain of the image in order to develop the theory of new media and technicity that he began in his multivolume *Technics and Time*.[57] Stiegler notes that in French, the word *langue* designates not only language but also the phonatory organ (tongue). The eye, like the tongue, must be "constructed" insofar as its strongest capacity is to contribute to a process of transindividuation through which the organ is organologically linked to linguistic organization—a linking that teaches the eye to think as well as to make. Stiegler's reorganization of the senses suggests that this process of learning "to see again" is part of a broader program of multiplying new libidinal economies in the face of "cultural industries and the psycho-technologies" that increasingly encroach upon our desires. Stiegler argues that these questions reveal a genealogy of the sensible inscribed in a general organology, and that something like a "tongue of the eye" allows us to conceptually reconsider the "history of art" as a process of engaged making and rediscovery.

Recall Jarman: the prayer to be released *from* image is a wish for an afterlife, for a domain of experience that the subject can survive, after the end of all images is accomplished. The wish of our volume marks a different kind of release—not a full evacuation of the category of the image itself, like a kite left behind, but rather an irruption of the multi-dimensionality of the concept. Images, then, not as coercive spectacles or representations, but as potentializing phenomena of our dwelling and thinking. Much has been said about the contemporary imagery of current new media, but we contend that there is still a great deal to be absorbed from a broader theoretical understanding premised on the position that an image should not be assumed as a given category, and attentive to the proliferations that it unleashes. Indeed, to release the image in the way that we are proposing means to short-circuit identificatory attempts to stabilize the image as a category of thought that is analogous to subject formation. Neither wholly reducible to its medium nor entirely "outside" its various projections, the image's philosophical trajectory suggests complex sites of speculation on embodied thinking.

Our three rubrics—origination of the image, new media images, and the image-concept—do not, of course, exhaust the possibilities and virtualities contained in the phrase *releasing the image*. For example, we would like to signal the fact that some of the most interesting scholarship devoted to exploring the relationship between identity and image emerges in the areas of gender and queer studies. While some of this work has been undertaken by scholars interested in questions of spectatorship or the representation of gender and sexuality "within" images (for example, the cinematic male gaze famously exposed by Laura Mulvey),[58] other critics have considered how "lived" or embodied experiences *through* the image are part of complex mediating processes that evoke gender and sexuality as modes of thought (rather than identity categories) that are undone by the image's phenom-enological potentiality.[59] Indeed, releasing the body is an adjacent project that is implied in the kind of destabilizing work that our volume seeks to do by complicating the semiotics of the image.

Though the essays here collectively map out something like a common direction for a philosophy of the image in the age of new media, there is nevertheless no "party line" to which all of these theories adhere. Instead, as if mimicking the very indeterminacy of the image for which we broadly ar-gue, the essays in our volume express a series of common nodes and points of contact around the importance of a method that emphasizes suspension, or arrest, and a thinking of the contemporary image in terms of life and after-life, iterability, temporality, virtuality, and inscription.

PART ONE

Origination and Auto-Origination of the Image

"Self-Generated" Images

PETER GEIMER

Translated by Michael Powers

1. *"Not by man's hand"*

One normally encounters the term "self-generated images" [*von selbst ent-standene Bilder*] in scare quotes. Such quotation marks are, as a rule, a means of establishing distance. One writes down a term and yet flanks it at the same time with quotation marks in order to make clear that a certain measure of precaution concerning the statement should be preserved. Quotation marks are insignia of inauthenticity, rhetorical separators, or—as Jacques Derrida formulated it—"speech act condoms, to protect our language from contamination."[1] In the case of "self-generated images," the unreasonable demand from which the scare quotes protect us exists in the presumption that an image (or a plurality of images) without any identifiable causation could be generated *of its own accord*. The image that "generates itself" seems to be a monstrosity, a non-thing [*Unding*], if one assumes that people produce images; that is, that images do not come into being absent an intentional act but are rather the results of conscious or unconscious intentions. Here, in this essay, this term will also be handled less as an empirical statement or historical finding, and more—like the quotation marks that accompany it—as an indicator of a problem area in image theory.

In *Homo Pictor*, philosopher Hans Jonas contends that "[t]he external intention of the maker lives on as intrinsic 'intentionality' in the product—the intentionality of representation, which communicates itself to the beholder."[2] This stream of intentionality is suspended in the case of self-generated images. The effects of an authorship that has become problematic take center stage whenever terms such as "automatically," "randomly," "naturally," or "self-generated" images are utilized: there, where a subject, a motif, a conscious or an unconscious intention is typically at work, a void emerges, and the need to elucidate this latter is provisionally occupied by the formula "self-generated." Who or what the possible cause may be remains undetermined at first—the only certainty being that *no person* was involved. In this respect, speaking of a "self-generated" image is, as a general rule, a *negative* discourse: it signifies who is *not* worth considering as the producer of the image, and marks first and foremost an *absence*.

In what follows, I will briefly discuss an early image-theological application of this concept, in order to then develop a more extensive examination of the "autonomy" of photographic image practice. The Byzantine image tradition is well acquainted with *acheiropoietoi*, images *not made by hand*.[3] It has been said of these images that they either miraculously generated themselves or arose through mere contact (with the countenance of Christ). Here already there are indications of an interest in the conditions of origination surrounding images. The question is not (or at least not exclusively), what does the image in question make visible? but rather, first and foremost, in what manner did the visible *materialize*? Both aspects, visibility and visualization, are inseparably interconnected to one another. The observation or veneration of the image draws life from the knowledge concerning its special mode of production; more specifically, from the knowledge concerning how it purportedly did *not* originate, through manual intervention. As Georges Didi-Huberman writes, it deals with "traces of the divine," whose meaning rests upon "non-contact of humans."[4]

No medium is more strongly implicated in this idea of automatism than photography. The first photographic images, produced in the 1830s, made use of this notion of self-generating images, here serving as a rather suggestive interpretive model: "[I]t is not the artist who makes the picture," noted William Henry Fox Talbot, the pioneer of photography, "but the picture which makes itself."[5] Once again, emphasis is placed on the *absent* intervention of the hand; again, the void initiated by the unique methods of production is occupied by supernatural and miraculous figures. The visibility of the image is ultimately bound to the specifics of its visualization. Photography, writes Talbot, is a "little bit of magic realized—of natural magic. . . . A person unacquainted with the process, if told that nothing of all this was executed by the hand, must imagine that one has at one's call the genius of Aladdin's lamp."[6]

Later variations on this theme show that such an understanding of photography should not be explained solely in historical terms, that is to say, as a consequence of interaction with a new medium that is still unusual and in need of explanation. According to Mary Ann Doane, the negative definition of photography was applied as early as Peirce's meditations on indexicality. As is well known, Peirce classified photographs under the "index" sign-type in his sign theory. Such signs stand in direct physical continuity with the object that they signify.

> The index is reduced to its own singularity; it appears as a brute and opaque fact, wedded to contingency. In this way, Peirce theorizes the index as potentially outside the domain of human subjectivity and meaning.[7]

In this respect, the photographic image is the perfect manifestation of the index. "In photography, for the first time, an aesthetic or spatial representation could be made by chance, by accident, without human control" (95). The following passage from André Bazin's meditations, "The Ontology of the Photographic Image" (1945), reads like a compressed, revised version of the thoughts already formulated by Talbot regarding photographic automatism:

> For the first time an image of the world is formed automatically, without the creative intervention of man. The personality of the photographer enters into the proceedings only in his selection of the object to be photographed and by way of the purpose he has in mind. Although the final result may reflect something of his personality, this does not play the same role as is played by that of the painter. All the arts are based on the presence of man, only photography derives an advantage from his absence.[8]

It is no coincidence that Bazin comes to speak in this context of the "the Holy Shroud of Turin," which "combines the features alike of relic and photograph" (8). The motif of the *acheiropoietoi* is invoked once again, this time in reference to the shroud preserved in Turin that allegedly contains the only authentic reproduction of Christ. Roland Barthes also considers photography to be "magic, not an art" and explicitly associates it with the image-theological tradition mentioned previously: "might we not say of it what the Byzantines said of the image of Christ which impregnated St. Veronica's napkin: that it was not made by the hand of man, *acheiropoietos*?"[9] In contrast to the effect of the *acheiropoietoi*, the autonomy implicit in photography is now considered as a purely *natural* phenomenon. The Byzantine images employed miracles as the proof of their authenticity. "That made it desirable for images to declare themselves authentic by performing miracles, the classic proof of authenticity" (*Likeness and Presence* 47). There are no known comparable incidents in the case of photographic images. Indeed, the origin of images, their cause, and authorship were all equally questionable to the pioneers of photography, albeit in a somewhat different manner. At first it was widely held that *they themselves* (i.e., the pioneers) brought the images onto paper or glass with the help of a camera, light, and various chemicals. They selected the motif, decided the camera position, determined the exposure time, and so on. And yet, the distinction from other more traditional forms of creating images was inescapable. A glimmer of that "self" from "self-generating" always remains in the photograph, a portion that is neither predictable nor entirely under control.

Countless details can *self*-position themselves into an image simply by being *on-site* at the moment that a photograph is taken and are therefore—whether consciously or unconsciously—recorded *alongside* the rest. This is what Walter Benjamin refers to as a "spark of chance . . . with which reality has, as it were, seared the character of the picture."[10] Roland Barthes refers to this same occurrence as the "not intentional": "it does not necessarily attest to the photographer's art; it says only that the photographer was there, or else, still more simply, that he could not *not* photograph the partial object at the same time as the total object" (*Camera Lucida* 147). Much about a photograph is calculable, foreseeable, and leaves open the potential for formal intervention. However, there are also modes of photography that demand the unpredictable. A photograph is, from this perspective, also an occurrence [*Vorfall*]. Something in the image *occurs* [*fällt vor*], or something unintended seems to fall into [*fällt ins*] the image. In his essay "Photography—Being and Expression" Rudolf Arnheim describes the most extreme degree of this partial passivity—a photographer who snaps an image, without looking at what appears in the viewfinder of his camera. For Arnheim this action participates in the "uncanny":

What is uncanny about photography is that the picture comes into being the moment one presses, without previously having been involved in any way, the trigger on the little machine. Neither the hand nor the eye needs to do anything further. And since the part played by the apparatus seems so great, and that played by the human being so small, one hesitates to call such a product a "photograph," if by that one understands something created by humans.

Here Arnheim describes, as he himself adds, an "extreme case" of image production. But its probability or empirical frequency is of little concern for his argument, for even the unlikely case of a blind photographer "illustrates a property that belongs to all photographs."[11] Arnheim points out that the photographer does not necessarily have to act consciously, see, or even be present at the moment of producing an image. It goes without saying that the creative interventions of the photographer are of deciding importance for an artistic assessment of photographic images; however, they do not represent a necessary prerequisite for the production of an image. The "part played by the apparatus" and the part played by the photographer complement one another, their respective emphases varying from case to case.[12] That Arnheim refers in the same text to "machinations . . . with which one falsifies photos at will by turning them into statements tinged with undeniable personal interest [*in bestimmt gefärbte Aussagen*]" makes clear that the emphasis on automatism does not necessarily include a theory of photographic objectivity (37). Like natural phenomena, the products of photography are by no means fraudulent, but when taken by themselves, they present no statement concerning that which is shown: "there is in photography always a certain opulence and contingency, just as there is in nature, for nature is not statement but being" (39).

Various authors and theorists of photography have developed different ways of filling in this void of the "self" in photography. Talbot's initial stance was that *the image* creates "itself." At another point in time he describes his house—portrayed in one of his first photographs, which he showed the members of the London Royal Society in 1839—as what he believes "to be the first that was ever yet known to have drawn its own picture."[13] A role reversal seems to take place, as *the object to be captured* in the photograph places "itself" in the image. With this same notion in mind, Barthes refers to the "matter itself," to an "emanation of the referent" (*Camera Lucida* 80). Finally, Rudolf Arnheim cites the stake of the *apparatus* in the picture-making process and so accentuates the technical agency involved in making a photograph.

At least three different agents of the "self" were made responsible for the specific form of photographic image-making: the image itself, the photographic "matter itself," and the "apparatus" that mediates between the two. The discussion concerning this issue in the theory of photography during the last decades either categorically dismisses the "self" in "self-generated" or takes the form of an undecided meandering back and forth between these poles.[14] The frequently encountered recourse to Peirce and his definition of the index has only further muddied the question. It seems extraordinarily difficult to arrive at a *positive* designation of photographic autonomy. As in the case of the *acheiropoietoi*, mostly *negative* definitions succeed: something in the image occurs and is obviously not made by hand. Against the negative determinations of photography one can doubtlessly object that they withdraw the medial aspects of photography from thought. Where one expects a positive explanation for the transfer of the object in the image, the negative explanations speak of unintentionality, unpredictability, and automatism. Moreover, Barthes's comparison with the non man-made images of Christ, Arnheim's appeal to the "uncanny" in photography, or Bazin's emphasis on their "irrational force" may in themselves already carry the features of a mythification or fetishization of the photographic image.[15] So long as the negative determination does not suddenly change over into metaphysics or a search for an unexplainable being *behind* the technology, it remains a legitimate indication of the partial inaccessibility of photography.

The art historian Wolfgang Kemp has recently criticized this as a "falling back" on an "archaic view" that sought to downplay the role of the photographer.[16] It is, however, by no means a matter of minimizing or denigrating the artistic and creative share in the image. That is to say, the "participation [*Beteiligung*] of the photographer" that Kemp mentions is not a static category. It varies according to author, intention, function, and method of image-capture. This is why Georges Didi-Huberman reminds us that a constructivist critique of photography runs the risk of "losing sight of photographic power itself, as well as the (problematic) point *where the image touches the real*."[17] This point is, as Didi-Huberman adds, "problematic" because the insistence on the efficacy of the real can easily make it seem as though the insights, already acquired, into the aesthetic, epistemic, historical, or social dimension of all things produced should be revoked on behalf of a new ontology. For Didi-Huberman, it is a matter of opposing "another mainstream" and countering the "radical skepticism of postmodern discourse . . . toward the image, even a photographic image" with a nuanced appreciation (70). In doing so he walks a thin line, which he indicates when he emphasizes that the photographic image *touches* [*anrühren*] the real (*l'image touche au réel*), instead of saying it *contacts* [*berühren*] the real. Thus photographic power does not allow one to *grasp* [*erfassen*] reality, but is rather an oscillation between the entry of the "real" into photography and the "formal procedures specific to this medium" that are resistant to further analysis. An image theory that attempts to encompass both technically created images as well as photographs just as equally must, in my opinion, contemplate *both* the "formal procedures" and "the real," that is, the intentionality of the producer, but also the partial unpredictability of that which cannot be produced.

In the case of photography, the virulence of our theme displays itself not only in the definition of the photographic image, but inevitably also in the historical challenge of naming its "origin." For the historical origin of the image, its "invention" or "discovery," always lies elsewhere depending on what one defines as a photographic image. The French photography historian Michel Frizot has spoken correctly in this regard of an "invention of the invention" of photography: "As if, because there is 'photography,' there also has to be, somewhere, its 'invention,' an 'invention' of that which did not exist before."[18] And so historians have pushed the inception of photography back and forth along the time axis, all the while complimenting, rectifying, or declaring false the genealogical accounts outlined by predecessors. At one point the German physician Johann Heinrich Schulze was regarded as the inventor of photography; at another it was the Frenchman Nicéphore Niépce or Jacques Louis Mandé Daguerre; finally, it was a scattered collective of photographers and "proto-photographers" who, as Geoffrey Batchen said, sensed a "desire to photograph" around the turn of the nineteenth century. It was rarely asked, in the course of such claims, which determinations underlay these stories of the invention and the inventors of the photographic image.[19] A more just portrayal of the state of affairs is yielded if one substitutes "history of sciences" with "history of photography" in the following remark by Georges Canguilhem: "Of what is the history of sciences the history? That this question has not been asked is related to the fact that it is generally believed that the answer lies in the very expression 'history *of* sciences' or of *a* science."[20] Similarly, the "history of photography" seems quite simply to be a history of that which established and cemented itself institutionally as "photography" during the course of the nineteenth century. From this point on, the origin and invention of photography are searched for retrospectively. The fixed localization of this historical origin has resulted in an inevitable further predefinition: the creation of a "prehistory," which only partially belongs to it. In the following, let us look at how this prehistory was founded and which features of photography should be relocated into this historiographical antechamber in order to pinpoint its actual "invention" in the first decades of the nineteenth century. In the process it should become clear that the majority of the theoretical difficulties involved in ascertaining the "origin" of photography are concerned with the at least partially "author-less" function in photography, which was mentioned earlier. This aspect of photographic recording could not be integrated into a manner of thinking that has always approached the image guided by central terms such as authorship, control, and intention.

2. Where Does Photography Begin?

On 18 July 1689, in the small French town of Lagny, lightning struck the church of Saint-Sauveur. The lightning pierced straight through the vault of the church building and struck the wide-open missal lying on the church altar. A bit later, as the remains of the ruined book were about to be removed, a peculiar sight presented itself: the text had been opened to a passage dealing with the events of the Last Supper, and the lightning had burned this scripture into the pallium on which the book lay at the time of the incident. The inverted, black words of the consecration were plain to read on the white pallium. However, to the great dismay of the clerics, precisely there, where the decisive words of the message of communion should have been legible—*Hoc est corpus meum / This is my body*—there was instead an enigmatic gap. The lightning had skipped over these words of consecration, causing many to proclaim the occurrence to be nothing less than a miracle. However, not long thereafter the scholar Pierre Lamy was called upon to investigate the matter and developed an exceedingly sober explanation for the strange occurrence. In the missal, the text of the Last Supper was written in black letters, and only the climax of the passage—the words *Hoc est corpus meum*—was inscribed in red ink. Lamy knew that black ink comprised four parts essence of turpentine and four parts oil, and was therefore extremely greasy. The red ink, on the other hand, contained considerably less oil and had had vermillion added to it, and was as a result very dry in comparison to the oily black ink. "Are there two things more dissimilar than these two inks?" asked Lamy. "And where else but in this difference should one seek the cause for the imprinting of black letters and the failure of the red letters to be imprinted by the flame of the thunder?"[21]

Whether this explanation sufficiently clarifies the events of July 1689 is of little concern to me. What is of interest, however, along with the described events, is the location thereof, which is called back into memory by Emmanuel Santini more than two hundred years later. Santini, editor of the popular scientific magazine *Science en famille*, reports on this occurrence in his text *La photographie à travers les corps opaques*. Santini's paper is one of many studies around the end of the nineteenth century that referred to the abilities and capacities of the photograph, some of which—contrary to the etymological determination of photography as a "light writing"—are not induced by natural light, but rather by physical radiation. As further causes of photographic recordings Santini cites electricity, cathode radiation, as well as the then recently discovered X-ray radiation (1895). Santini ends by summarizing the photograph's image-inducing effect under the then common term "photography by means of an opaque body."

The fact that a lightning strike in a French nave, which had occurred more than 150 years before the official invention of photography, was recalled into memory at the end of the nineteenth century as an occurrence belonging to the history of photography certainly merits attention. Measured against the official French reading of photographic history—the first photograph produced by Nicéphore Niépce in 1822, and the issue of a patent for the process in 1839—the lightning-like emergence of photographic images in these earlier examples predates photography's official inauguration by 150 years. Moreover, the numerous other causes on which Santini reports, with this purpose in mind, demonstrate that such natural images have probably always existed. According to this account, photography would not be something that was invented, since it had always existed as a sort of natural system of writing.

Santini was not alone in proposing such a genealogy gone awry. The French astronomer Camille Flammarion also treats "pictures made by lightning" in his 1905 writing *Les caprices de la foudre*. Flammarion also names a series of other comparable occurrences: for example, a lightning bolt that "imprinted" the metallic letters initialed onto a wallet ("two *D*s intermingled") through the clothing and onto the thigh of an unsuspecting victim; another lightning bolt, which tore the pants and footgear of a day laborer who was caught by surprise in an open field during a thunderstorm, the lightning leaving an outline-like "representation of a pine-tree" on his skin ("like a tattooer making use of photography").[22] Not only is a mirror image of several letters supposedly brought about in the one case by the direct physical contact of object and image carrier, but in the other, a proper image of the landscape was purportedly produced, an image carried over a wide distance onto the skin of the person concerned, where it was then fixed. Flammarion leaves open whether he believes these often fantastic-sounding reports, and we will follow suit. More crucial than the historical *validity* of the reports is the fact that Flammarion and Santini describe these phenomena as genuine photographic processes. In order to describe the "temperaments" of lightning, Flammarion falls back upon the explanatory model employed by Santini: the lightning "photographs," so to speak. The images that it creates are "reproductions," the skin of those affected serving as the "sensitive photographic paper" of the natural reproduction process. Behind this explanation of the lightning image as a light-writing lies the following minimal definition of photography: "a body inscribes its image onto another body."[23] This process of creating a copy can occur either through direct physical contact or from a distance. Its medium is first and foremost lightning, but this photography occurs in a natural manner; that is to say, without human assistance, "by itself" (*spontané*).

If lightning does indeed "photograph," if it was indeed the photographic copy of a book page that appeared on a pallium in 1689, then the history of photography is as old as lightning itself. The photographic process, a natural photography devoid of the camera, without an optical system or the addition of light-sensitive substances, would then have *preceded* actual photography. This natural "photography" would have been able to lay claim to its name long before the inventors of the new medium reclaimed it for themselves in the beginning of the nineteenth century. It would have been a light-writing that had been present all the while, a process that no person had invented and that was instead simply part of an endless series of "self-generated images," lacking a clearly datable origin. It is therefore evident that the question of the beginning of photography cannot be resolved with a simple chronicle of incidents or an exact dating, but instead, a much more fundamental issue must first be resolved: what exactly should, and should not (yet), be counted as photography?

I will first cite another example. In 1737 the members of the Parisian Académie des Sciences received a report on the different effects of sunlight: "Among the examples that I could cite," writes the author Dufay, "is one that I wish to mention, of a crimson colored taffeta curtain which hung for a long time before a window; all parts which had hung exactly opposite the windowpanes were entirely decolorized, while those parts opposite the window frame were not bleached nearly so much."[24] One can easily imagine the appearance of this drape: a rectangle of faded, light material on which the framework of the window had inscribed itself as a red marking. Indeed no recognizable intention of design lay at the basis of this image, but it can nonetheless be said that on the window of Captain Dufay, a lasting light image was produced. One could have taken the faded fabric from the wall to a different location and demonstrated it to be a—more or less clear—reproduction of the window.

Initially, what is most evident is a difference between this process and what would later be called "photography." While Niépce and Talbot employed sunlight for the *blackening* of light-sensitive material more than one hundred years after Dufay, the phenomenon described in the case of Dufay produced the reverse effect of *fading*. At the same time, though, this light image captured in Dufay's curtain anticipates the basic principles of later photograms, which originally served to make Talbot famous as one of the first inventors of photography. Furthermore, in neither case was it a matter of a projected image from a camera obscura fixed onto paper, but rather the direct outline of an object that had itself come into contact with its respective canvas. Like the photograms, the motif also appeared as a negative image in the case of Dufay's drape; namely, there where its outline had been, it had been *shielded* from the influence of light—the red crossbar of the window on an otherwise sunlight-faded fabric, similar to the effects produced by projecting through a negative onto photosensitive paper.

It is not my intention to recall an involuntary sketching on a curtain from the eighteenth century as a forgotten incunabulum of photographic history, nor is it my intention to accord Dufay the honor of being the unrecognized pioneer of photography. The example does show quite plainly, however, where the boundary between the "history" and "prehistory" of photography lies. The diapositive captured in Dufay's drape possessed two of the qualities that match the later conventional definition of photography: even if it had not actually been fixed, the impression did indeed have a certain temporal permanence. Second, the image had a mimetic quality attached to it, no matter how limited: the outline was recognizable as the image of a window. Despite this, Dufay (or any other observer of these same phenomena) never came into consideration in any of the numerous *histories of photography* as the inventor of the process. We cannot account for this circumstance simply by the fact that his report has sunk into oblivion. Rather, it has much more to do with the fact that he did not *willingly* effectuate the phenomenon in question. The window crossbar was not an "intentional image." Like the "photographic" effects of lightning described by Flammarion and Santini, this light-sketch came into being "*of its own accord*"—in any case, not as the result of an intentional process of depiction. Dufay reported a phenomenon to the Académie des Sciences that he had *found* and that had undoubtedly been occurring for a long time at innumerable locations without receiving any further comment.

In the *Imagerie d'Epinal*, released in 1880, a comic strip of sixteen images deals with "the history of photography." "Incidentally," so the commentary reads, "everything is sensitive to the action of the sun: the window-curtains, which to the despair of the mistress of the house lose their color, dresses, fabrics, tapestries, wallpaper—all change in tone because of light. The silver salt is simply more sensitive than anything else."[25] In contrast to his successors—the historiographers of the twentieth century—the anonymous illustrator of this comic strip is prepared to cite such automatic changes to fabric in sunlight under the title "History of Photography." Indeed, the reports from Dufay, Flammarion, and Santini are by no means anecdotes or peripheral phenomena from the early days of photography. The questions that they provoke concern no less than the determination of the historical "origin" of photography and thereby also the question, what exactly should, and should not (yet), be counted as photography?

3. Invention or Discovery?

Neither should the appearance of the "first" and "proper" images be transferred to another scene in history, nor should the position of "inventor of photography" be filled with new, unknown names. Of much more interest here are the theoretical course-settings that were connected to the search for the historical origin and invention of photography. An invention, says Derrida, designates "a place of creation, art, and invention. . . . It's a matter of finding, of bringing out, of making what is not yet here come to be."[26] With the entrance of this new thing, the question also emerges, *whence* did the unexpected become possible? "[I]f the structure of the field makes an invention possible (at a given point in time a given architectural invention is possible because the state of society, architectural history, and architectural theory make it possible), then this invention is not an invention. Precisely because it's possible. It merely develops and unfolds a possibility, a potentiality that is already present" (450). The discourse surrounding the invention of photography is enmeshed in this paradox. As soon as the beginning of photography was determined, there was a history and a prehistory, an invention and its imperfect "prehistory." In this antechamber of photography, everything that does not count in the official history of photography, but yet in another complicated turn still does seem to belong to it, has been collected. And so the questions begin anew: does an invention play a role at all in photography? Or, was it simply *discovered* in the first decades of the nineteenth century? Is the design of a technology, which had never previously existed, the real matter of concern? Or, the *discovery* and finding [*vorfinden*] of a natural process, which had always already existed in the long history of natural discoloration, blackening, and photochemical traces?

The term "discovery" is no less problematic than a story of a great inventor. As "part of a positivistic lexicon," it sketches out a science, which finds its objects in a world without a history.[27] These phenomena would also always have been available (in existence) *before* their discovery, and researchers would simply have uncovered their availability, so to speak. Through the example of Louis Pasteur's "discovery/invention/construction of milk enzymes," Bruno Latour expounded on the peculiar tension between the datability of a discovery and the apparent timelessness of that which is discovered. Pasteur's "discovery" of the lactic acid enzyme in 1857 showed that it "has always already been there, from Neolithic times in the gourds of homo sapiens."[28] In contrast with "the inventor," "the discoverer" is simply someone who arrived and uncovered what had long been in existence without his aid and even before he had come to be. Thus the object of the researcher can only be represented in one of two opposing modes: it either falls in the "catchment area [*bassin versant*] of human inventiveness, whose history is easily written . . . , or it falls in the catchment area of nature, of objects without history which have always already been there and which humans can at most discover."[29] Latour suggests as a solution historicizing *both*: not just the local context, motives, and acts of human actors, but also the activity of the objects involved. "[A]ction is not simply a property of humans *but of an association of actants*."[30] This thought articulates itself in Latour's attempt to situate his descriptions within a space that is "unable to differentiate as yet between . . . subjective and objective." Therefore, an occurrence such as the discovery of milk enzymes transpires in a "collective of humans and nonhumans" (20, 173). The actors of this collective do not stand opposite one another as subjective and objective monads, but rather operate in a mutual game of relations: "the more activity there is from one, the more activity there is from the other" (147). For Latour, it is important that this thinking in terms of relations should not designate "a sort of golden mean or dialectic between objectivity and subjectivity." Rather, it revolves around that position "left empty by the dichotomy between the object and the subject or the external world": "the blind spot in which society and matter exchange properties" (303, 190).

Without my going too deeply into the epistemology underwriting the premises and problems of his deliberations, Latour's theory of hybrid authorship can be at least partially transferred to photographic theory and history. Photography was neither brought into the world as an unexpected human invention, nor was it discovered one day in its natural, always existing latency. Photography would have never come into being without the construction of mobile cameras and light-intensive lenses, without successful experimentation and reflection, without information being passed down, without correspondence or meetings. Equally important presuppositions include that which cannot be invented, such as wavelengths of light, or the reaction of salts. Niépce, Daguerre, Talbot, and others were therefore just as involved in its facilitation as mercury vapor, lavender oil and gallic acid, or the lighting conditions in Chalon-sur-Saône in the spring of 1822. Parts of this historical amalgam made an appearance in the beginning of the nineteenth century; other parts had already been present for a long time beforehand. A complete listing of all the factors that were of significance for the development of photography would be an inane and impossible undertaking. Such an attempt would fare no better than the hero of Sterne's novel *Tristram Shandy*, who in the narration of his life story does not even reach adolescence because he believes he needs to expound on the circumstances of his procreation, the midwife, and so on. It would therefore be a mistake to accuse the numerous published histories of photography's emergence of not reaching such completeness and developing their genealogical concepts from a specific standpoint. Indeed, it is worth remembering that the search for a datable beginning of photography was connected to *establishing* photography, which was initially neither self-evident nor resistant to further analysis. The search for an origin is, as Foucault remarks, "an attempt to capture the exact essence of things, their purest possibilities, and their carefully protected identities."[31] Photography is, however, not an object that has been in existence since 1727, since 1822 or 1839, after having dwelled for several centuries in the seclusion of its meager "prehistory." The "history of photography" as a history of intended, lasting, and mimetic images only came to be at the expense of situating the non-intended, transient, and "object-less" [*gegenstandslosen*] light-sketches as paradoxical forerunners of photographic history. On the other hand, if one does not untangle the history of photography from its alleged past and allows it to commence before its "invention," then the legendary view from Niépce's window should not be situated as first, but rather that place should be held by the countless discolorations and traces of light, the ephemeral pictures from Wedgwood and Davy, or the photochemical haze of Talbot's early experiments.

4. The Unforeseen

The decision to designate as photographic images not just intended and durable representations, but also early traces, conforms to "an inflection of the word [image] that speaks neither of imagery, nor of reproduction, nor of iconography, nor even of 'figurative' appearance. It would be to return to a questioning of the image that does not yet presuppose the 'figured figure'—by which I mean the figure fixed as representational" (*Confronting the Image* 141). From this perspective, the evolutionary history of photography appears not simply as a success story of photographic representation, but also as a long story of discoloration, bleaching, and destruction. This knowledge seems to have been much more present in the decades around 1900 than in the later—in most cases teleological—representations of the history of photography. For instance, the chemist Gaston-Henri Niewenglowski, editor of the magazine *La Photographie*, remarks: "The number of reactions that can be provoked by light is considerable; some have been well-known for some time, such as the destruction of various colored materials by the prolonged action of sunlight."[32] Light is portrayed as something that possesses image-giving qualities, but also as a factor against which substances and materials must be protected. What later became the "basis for a new scientific media-technology" was at first an "error or nuisance" for several centuries.[33] That being said, it should in no way be claimed that the photography of the nineteenth century was already "available" in these processes of discoloration, darkening, and bleaching. An image produced unintentionally on a drape at a certain point in the eighteenth century is not a latent prefiguration of a photography that is still to arrive. Such a point of view would drive the teleological contemplation, which dominates numerous studies in the history of photography, into a boundless infinity. In terms of Latour's conception of the hybrid actors, however, it can be said that photography consists of the collaboration of conscious and unconscious, of cultural and natural, factors, and that some of these factors already existed long before the nineteenth century, though without an original or causal connection to their later photographic employment. These deliberations demonstrate not only that the bisection of the history of photography into a valid and a preliminary history, which later did not fully count, is neither obligatory nor compelling. They also serve to remind us that the history of photographic representations is accompanied by a history of contaminations, disturbances, and deteriorations. Johann Heinrich Schulze, who has been repeatedly acknowledged as the inventor of photography, garnered this experience for himself in his 1727 experiments. Because Schulze did not possess a fixing agent, light destroyed his fragile trial samples. "Darkened by the sun"—this is how Schulze designated the effect of making invisible and named his invention "Scotophorus" ("carrier of darkness"): as though he did not discover the capacity to produce a light drawing, but rather its progressive obfuscation. Schulze's neologism describes the ambivalence of a process that both created and destroyed images. Portions of the salt compound must be *exposed* to sunlight, and then the same portions must be later kept away from the sunlight. One and the same cause effectuated the appearance and disappearance of an image. Whether a photographic image is produced or destroyed is a question of time, for the "carrier of darkness" produces darkness until one interrupts its chemical effect. The blackening of the images is therefore no accidental matter, no mishap that would have befallen photography from outside, but rather its integral component. Photography's accident was photography itself. The cause of images is light; the cause of their vanishing is too much light.

Given artistic and cultural-historical traditions of interpretation, which have above all trained their methods on intended, composed, and meaningful images, a concept of images that can also incorporate contingency, occurrence, and the "uncomposed" seems necessary. The investment of the photographer in the image is not a static category, resistant to further analysis. It varies according to author, function, and photographic technique. There are photographs, such as the pictorialist manual photochemical printing process, in which everything centers on the development of a personal style of handwriting, and in so doing, seeks to eliminate as much as possible in the process the contingencies of motif and material. The invasion of the manual can be so determining for the image that the effect of the image is hardly discernible from that of a painting or drawing. At the same time, other, more scientific methods of application are being tested, which make use of the sensorium of photographic plates in order to achieve a reverse effect and produce images of what before remained *unforeseen*. In such instances, the partial autonomy of the photographic apparatus is purposefully utilized in order to bring about something that was not already clearly contoured. The author of such pictures sets a plan and follows it through, but also leaves a part of the experiment to itself. He controls and intervenes, but also excludes himself from certain portions of the experimentation, all according to plan.[34] As a rule, he first sees what the apparatus has brought forward under his guide only after it has created its effect—often without knowing exactly what he is dealing with in the image. A controllable, formable, predictable photographic process would be redundant from this perspective. An experimental arrangement must facilitate "unpredicted signals": the appearance of "things and concatenations not sought for" (*Toward a History* 80, 134). Borrowing a formulation from the French physiologist Claude Bernard, one could speak here of a *faire apparaître*, of a "bringing into appearance," or of a literal "making appear." The photographer described in such experimental conditions "makes an *appearance*." He makes something come to the surface that would have remained invisible without his doing, something that is in itself, however, not "make-able" [*machbar*]. Numerous photographs are based on the interaction between control and disorientation, formation and coincidence, intervention and unpredictability, contribution on the behalf of the photographer and on the behalf of the machine. They demand a description that leaves behind the classical oppositions between "intentional," and "subjective" images on the one side, and "naturally caused" and "objectively produced" on the other.

Cézanne's Certitude

JEAN-LUC MARION

Translated by Deborah S. Reisinger, with Nathan Phillips

My grand principle, my certitude, my discovery.

—Cézanne, *Conversations avec Cézanne*[1]

Shouldn't we agree to refrain from speaking about Cézanne who himself warned that "talking about art is *almost* useless"?[2] The caveat "almost" will authorize our hopes of justifying a new attempt to "converse" about Cézanne. But there is more: in order to have even the most banally accurate vision of Cézanne's painting, we would have to see it as Cézanne himself intended for us to see it, that is to say, to see it as he painted it. Now a simple vision of this painting already requires that we not see it as those who did not paint like Cézanne saw it (or rather did not see it). And therefore, since, during his lifetime, only Cézanne painted like Cézanne, that we see in the way Cézanne explained how he himself saw what he painted, in order to succeed, always with difficulty, in making it seen. The achievement of this vision is not self-evident, because Cézanne wrote strangely, as strangely as he painted, but especially because he lacked the concepts with which to think it. Not that he thought in a confused, approximate, or naïve fashion: rather, what he attempted to say and to make seen could not be authorized by any evidence already acquired nor by any previously established aesthetic doctrine, so that he had to think with his force alone and in as solitary a fashion as he also painted. This struggle to paint was redoubled by an equivalent struggle to speak—so as to think the effort of painting. We will not attempt to speak of this or that one of Cézanne's paintings (which others have done with greater competence), but to reconstitute the thought Cézanne had conceived of their visibility, of their mode of presence, and of their phenomenological status.

I

Let us begin with one of Cézanne's most famous assertions: "Let me repeat what I told you when you were here: Render nature with the cylinder, the sphere, and the cone, arranged in perspective" (*Conversations*, 27; *CC*, 29). Although it is often cited, the meaning of this formula is not readily apparent, and in fact, it poses a considerable challenge. One does not need great training in philosophical history or in the sciences to hear an echo, almost a direct quotation from Descartes's and Galileo's theses concerning the way in which the world is written in mathematical language:

> Philosophy is written in this vast book, which is constantly held open before our eyes (I mean the universe), but we cannot understand it if we do not first learn the language and understand the characters in which it is written. For it is written in mathematical language and its characters are triangles, circles, and other mathematical figures, without which we wander in vain through an obscure labyrinth.[3]

There is nothing forced about linking Galileo with Cézanne, and some arguments even corroborate their connection. First of all, Cézanne evokes nature consistently in opposition to the book of the Louvre: "The Louvre is a good book to consult, but it should only be an intermediary. The real and prodigious study to undertake is the diversity of the picture of nature."[4] Thus the Galilean (and medieval) parallel between the book of nature and that of Scripture (the Bible) can be found in a parallel between the book of the Louvre and this nature that must also be read: "Lire la nature."[5] Some, moreover, do not hesitate to make such a connection. Maurice Denis thus evokes "the mathematical conception of art" of Sérusier, for whom synthesis [which Cézanne would practice] "consists of making all perceived shapes conform to the small number of shapes that we are capable of imagining— straight lines, a few angles, arcs of circles and of ellipses. Apart from that we get lost in the ocean of variety."[6] A similar interpretation can be found in all the genealogies that trace Malevich or Mondrian, even Léger and modern industrial painting, to Cézanne.[7] This would perfectly confirm Cézanne's rejection of common impressionism and also of Gauguin, as well as his obsessive interest for the "geological strata" of Mount Saint-Victoire, especially as it displays "'geometry,' which 'measures the earth,' stubborn geography [*sic*]."[8] In this reading, Cézanne would try to undo the things in themselves, in order to reconstitute them in so many objects, starting with geometrical figures and more generally from order and from measure, ending finally with concepts of the understanding. We would then clearly inscribe him not only in the modern tradition of mathematically interpreting nature, but within the genealogy of deconstructing the visible.

And yet, we must totally reject this comparison for an obvious reason: Galileo and Descartes's project results in and aims only for the constitution of objects, which are completely transparent to human understanding. Whereas this effort constructs objects exclusively from self-evident and certain elements, Cézanne's entire effort aspires only to destroy objects and to free the gaze, and in a way, to free the things themselves so that they can appear *as* themselves *from* themselves. The difference between the object and the thing is actually quite radical. The object confronts consciousness, its intentionality or its aim, by unconditionally alienating itself; the thing, on the other hand, occurs from itself, at its own initiative, being self-sufficient enough to impose itself on any subject, which, paradoxically, it will end up constituting. Merleau-Ponty perfectly expressed how Cézanne tried, obstinately and painfully, to undo the objects that conform to the gaze, and to make the things themselves visible: "The lived thing [*chose vécue*] is not rediscovered or constructed on the basis of the contributions of the senses; rather, it presents itself to us from the start as the center from which these contributions radiate."[9] The thing does not come from what we perceive but precedes it and thus alone makes it possible. To cite Rilke: "to achieve the conviction and substantiality of things, a reality intensified and potentiated to the point of indestructibility by his experience of the object, this seemed to him [Cézanne] to be the purpose of his innermost work."[10] We could correct Rilke's statement in this way: the indestructible reality of the seen thing exempts vision from all work that is *creation*, to such an extent that the object disappears and literally becomes *without object*, while the thing's appearance is its own concern.

This will be our hypothesis. It obviously requires that we reread the statement in a non- Galilean (and non-Cartesian) way, but in order to reach this goal, "the artist must stand firmly on the ground of observation and analysis, forgetting existing works of art, in order to create the unexpected, derived from the bosom of God's creation" (*Conversations*, 35; *CC*, 38). But can we ever see in a manner like that in which God creates?

II

Let us return to the "book of the Louvre," which contrasts nature since nature is also "to be read" (*à lire*). But to the extent that reading the Louvre amounts to "consulting" it to our liking, so "the real and prodigious study to undertake is the diversity of the picture that nature presents" (*Conversations*, 28; *CC*, 30). What does this "diversity" mean? It is not a question of it being one characteristic among others, as if accidental, but of it being a "masterpiece": "Q: In your opinion, what is the great masterpiece of nature? A: Its infinite diversity" (*Conversations*, 103; *CC*, 102). Diversity character-izes nature in itself, that is to say, as its own self, without which its essence would no longer be its own. Nature is not a tableau, but a prodigious diver-sity. Here diversity means that this painting cannot be reduced to a single unity, at least not to the unity that *we* impose upon it, precisely because we are not capable of as prodigious a diversity. The "masterpiece" of na-ture, "its infinite diversity," puts us outside the work, for we are finished. In contrast to the Louvre, which remains at our level because we constructed and populated it, this other book, nature, cannot become a simple text for us, whose univocal meaning could yield to an exact interpretation. But if this is the case, how was Cézanne able to ask to "render nature with the cylinder, the sphere, and the cone, arranged in perspective"? (*Conversations*, 27; *CC*, 29). Is not the use of these geometric figures (like all other models) precisely an attempt to reduce the "infinite diversity" of nature to simple figures, as barely differentiated as they are, simply reproduced and indefi-nitely combined in every imaginable disposition without any "unforeseen" work ever appearing (Galileo and especially Descartes had admitted this very intention)? It is because in contrast to the common reading that we just followed, Cézanne does not seek to *reduce* nature *to* cylinders, to spheres, and to cones (as might some Cubists), but to "render nature with the cyl-inder, the sphere, and the cone" (*Conversations*, 27; *CC*, 29). The difference is not negligible: it is no longer about constructing and constituting nature from objects, but of "seeing it beneath the veil of interpretation," beginning from itself, for here "everything in nature *is modeled after* the sphere, the cone, and the cylinder . . . *according to* these simple figures" (*Conversations*,

36; *CC*, 39, emphasis added). Henceforth, the sphere, the cone, and the cylinder no longer impose themselves on the thing, but the thing models *itself*, then phenomenalizes itself, according to, or rather, *as* the forms that are presented to it. It is no longer a question of using categories or models to reduce the visible to objects, but of letting the things ("nature") render *themselves* visible thanks (through, upon, according to) these figures.

But then another question arises: how do these same figures (the sphere, the cone, and the cylinder) themselves shift from one function to another? Undoubtedly because it is precisely *not* a question of the same figures. A clue to the difference between Galileo's and Cézanne's figures can actually be found in the list of figures provided by Émile Bernard: "the cone, *the cube*, the cylinder, the sphere" (*Conversations*, 163; *CC*, 162).[11] This addition, which has been often cited, is quite noteworthy: it introduces to the list of Cézanne's figures, which are *all curved*, a rectilinear figure—one even raised to the third power, rectilinear cubed, since the form in question is a parallelepiped. And yet this single unwarranted figure is enough to confound the essential determination of the Cézannian optic, its sphericity, which has been called "the theory of the sphericity of objects in relation to the eye."[12] Which Cézanne himself repeats: "I apply myself, . . . to rendering the cylindrical aspect of objects . . . everything is spherical and cylindrical" (*Conversations*, 88; *CC*, 87). "I look for light—the cylinder and the sphere."[13] "All the bodies which are seen in space are convex" (*Conversations*, 16; *CC*, 17). Where does this thesis originate, and which facts support it? One can, as with Maurice Denis (who encroaches here on Malevich), see it as nothing more than an admission of impotence, as Cézanne's failure to abstract form to the level of true geometry:

> [A]ll his faculty of abstraction goes only so far as to distinguish "the sphere, the cone, and the cylinder" as notable forms. All shapes lead back to these, the only ones he is able to consider . . . However, he does not go so far as the idea of the circle, *triangle*, or *parallelogram*. Those are abstractions which his eye and his brain refuse to accept. For him, forms are volumes. (*Conversations*, 177; *CC*, 176, emphasis added)

In other words, Cézanne would actually maintain a Galilean and Cartesian project without ever being able to fulfill it, because he did not push geometrization to its final elements.

III

This explanation is not viable, however, as the sphericity of the forms ("Forms are for him only volumes") is not the negative result of a lack of abstraction, but rather a positive outcome of one of Cézanne's essential discoveries. When he was asked what one should study in order to learn how to paint, he responded "copy your stovepipe." In other words,

> he considered it essential to observe carefully the modulation thanks to which reality of form can be expressed by following this process: highlight, gradation, half-tone, shadow, reflection. The stovepipe was *not*, for Cézanne, *the cylinder of geometry*, but a cylindrical metal object, made by a tinsmith.[14]

What makes the pipe visible is not the figure's geometrization, but rather the cylindrical form's ability to resist all construction by making itself appear from its first light (the luminous point), and from there on, in allowing itself to modulate its curved surface. The cylindrical pipe (and not the actual *figure* of the cylinder) phenomenalizes itself from its very center, which defines its point of visibility and maximum light; absent this point, the thing would never appear from itself and would on the contrary reduce itself to an object constituted by geometrization. Even in its geometric appearance, the form is not the result of a constructivist abstraction, but of a point of maximum visibility whose surfacing raises the thing into its own light and spreads it [*déployer*] out through an intrinsic modulation.

Herein lies one, indeed *the* essential discovery of the Cézannian optic, a discovery that was indeed difficult and slow:

> For a long time I was powerless, I didn't know how to paint Saint-Victoire, because I imagined, just like all the others who don't know how to see, that shadows were concave. But look—it is convex; its edges recede from its center. Instead of becoming stronger, it evaporates, becomes fluid. (*Conversations*, 112; *CC*, 114)

Or, put another way,

> I need to know geometry, planes, everything that keeps my mind straight. I ask myself, "Is shadow concave? What's that cone up there? Wait. Is it light?" I realized that shadows on Sainte-Victoire were convex, bulbous. You see it as I do. It's incredible! It's as I said. (*Conversations*, 122; *CC*, 123)

What is so incredible here? Not only the "cylindrical side of objects" but the fact that the light always diffuses following a cone's curve, or more precisely, from a luminous and central dominant point that spreads out [*s'étend*] in all directions to illuminate itself within one form—which becomes convex *from this point onward*. What we must still grasp is the incredible and yet undeniable fact: the shadow, which is first of all light, is not swallowed up or sucked back inside as if by a black hole so dense as to prevent light from diffusing outward (a sort of anti-matter of the concavity), but rather it escapes from its center, and in a centripetal motion, and is diffused by creating the appearance of a convex surface, of a curved exterior. In other words, we are still unsure why and how light manifests itself outwardly as sphere, cone, and cylinder—*lumen diffusivum sui*, from a sloped diffusion where the "light escapes from its center."

Actually, it is not as important to understand this as to establish it—to establish that "no two points of the same visual ensemble, no more than any two points of the same shape, can reflect the same amount of light" and to understand "the maximum point of luminous intensity in the painting."[15] In something that is visible, whether it be simple or composite, our gaze always sees a point that is more luminous than the others, and it makes itself known by imposing itself as the most visible point, as "a culminating point; and this point is always . . . the closest to our eye."[16] In this way, the thing spreads itself out [*se déploie*] from an incontrovertibly high point, for it is closest to the eye, and extends dashes of color (from this point and along its sides) that little by little delineate a form, depending on whether the colors modulate the form by partially superimposing themselves one upon the other, uncoiling the form toward the exterior from itself. The thing appears little by little, according to the rhythm of its colored variations and from the convex form that they generate. But this appearance is not organized around a vanishing point defined for *my eye* (the eye of the supposedly impartial spectator), that is to say, in geometric perspective; on the contrary it materializes according to the (convex) curvature of the dashes of color, which are intimately connected with one another, each one in the service of another, beginning from a point of maximum light on which my eye does not choose to focus, but rather that is imposed on my eye. As a consequence, my gaze can no longer command, organize, or constitute what appears in its empty view, which traverses geometric space; it must patiently and sometimes painfully follow the manner in which the escape of the form from the culminating point materializes in a blossoming of colors.

The thing (for it henceforth ceases to be a question of an object, but of a thing) no longer conforms to the rectilinear aim of the gaze, but is imposed on the eye by organizing itself according to the convexity of its luminous diffusion: "only nature and an eye trained by contact are required. All this becomes concentric by dint of looking and working" (*Conversations*, 120; *CC*, 121).[17] The eye is curved according to the volume of the thing, rather than the thing being staged as an object of the gaze.

And "when you have understood that," "my certitude" becomes evident, Cézanne's certitude (*Conversations*, 120, 159; *CC*, 121, 158).

IV

Now that we have addressed the objectivist interpretation of Cézanne, we can return to the formula, which served as a point of departure, and continue reading the text it so effectively introduced:

> Let me repeat what I told you when you were here: Render nature with the cylinder, the sphere, the cone, arranged in perspective so that [*soit*] each side of an object or a plane is directed toward a central point . . . Lines parallel to the horizon give breadth, that expanse of nature—or if you prefer, of the landscape—that the *Pater omnipotens, aeterne Deus*, spreads out before our eyes.[18] Lines perpendicular to the horizon give depth—Now nature exists for us humans more in depth than on the surface. Therefore, into vibrations of light, represented by the reds and yellows, we need to introduce sufficient blues to make one feel the air. (*Conversations*, 27; *CC*, 29)[19]

This text, which is already poorly punctuated, is somewhat garbled: the balancing of the two "soit" is thwarted, if not contradicted, by the breaks of the sentences (the ellipses and dashes after "central point" and "depth"). This very uncertainty makes it all the more indispensable to attempt a reading, as risky as it may be. Thus we propose to understand this text by organizing it in three moments: (a) Nature treated by the cylinder, the sphere, and the cone can first ("so that") be seen according to perspective. In this case, the object is organized around a "central point," the one that is located precisely where the "sides" are concentrated; but, in fact, here the "plane" only shows "breadth," following the measure of the "lines parallel to the horizon." As a result, no depth can appear as such. (b) There is another possibility ("that expanse of nature"): taking the viewpoint of God, who sees the world as it is (geometrically); for Him, and for Him alone, "perpendicular lines" join themselves to the preceding "lines parallel to the horizon," this time to cross and, finally, to give "depth." The depth actually appears, but only because the absolute gaze of God (a sort of divine bird's-eye view) can make a "show" of all nature. This possibility of course remains closed to any finite view. (c) A final moment remains, one that is at once aporetic and Cézannian. First, the aporia: for us humans, either depth does not truly reveal itself (first moment, insufficiency of perspective), or it evokes a divine gaze (second moment). And yet, "nature exists for us humans more in depth than on the surface," which means that nature is best revealed to us in depth, a depth that we cannot see, a depth that cannot be attained through impractical "perpendicular lines."

At this point, the Cézannian breakthrough occurs. All that remains is to attain depth through color without perspective, because there is no "perpendicular" line: to introduce into our "vibrations of light" (reds, yellows) enough blueness "to make one feel the air." The blue of the air is capable of giving depth without recourse to line, to perspective, or to God, which means—without intent.

This reading in three moments finds confirmation if we consider Cézanne's text as a radical contestation of the theories of Charles Blanc.[20] Studying the "laws of perspective" so that the painter can "submit to them," Blanc encounters precisely the aporia that Cézanne described: painting must "hollow fictitious depths upon a smooth surface, and . . . give to these depths the same appearance as they would have in nature." But the challenge of perspective intensifies: not only can it not reach a fictive depth, but it can only function within the limits of "the representation of a scene of which the whole can be embraced at one glance."[21] Yet this representation must remain finite, because "experience teaches us that our eyes can take in an object at one look only at a distance equal to about three times the greatest dimension of the object" (*GAD*, 480; *GPE*, 51). Therefore, despite any "*tricks* favorable to the view," its weakness trumps the painters' talent, and in the end "only the eye of God can see the universe geometrically" (*GAD*, 484; *GPE*, 59, 67). For "man can see in their true size, that is *geometrically*, only the things that are perpendicular to his retina, and at a certain distance; for the geometrical image of an object is that seen in its real dimensions by an eye as large as it." Blanc draws the same conclusion as Cézanne: "Perspective is, so to say, the ideal of visible things . . . [b]ut this ideal . . . ceaselessly flies and escapes us" (*GAD*, 488; *GPE*, 66, 67). Would Cézanne then follow Blanc?

Undeniably, he takes up the question: strictly speaking, perspective is only possible for the gaze of God, who alone sees the world geometrically; moreover, Cézanne uses the same terms as Blanc:

> The masters used geometry, geometries, and perspective as a base . . . Geometry evaluates solid bodies and determines their surfaces; flat projections establish the values of height, width, and depth; and perspective outlines contours according to their distance from the spectator. (*Conversations*, 163; *CC*, 162)[22]

But Cézanne's conclusion utterly contradicts that of Blanc: because perspective only gives a false sense of depth, because real depth assumes a geometrical spectacle and only reverts back to God's gaze, but moreover because the painter, like "us humans," *must* see nature "more as depth than as surface." What remains is to render this depth without recourse to lines (neither in perspective, nor geometrically), and instead to treat it by means of what remains, in order to "give the feel of air"—color, as least as it modulates form.

Painting is always accomplished in finitude. It must accordingly attain its end by no longer entrusting its destiny to the power of lines; it must rely on the power of color.

V

After the decision to favor color, it was logical for Cézanne to abandon perspective. Maurice Denis saw this almost as a failure: "His system certainly excludes affinities of value in the scholarly sense of the word, that is in the sense of atmospheric perspective."[23] But since resorting to perspective means that depth is confined to lines (in this case, perpendicular lines), the primacy of drawing is also questioned.

How much weight should we give Cézanne's arguments against the primacy of drawing? We know that they are in part a response to the constant critique of Ingres, who "in spite of his 'estyle' (Aixian pronunciation) and his admirers, is only a very small painter" (*Correspondance*, 304; *PCL*, 305), "pernicious,"[24] even "dangerous" as he remains indisputably "talented, very talented" (*Conversations*, 135; *CC*, 136).[25] The power of drawing accentuates the danger of believing that form could either dispense with depth or attain it by a simple game of lines, without passing through the work and the spreading out of color. But Ingres and David threaten painting even more, for they maintain the "superiority of drawing over color," just as Charles

Blanc also wishes to reestablish it. Blanc's principal argument is that architecture and sculpture, which dispense with color, cannot forgo drawing; and so by analogy, painting itself, without forgoing color, should at least subordinate color to drawing, line, and form. In fact, when Cézanne declares that "pure drawing is an abstraction," he discovers Blanc's position (barring its negative connotation), which assures the privilege of drawing over its own abstraction.[26] But this tacit agreement offers a terrain of fundamental disagreement because the hierarchy that Blanc establishes supposes that drawing (form) and color are different from one another: "Drawing is the masculine side of art, color the feminine" (*GAD*, 53; *GPE*, 146).[27] This is precisely and essentially what Cézanne contests: "Drawing and color are not distinct from one another; gradually as one paints, one draws. The more harmonious the colors are, the more precise the drawing will be. Form is at its fullest when color is at its richest" (*Conversations*, 36; *CC*, 39).[28] Indeed, since form no longer depends on perspective (from the perpendicular line and from drawing), it is traced by the same movement as the one in which color materializes. Cézanne's coherence seems perfect here: the painter does not draw any more than he constructs perspective or does a colorist's work; he paints the form of the color indissolubly, because both form and color are born from the "culminating point."

But then why criticize Gauguin—"Gauguin wasn't a painter, he only made Chinese pictures" (*Conversations*, 63; *CC*, 63)? Can we accuse this eminent colorist of having misread color? Did he not subordinate form to it? But it is not enough to practice color just so it generates the form being realized; color must also and above all not remain flat, so that it can assume the convexity of things. Gauguin's use of color lacks precisely that which makes it capable of evoking form: it lacks a model of depth, as this decisive sequence asserts: "Form is at its fullest when color is at its richest. The secret of drawing and *modeling* lies in the contrasts and affinities of colors" (*Conversations*, 36; *CC*, 39, emphasis added). Gauguin is content to use color without spreading it out [*déployer*]; he paints flat. And so the virtuosity of the colorist is worthless, because it does not give form to anything. Here, the counter-example of Matisse illuminates perfectly what Cézanne means: even with Fauvist colors, even those that are pure, it is still possible that their plenitude be realized in a form, up to the extreme cases of *découpage*, where paradoxically the scissor follows the pressures of the color to outline a form, and not the other way around. For color is only important to Cézanne and only merits primacy when it models: thus color can trace the form of its own completion only when it spreads out [*se déployant*] according to the original convexity of the visible. One has thus rightly spoken of a "chromatic concept of modeling."[29] Or more precisely, that it modulates. "One should never say 'model'; one should say 'modulate'" (*Conversations*, 36; *CC*, 39).[30] The line that frees the form spreads out [*se déploie*] like a line of music, where each tone does not juxtapose itself to the preceding one (despite the metaphor of *tuilage*) as much as it follows it in time—in the time of the gaze, which follows the production of each stroke that has been colored by the former, all from a "culminating point," an original light that opens the flux of the others, just as the original impression inaugurates the consciousness of time. A painting by Cézanne seeks an explicit *time* to be seen: not because the gaze will displace itself to follow it, but because it must wait for the emergence of all the strokes that modulate, beginning with the first point of light, which ultimately gives form to the form (of a mountain, of a house, or of a tree).

VI

If this was in fact Cézanne's certitude—that the thing surges toward the light from the "dominant point" and reveals its convex form of color strokes from this point—then the painter's efforts would be an essentially negative labor. We must first let modulation create itself, without perspective or drawing—that is, the voyeur's point of view—getting in the way. This includes the painter's point of view. Cézanne understood this negative labor with a clear nuance:

> There are three things that make up the basis of our craft, which you will never have and toward which I have been working for thirty-five years, three things: scruples, sincerity, submission. Scruples before ideas, sincerity before myself, submission before the motif . . . absolute submission to the object. (*Conversations*, 151; *CC*, 151)

But submission to the object does not just signify his revenge on the subject, precisely because there is no longer any reason to speak of a subject, since the thing that makes itself visible does not depend on one, and in fact does not correspond to any object. Moreover, the object as understood in its pictorial meaning (chosen by the painting subject) also disappears: "'You must notice one thing,' Sérusier adds. 'It is the absence of a subject. In his first style, his subject was unimportant, sometimes childish. After his evolution, the subject disappears; there is only a *motif* (*Conversations*, 173; *CC*, 173).[31] The painting subject and the painted object disappear together in one fell swoop; the only thing left is the spreading out [*le déploiement*] of the thing from its first light, under the consenting and humble eye of that which allows (itself) to be painted. If according to Guérin's formula, "the thing kills the object," then we must conclude that Cézanne establishes the thing at the cost of putting the object to death.[32]

The death of the object of course also implies the death of the painting subject. Cézanne literally asks that the painter diminish his role and stop organizing the visible to simply take it in and record it:

> But if I have the least distraction, the slightest lapse, if I interpret too much one day, if today I get carried away with a theory that contradicts yesterday's, *if I think while I am painting, if I intervene, then bang! All is lost* . . . An art-ist is only a receptacle for sensations, a brain, a recording device . . . His entire will must be silent. He must silence all prejudice within himself. He must forget, forget, be quiet, be a perfect echo. Then the full landscape will inscribe itself upon his photographic plate. (*Conversations*, 109; *CC*, 111, emphasis added)[33]

If the motif no longer occupies the rank of object, but is instead the driving force that puts the painting into movement, then in order to surrender to it, Cézanne "must adapt [his means of expression] to his motif. He must not force it to conform to him, but he should conform to it, let it be born, let it germinate from within."[34] To surrender to the thing, the motif must become the painter's sole motivation, and therefore he must not so much paint as he must let himself paint (as one "lets happen") under the motif's control. To the extent that the painter only paints correctly if he is not thinking: "I am sure that in painting he thinks nothing."[35] We must read this expression rigorously: no longer thinking means leaving the rank of reasonable animal to become an animal without reason, a brute: "I am a brute. Very happy if I can be a brute" (*Conversations*, 116; *CC*, 118).[36] It may be important to read this even more radically: if I exist only to the extent that I think, and since I paint on the very condition that I think about nothing (neither theory, nor interpretation, nor willful intervention), almost *not* thinking, then I paint correctly when I do not exist. A thesis less unthinkable than it seems, since painting consists in seeing what no one has seen: "To see as one who has just been born!" to know by "forgetting everything that has come before," "as if nobody has seen it [nature] before us," "*with a vision heretofore un-*

known.[37] And no one has seen it since it is not only about what has not yet been seen, but about the unseen itself, glimpsed at the exact moment where the first visible point bursts forth, at the moment of its entry into visibility, almost *before* its visibility.

In a more banal framework, one assumed to be perfectly well framed, it is not about the domain reserved to and controlled by the painter, but of the volcano's mouth, where the irrepressible and unpredictable visible (which is never predictable in advance) leaps forth into a pure state of self-demonstration. The real painter does nothing; he sees: or rather, the visible becomes clear to him, and it does this without the painter's intervention. For example, "Monet is an eye, the most prodigious eye in the history of painters. I take my hat off to him. Courbet had his image already composed in his eye."[38] In fact, like the visibility of the "culminating point," "by themselves they will establish harmony," "when they [the tones] are juxtaposed harmoniously and when they are all present and complete, the painting models itself," "they [the colors] arrange themselves haphazardly, as they please. Sometimes that makes a painting" (*Conversations*, 16, 36, 116; *CC*, 18, 39, 118). In order to explain how the painted thing self-manifests from itself and itself alone, Cézanne uses a term that he over-determines: *realization*. For the realization is not a fabrication, especially not the fabrication of an ideal form materialized as an object. It consists instead of *realizing* a good, a sum, or a financial operation, that is, to provoke or to allow the mutation of an immaterial (profit, credit, "hope") to become a visible, autonomous, unexceptional thing. Thus the painter allows the unseen to be realized both by and as itself in the visible, by "the obstinacy with which I pursue the realization of that part of nature, which, spreading out before our eyes, *gives us the picture.*" In fact the realization does not create the visible but allows it the opportunity to give itself, "to re-create the image of what we see, forgetting everything that has gone before" (*Conversations*, 46; *CC*, 48, translation altered and emphasis added).[39] At least once, Cézanne evoked Kant's authority (or at least what he understood by this name) to more clearly define "realization":

> The other night, returning to Aix, we spoke about Kant. I tried to put myself in your mind [that of Gasquet]. Sensitive trees? What do we have in common with a tree? What is there in common between the way a pine tree appears to me and the way a pine is in reality? Hmm, if I painted that . . . wouldn't it be nature giving us our painting?[40]

We can reconstitute the argument like this: in assuming Kant's position, we must distinguish the phenomenon of the tree for us from the tree in itself; but the painter's ambition inspires him to make the pine visible in its *reality*, to make it seen as a *thing*, and if this project were to achieve its goal, it would imply the realization of a part of the phenomena becoming *things* before our eyes—and this is what the painting shows, or rather the *what* that the painting shows.

What is at play in this understanding of realization indisputably concerns phenomenality, in its most precise meaning. Cézanne maintains that painting, at least painting where color engenders form by modulating from an originating visible point, succeeds in phenomenalizing the thing as it exists, resulting in a gift of the visible from itself.[41] We cannot avoid relating this endeavor to Heidegger's definition of the phenomenon: that which shows itself, the self-showing, the manifest (*das, was sich zeigt, das Sichzeigende, das Offenbare*), what shows-itself-in-itself (*das sich-an-ihm-selbst-zeigende*).[42] The phenomenon shows nothing more than itself (and precisely this thing-in-itself), thus concealing either this other or itself. Nor is this based on an initiative of an other of the self (the transcendental subject), which would alienate it outside itself, but it manifests as it is, because it is revealed only through its own initiative. This can be put another way: if the painting is realized as it is phenomenalized, that is, as *and by itself*, this latter part is not accomplished by the painter, who at best assists and witnesses its apparition, but by the painting itself. No human hand has ever made a Cézannian painting; *this* painting always appears as an *acheiropoieta* (not made by a human hand). Even so, it does not possess an iconic status. It does not so much lack the glory of God (which bathes painted creation), nor the likelihood that God shows his face [*prendre visage*] in visibility as Christ did, but it lacks the general possibility of painting a face. For the face remains an undecided aporia for Cézanne: the face cannot and must not be envisaged from itself, because it is intentionally (or more likely unintentionally) destined to another face, one that has the power and the right to deface it. And here Cézanne encounters one *more* uncertainty.

In all these other cases, truth in painting remains. The promise ("I owe you the truth in painting and I shall give it to you") has been kept.[43] But this is not about truth being restored to itself, nor is it a portrait of truth, truth in a pictorial mode, or the truth about painting. It is about truth by means of the visible.[44] The thing appears in its truth, because it stages its own phenomenon. That the painting itself produces this changes little; for the painting, this creation not created by human hands, abolishes the difference between the thing and its phenomenon, even pictorially. The painter reestablishes the *natural* attitude because he rendered visible things visible by returning to them their own visibility. We do not look at Cézanne's paintings, but we are there; we are in what they allow to appear. It is always Tintoretto's Paradise: "The miracle is within, the water changed into wine, the world changed into painting. We swim in the truth of painting. We are drunk. We are happy" (*Conversations*, 134; *CC*, 134). Without doubt.

THREE

Nymphs

GIORGIO AGAMBEN

Translated by Amanda Minervini

> It is quite true they are all females, but they don't piss.

—Boccaccio

I

In the first months of 2003 the Los Angeles Getty Museum showed a video exhibit by Bill Viola entitled *Passions*. During a stay at the Getty Research Institute, Viola had worked on the expression of passions, a theme codified by Charles Le Brun in the seventeenth century and taken up again in the nineteenth century by Duchenne de Boulogne and by Charles Darwin on a scientific and experimental basis. The videos presented at the exhibition were the results of this period of research. At first sight, the images on the screen appeared to be still, but, after a few seconds, they started to become animate, almost imperceptibly. The spectator then realized that the images had always been in movement and that it was only the extreme slowdown that, by dilating the temporal moment, had made them appear immobile. This effect explains the impression of at once familiarity and strangeness [*estraneazione*] that the images stirred up. It was as if one entered the room of a museum and the old masters' canvas miraculously started to move.

At this point, the spectator familiar with art history would have recognized in the three extenuated figures of *Emergence* Masolino's *Pietà*; in the astounded quintet of *Astonished, Christ Mocked (The Crowning with Thorns)* by Bosch; and in the weeping couple of the *Dolorosa*, the diptych attributed to Dieric Bouts of the National Gallery of London. However, what was decisive each time was not so much the transposition of the figure into a modern setting, as the setting in motion of the iconographic theme. Under the incredulous eyes of the spectator, the *musée imaginaire* becomes the *musée cinématographique*.

Because the event that they present can last up to twenty minutes, these videos require a type of attention to which we are no longer accustomed. If, as Benjamin has shown, the reproduction of the work of art is content with a distracted viewer, Viola's videos instead force the spectator to wait—and to pay attention—for an unusually long time. The spectator who arrived at the end—as one used to do at the movies as a child—would feel obliged to re-watch the video from the beginning. In this way the immobile iconographic theme is turned into history. This appears in an exemplary fashion in *Greetings*, a video exhibited at the *Venice Biennale* in 1995. Here the spectator could see the female figures that appear entwined in Pontormo's *Visitazione* as slowly moving toward each other and ultimately recompose the iconographic theme of the canvas of Carmignano.

At this point, the spectator realizes with surprise that what caught his attention is not just the animation of images that he was used to considering immobile. It is, rather, a transformation that concerns the very nature of those images. When, in the end, the iconographic theme has been recomposed and the images seem to come to rest, they have actually charged themselves with time, almost to the point of exploding. Precisely this kairological saturation imbues them with a sort of tremor that constitutes their particular aura. Every instant, every image virtually anticipates its future development and remembers its former gestures. If one had to define the specific achievement of Viola's videos with a formula, one could say that they insert not the images in time but time in the images. And because the real paradigm of life in the modern era is not movement but time, this means that there is a life of images that it is our task to understand. As the author himself states in an interview published in the catalogue: "the essence of the visual medium is time . . . images live within us. At this moment we each have an extensive visual world inside of us . . . We are living databases of images—collectors of images—and these images do not stop transforming and growing once they get inside us."[1]

II

How can an image charge itself with time? How are time and images related? Around the middle of the fifteenth century, Domenico da Piacenza composed his essay *Dela arte di ballare et danzare* (1460) (*On the Art of Dancing and Conducting Dance*). Domenico—or rather Domenichino, as his friends and disciples called him—was the most famous choreographer of his time, a master of dance at the Sforza court in Milan and at the Gonzaga court in Ferrara. Although at the beginning of his book, quoting Aristotle, he insists on the dignity of dance, which requires "as much intellect and effort one can find," Domenico's treatise is situated on a middle ground between a didactic handbook and an esoteric compendium derived from the oral tradition passed down from teacher to student. Domenico lists six fundamental elements of the art: measure, memory, agility, manner, measure of the ground, and "phantasmata." This last element—in truth, the absolutely central one—is defined as follows:

> I say that whoever wants to learn this art, needs to dance through phantasmata; note that phantasmata are a kind of corporeal swiftness that is controlled by the understanding of the measure. . . . This necessitates that at each *tempo* you appear as if you had seen Medusa's head, as the poet says; after having performed the movement, you should appear entirely made of stone in that instant and in the next you should put on wings like a falcon moved by hunger, according to the above rule, that is to say, employing measure, memory, manner with measure of ground and air.[2]

Domenico calls "phantasm" (*fantasma*) a sudden arrest between two movements that virtually contracts within its internal tension the measure and the memory of the entire choreographic series.

Dance historians have wondered about the origin of this "dancing through phantasmata," "a simile with which," according to his disciples, the teacher meant to convey "many things that one cannot tell." It seems certain that this doctrine derives from the Aristotelian theory of memory, condensed in the brief essay *On Memory and Recollection*, which had a determinant influence for medieval and Renaissance psychology. Here the philosopher, by tightly binding time, memory, and imagination together, affirmed that "only the beings that perceive time can remember, and they do so with the same faculty with which they perceive time," that is, with imagination. Indeed, memory is impossible without an image (*phantasma*), which is an affect, a *pathos* of sensation or of thought. In this sense, the mnemic image is always charged with an energy capable of moving and disturbing the body:

> That this condition affects the body, and that recollection is the search for an image in a corporeal organ, is proved by the fact that many persons are made very restless when they cannot recall a thing, and when quite inhibiting their thought, and no longer trying to remember, they do recollect nevertheless, as is especially true of the melancholic. For such persons are most moved by images. The reason why recollection does not lie within our power is this: just as a person who has thrown an object can no longer bring it to rest, so too one who recollects and goes in search of a thing, sets a corporeal something in motion, in which the desired experience resides.[3]

Therefore, for Domenichino dancing is essentially an operation conducted on memory, a composition of phantasms within a temporally and spatially ordered series. The true locus of the dancer is not the body and its movement, but rather in the image as a "Medusa's head," as a pause that is not immobile but instead simultaneously charged with memory and dynamic energy. This means, however, that the essence of dance is no longer movement but time.

III

It is not improbable that Aby Warburg knew the treatise by Domenico (and his pupil, Antonio da Cornazano) when he prepared his study *Theater Costumes for the 1589 Intermedi* during his sojourn in Florence. Certainly nothing resembles his vision of the image as *Pathosformel* more than the "phantasmata" that contracts within itself in an abrupt stop the energy of movement and memory. The resemblance also extends to the spectral, stereotypical fixity that seems to accord as much with Domenico's "phantasmatic shadow" (in the words of Antonio da Cornazano, who misunderstands his teacher) as with Warburg's *Pathosformel*. The concept of the *Pathosformel* appears for the first time in the 1905 essay *Dürer and Italian Antiquity*, which traces back the iconographic theme of one of Dürer's etchings to the "pathetic gestural language" of ancient art. Warburg gives evidence for such a connection by retracing a *Pathosformel* in a Greek vase-painting, in an etching by Mantegna, and in the xylographs of a Venetian incunabulum. First of all, it is important to pay attention to the term itself: Warburg does not write, as he could have, *Pathosform*, but *Pathosformel*—pathos *formula*—thus emphasizing the stereotypical and repetitive aspect of the imaginal theme with which the artist had to grapple in order to give expression to "life in movement" (*bewegtes Leben*). Perhaps the best way to understand its meaning is to compare it with the usage of the term "formula" in Milman Parry's studies on Homer's formulaic style, published in Paris during the same years that Warburg was at work on his *Mnemosyne Atlas*. The young American philologist had renewed the field of Homeric philology by showing how the oral composition technique of the *Iliad* and of the *Odyssey* was based on a vast but finite repertoire of verbal combinations (the famous Homeric epithets: "the swift-footed Achilles," "Hector flashing helmet," "Odysseus of many turns," etc.). These formulae are rhythmically configured so that they can be adapted to portions of the verse; they are themselves composed of interchangeable metrical elements that allowed the poet to vary syntax without changing metrical structure. Albert Lord and Gregory Nagy have shown that formulae are not just semantic filler destined to occupy a metrical slot, but that, to the contrary, the meter probably derives from the formula traditionally passed down. Along the same lines, the formulaic composition entails the impossibility of distinguishing between creation and performance, between original and repetition. In Lord's words: "an oral poem is not composed for but in performance."[4] This means that formulae, exactly like Warburg's *Pathosformeln*, are hybrids of matter and form, of creation and performance, of first-timeness [*primavoltità*] and repetition.

Let us consider the *Pathosformel* "Ninfa" to which the forty-sixth plate of the *Mnemosyne Atlas* is devoted. The plate contains twenty-six photographs, starting from a seventh-century Longobard relief to a fresco by Ghirlandaio in S. Maria Novella (this latter portrays the female figure that Warburg jokingly called "Miss Quickbring" and that, in an exchange about the nymph, Jolles characterizes as "the object of my dreams that turns each time into an enchanting nightmare").[5] The same table also contains figures from Raffaello's water carrier to a Tuscan peasant woman photographed by Warburg in Settignano. Where is the nymph? In which one of the table's twenty-six apparitions does it reside? To search among them for an archetype or an original from which the others have derived would amount to misreading the *Atlas*. None of the images is the original; none is simply a copy. In the same sense, the nymph is neither passional matter to which the artist must give a new form, nor a mold into which he must press his emotional materials. The nymph is an indiscernible blend of originariness and repetition, of form and matter. But a being whose form punctually coincides with its matter and whose origin is indissoluble from its becoming is what we call time, which Kant, on the same basis, defined in terms of self-affection. *Pathosformeln* are made of time: they are crystals of historical memory, crystals that are "phantasmatized" (in Domenico da Piacenza's sense), and around which time writes its choreography.

IV

In November 1972 Nathan Lerner, a Chicago photographer and designer, opened the door of the room at 851 Webster Avenue in which his tenant, Henry Darger, had lived for forty years. Darger, who had left the room a few days earlier to move to an assisted-living home, was a quiet but certainly bizarre man. He had supported himself until that moment washing dishes in a hospital, always on the verge of poverty; his neighbors sometimes had heard him talking by himself imitating a feminine voice (a little girl?). He would go out rarely, and in the course of his strolls he had been seen rummaging in the trash like a bum. In the summer, when the temperature in Chicago turns sultry all of a sudden, he used to sit on the outside steps, staring into the void (this is how his only recent picture portrays him). But when, in the company of a young student, Lerner entered the room, he found an unexpected scene before him. It had not been easy to find his way through the piles of all kinds of objects (balls of string, empty bismuth bottles, newspaper clippings), but heaped up in a corner on an old chest, there were about fifteen hand-bound typed volumes that contained a sort of romance, almost thirty-thousand pages long, eloquently entitled *In the Realms of the Unreal*.[6] As the front cover explains, it tells the story of seven little girls (the Vivian girls) who lead a revolt against cruel adults (the Glandolinians) who enslave, torture, strangle, and eviscerate the girls. It was even more surprising to discover that the solitary tenant was also a painter who for forty years had patiently illustrated his novel in dozens and dozens of watercolor canvas and paper panels, at times almost ten feet tall. In them the naked girls, who usually have a little male organ, wander in self-absorption or play among flowers and marvelous winged creatures (the Blengiglomean serpents) in idyllic landscapes; these images alternate with sadistic scenes of inconceivable violence in which the bodies of the little girls are tied, beaten, strangled, and, in the end, opened in order to carve out the bloody viscera.

What interests us the most is Darger's ingenious compositional procedure. Since he could not paint and even less draw, he would cut images of little girls from comics or newspapers and copy them on tracing paper. If the image was too small, he would photograph it and have it magnified to suit his purpose. In this way, the artist ultimately had at his disposal a formulaic and gestural repertoire (serial variations of one *Pathosformel* that we can call *nympha dargeriana*) that he can freely combine in his big panels by means of collage or tracing. Darger thus offers the extreme case of an artistic composition solely made of *Pathosformeln*, one that produces an extraordinary effect of modernity.

But the analogy with Warburg is even more essential. The critics who have commented on Darger have underlined the pathological aspects of his personality, which presumably had never overcome infantile traumas and which undoubtedly exhibited autistic traits. However, it is much more interesting to inquire into Darger's relationship to his *Pathosformeln*. Certainly he lived for forty years totally immersed in his imaginary world. Like every true artist, he did not want to construct the image of a body, but a body for the image. His work, like his life, is a battlefield whose objective is the *Pathosformel*: "the Dargerian nymph." The nymph was enslaved by evil adults (often represented as professors with caps and gowns). The images that constitute our memory tend incessantly to rigidify into specters in the course of their (collective and individual) historical transmission: the task is hence to bring them back to life. Images are alive, but because they are made of time and memory their life is always already *Nachleben*, after-life; it is always already threatened and in the process of taking on a spectral form. To free images from their spectral destiny is the task that both Darger and Warburg—at the border of an essential psychic danger—entrust to their work: one to his endless novel, the other to his nameless science.

V

Warburg's research is contemporaneous with the birth of cinema. At first sight what the two phenomena seem to have in common is the problem of the representation of movement. But Warburg's interest in the representation of the body in movement—the *bewegtes Leben* that finds its canonical example in the nymph—was not so much motivated by technico-scientific or aesthetic reasons as by his obsession with what one could call "the life of images." This theme (whose relations to cinema are yet to be investigated) delineates a current that is not of secondary importance in the thought and the poetics (and perhaps in the politics) of the beginning of the twentieth century—from Klages to Benjamin, from Futurism to Focillon. From this perspective, the proximity of Warburg's research to the birth of cinema acquires a new significance. In both cases the effort is to catch a kinetic potentiality that is already present in the image—whether as an isolated film still or a mnestic *Pathosformel*—and that has to do with what Warburg defined with the term *Nachleben*, posthumous life (or after-life).

It is well known that the origin of the precursors to cinema (Plateau's phenakistoscope, Stampfer's zoetrope, or Paris's thaumatrope) was the discovery of the persistence of the retinal image. As we read in the explanatory brochure of the thaumatrope,

> it has been now experimentally proven that the image received by the mind in this way persists for about one eighth of a second after the image has been removed . . . the thaumatrope is based on this optical principle: the impression left on the retina by the image drawn on paper is not erased before the image painted on the other side has reached the eye. The consequence is that you will see the two images at the same time.

The viewer looking upon a disk of moving paper with a bird drawn on one side and a cage on the other would see the bird entering the cage because of the fusion of the two retinal images separated in time.

It can be affirmed that Warburg's discovery consists of the fact that, alongside the physiological *Nachleben* (the persistence of retinal images), there also exists a historical *Nachleben* of images based on the persistence of a mnestic charge that constitutes them as "dynamograms." He is the first one to have noticed that the images passed down by historical memory (Klages and Jung are interested instead in meta-historical archetypes) are not inert and inanimate but possess a special and diminished life that he calls, indeed, posthumous life, after-life. And just as the phenakistoscope—and just as later, in a different way, cinema—must succeed in catching the retinal after-life in order to set the images in motion, so the historian must be able to grasp the posthumous life of *Pathosformeln*, in order to restore to them the energy and temporality they once contained. The after-life of images is not in fact a given but requires an operation: this is the task of the historical subject (just as it can be said that the discovery of the persistence of retinal images calls for the cinema, which is able to transform it into movement). By way of this operation, the past—the images passed down from preceding generations—that seemed closed up and inaccessible is reset in motion for us and becomes possible again.

VI

Starting from the mid-1930s, while at work on his Paris book and then on his study of Baudelaire, Benjamin elaborates the concept of dialectical image (*dialektisches Bild*) that was to provide the pivot for his theory of historical knowledge. Perhaps in no other text is Benjamin so close to giving a definition of the concept as he does in a fragment of the *Arcades Project* (N,3,1). Here he distinguishes the dialectical image from the "essences" of Husserl's phenomenology. While the latter are known independently from every factual given, dialectical images are defined by their historical index, that which refers them to the present. And while for Husserl intentionality remains the presupposition for phenomenology, in the dialectical image truth appears historically as "death of the *intentio*." This means that Benjamin assigns to dialectical images a dignity comparable to that of the *eide* in phenomenology and to that of ideas in Plato: philosophy deals with the recognition and construction of such images. Benjamin's theory contemplates neither essences nor objects but images. However, for Benjamin it is decisive that images be defined through a dialectical movement caught in the moment of its standstill (*Stillstand*): "It is not that what is past casts its light on what is present, or what is present its light on what is past; rather, image is that wherein what has been comes together in a flash with the now (*Jetzt*) to form a constellation. In other words, image is dialectics at a standstill" (*Stillstand* does not indicate simply arrest but a threshold between immobility and movement).[7] In another fragment, Benjamin quotes a passage by Focillon in which classical style is defined:

> A brief, perfectly balanced instant of complete possession of forms . . . a pure, quick delight, like the akmé of the Greeks, so delicate that the pointer of the scale scarcely trembles. I look at this scale not to see whether the pointer will presently dip down again, or even come to a moment of absolute rest. I look at it instead to see, within the miracle of that hesitant immobility, the slight, inappreciable tremor that indicates life.[8]

As in Domenico da Piacenza's "dancing through phantasmata," the life of images consists neither of simple immobility nor of the subsequent return to motion but of a pause highly charged with tension between the two.

"Thinking involves not the flow of thoughts, but their arrest as well. Where thinking suddenly stops in a configuration pregnant with tensions," we read in the seventeenth thesis on the philosophy of history, "it gives that configuration a shock, by which it crystallizes into a monad."[9]

The exchange of letters with Adorno in the summer of 1935 clarifies the sense in which the extremes of this polar tension are to be understood. Adorno defines the concept of dialectical image starting from Benjamin's notion of allegory in the *Trauerspielbuch*, which speaks of a "hollowing out of meaning" carried out in objects by the allegorical intention.

> With the vitiation of their use value, the alienated things are hollowed out and, as ciphers, they draw in meanings. Subjectivity takes possession of them insofar as it invests them with intentions of desire and fear. And insofar as defunct things stand in as images of subjective intentions, these latter present themselves as immemorial and eternal. Dialectical images are constellated between alienated things and incoming and disappearing meaning, are instantiated in the moment of indifference between death and meaning.[10]

Copying this passage onto his note cards, Benjamin comments: "with regard to these reflections, it should be kept in mind that, in the nineteenth century, the number of 'hollowed-out' things increases at a rate and on a scale that was previously unknown, for technical progress is continually withdrawing newly introduced objects from circulation."[11] Where meaning is suspended, dialectical images appear. The dialectical image is, in other words, an unresolved oscillation between estrangement and a new event of meaning. Similar to the emblematic intention, the dialectical image holds its object suspended in a semantic void. Hence its ambiguity, criticized by Adorno ("the ambiguity must absolutely not be left as it is").[12] Adorno, who is ultimately attempting to bring the dialectic back to its Hegelian matrix, does not seem to understand that for Benjamin the crux is not a movement that by way of mediation leads to the *Aufhebung* of contradiction, but the very moment of standstill—a stalling in which the middle-point is exposed like a zone of indifference between the two opposite terms. As such it is necessarily ambiguous. The *Dialektik im Stillstand* of which Benjamin speaks implies a dialectic whose mechanism is not logical (as in Hegel) but analogical and paradigmatic (as in Plato). According to Enzo Melandri's acute intuition, its formula is "neither A nor B," and the opposition it implies is not dichotomous and substantial but bipolar and tensive: the two terms are neither removed from nor recomposed in unity but kept in an immobile coexistence charged with tensions.[13] This means, in truth, that not only is dialectic not separable from the objects it negates, but also that the objects lose their identity and transform into the two poles of a single dialectical tension that reaches its highest manifestation in the state of immobility, like dancing "through phantasmata."

In the history of philosophy this "dialectic at a standstill" has an illustrious archetype. It is a passage in the *Posterior Analytics* in which Aristotle compares the sudden arrest of thought that produces the universal to a fleeing army in which a single soldier abruptly stops, followed by another and then another, until the initial unity is reconstituted. In this instance, the universal is reached not inductively but analogically in the particular, by way of its arrest. The multiplicity of the soldiers (that is to say, of thoughts and perceptions) in disorderly flight is suddenly perceived as a unity in the same way that Benjamin described the sudden arrest of thought in a constellation—in an image deriving from Mallarmé's *Coup de dés* in which the written page is elevated to the power of the starry sky and, at the same time, to the graphic tension of the *réclame*. For Benjamin this constellation is dialectical and intensive, that it to say, capable of placing an instant from the past in relation to the present.

In a 1937 etching the great art historian Focillon, who had inherited a passion for prints from his father, seems to have wanted to freeze this suspended restlessness of thought in an image. The etching represents an acrobat hanging from his trapeze, swinging back and forth over the illuminated arena of a circus. At the bottom right the author wrote its title: *La dialectique.*

VII

The influence exercised on young Warburg by Friedrich Theodor Vischer's essay on the symbol is well known.[14] According to Vischer, the proper space of the symbol is situated between the obscurity of mythical-religious consciousness, which more or less immediately identifies image (*Bild*) and meaning (*Bedeutung, Inhalt*), and the clarity of reason, which keeps them distinct at every point. "We call symbolic," writes Vischer, "a once believed mythical element, not objectively believed, yet with the lively backward transposition of a belief that is assumed and taken up as freely aesthetic— not an empty but rather a meaningful phantasmic image (*sinnvolles Schein-*

bild)" (306). Thus, between mythical-religious and rational consciousness, one must introduce

> now a second fundamental form that lies in the middle between free and unfree, light and dark, in order first to let the entirely free and light to result as a third element. . . . The *middle* [*die Mitte*]: we can also designate what concerns us now as a peculiar *twilight* [*Zwielicht*]. It is the involuntary and nevertheless free—unconscious and in a certain sense still conscious—natural animation [*Naturbeseelung*], the granting act through which we subject our soul and its moods to the inanimate. (307)

Vischer calls *vorbehaltende* (suspending) this intermediate state in which the viewer no longer believes in the mythical-religious power of images yet, nonetheless, continues to be somehow connected to them, keeping them suspended between the efficacious icon and the purely conceptual sign.

The influence that these ideas were to exercise on Warburg is evident. The encounter with images (the *Pathosformeln*) happens in this neither conscious nor unconscious, neither free nor unfree zone in which, nevertheless, human consciousness and freedom are at play. The human is thus decided in this no-man's-land between myth and reason, in the ambiguous twilight in which the living being accepts a confrontation with the inanimate images transmitted by historical memory in order to bring them back to life. Like Benjamin's dialectical images and Vischer's symbol, the *Pathosformeln*, which Warburg compares to dynamograms full of energy, are received in a state of "unpolarized latent ambivalence" (*unpolarisierte latente Ambivalenz*) and only in this way—in the encounter with a living individual—can they obtain polarity and life.[15] The act of creation in which the individual—the artist or the poet, but also the scholar and even every human being—confronts images takes place in this central zone between two opposite poles of the human (Vischer calls it "the middle" [*die Mitte*], and Warburg never tires of warning that "the problem lies in the middle" [*das Problem liegt in der Mitte*]).[16] We could define it as a zone of "creative indifference," with reference to an image from Salomon Friedländer that Benjamin liked to quote.[17] The center in question here is not geometrical but dialectical: it is not the middle-point separating two segments on a line but the passage of a polar oscillation through it. Like Domenico da Piacenza's "phantasmata," this center is the immobile image of a being in transition [*di un essere di passaggio*]. This also means, however, that the operation Warburg entrusts to his *Mnemosyne Atlas* is exactly the opposite of what is usually understood to belong under the rubric of "historical memory": according to Carchia's insightful formula, "historical memory ends up revealing itself, in the space of memory, as an authentic collapse of meaning, the place of its very failure [*mancamento*]."[18]

The atlas is a sort of depolarization and repolarization station—Warburg speaks of "disconnected dynamograms" (*abgeschnürte Dynamogramme*)—in which the images from the past that lost their meaning and now survive as nightmares or specters are kept suspended in the shadows where the historical subject, between waking and sleep, engages with them in order to bring them back to life, but also, sooner or later, to awaken from them.[19]

Among the sketches retrieved by Didi-Huberman from the excavations of Warburg's manuscripts, besides various schemes of pendular oscillations, there is a pen drawing showing an acrobat walking on a plank kept in precarious equilibrium by two other figures.[20] The acrobat, designated by the letter *K*, is perhaps the cipher of the artist (*Kunstler*) suspended between images and their content (elsewhere Warburg talks about a "pendular movement between the position of causes as images and as signs").[21] The image may also be intended as the cipher of the scholar who (as Warburg writes about Burkhardt) acts like "a necromancer, who is fully conscious; thus he conjures up specters which quite seriously threaten him."[22]

VIII

"Who is the nymph; where does she come from?" Jolles asked Warburg in their 1900 Florence exchange regarding the female figure in movement painted by Ghirlandaio in the Tornabuoni chapel (108). Warburg's response sounds peremptory, at least superficially: "As a real being of flesh and blood she may have been a freed slave from Tartary . . . but in her true essence she is an elemental spirit (*Elementargeist*), a pagan goddess in exile. . . . " (124). The second part of the definition (a pagan goddess in exile), upon which scholarly attention has mostly lingered, inscribes the nymph in the most proper context of Warburg's research on the *Nachleben* of the pagan gods. It has not been noted, however, that the first part of the definition (the term *Elementargeist*) signals an esoteric branch in the genealogy of the nymph, a lineage that, although hidden, could not possibly be unknown to both Warburg and Jolles. For the term perspicuously refers to the Romantic tradition that, through La Motte Fouqué's *Undine*, stems from Paracelsus's essay *De nymphis, sylphis, pygmeis et salamandris et caeteris spiritibus*.[23] In this derivation, at the crossroads among different cultural traditions, the nymph names the object par excellence of amorous passion (which she certainly was for Warburg: "I should like to be joyfully whirled away with her," he writes to Jolles).[24]

Let us now consider the essay written by Paracelsus directly recalled by Warburg. Here the nymph is inscribed in Paracelsus's doctrine of the elemental spirits (or spiritual creatures), each of whom is connected to one of the four elements: the nymph (or undine) to water, sylphs to air, pygmies (or gnomes) to earth, and salamanders to fire. What defines those spirits, and the nymph in particular, is that even if they resemble humans in every respect, they were not fathered by Adam but belong to a second branch of creation: "they are more like men than like beasts, but are neither."[25] There exists, according to Paracelsus, a "twofold flesh": one coarse and earthly, springing from Adam, the other subtle and spiritual, from a non-Adamic ancestry (227). (This doctrine, implying a special creation for some creatures, seems the exact counterpart of La Peyrère's proposal on the pre-Adamic creation of heathens.) What defines the elemental, in every case, is the fact that they do not have a soul and hence are neither men, nor animals (since they possess reason and language), nor are they properly spirits (since they have a body). More than animal and less than human, hybrids of body and spirit, they are purely and absolutely "creatures": created by God among the material elements and as such subject to death, they are forever excluded from the economy of redemption and salvation:

> Although they are both spirit and man, yet they are neither [one nor the other]. They cannot be man, since they are spirit-like in their behavior. They cannot be spirits, since they eat and drink, have blood and flesh. Therefore, they are a creation of their own, outside the two, but of the kind of both, a mixture of both, like a composite remedy of two substances which is sour and sweet, and yet does not seem like it, or two colors mixed together which become one and yet are two. It must be understood further that although they are spirit and man, yet they are neither. Man has a soul, the spirit not. . . . This creature, however, is both, but has no soul, and yet is not identical with a spirit. For, the spirit does not die, but this creature dies. And so it is not like man, it has not the soul; it is a beast, yet higher than a beast. It dies like a beast and the animal body has no soul either, only man. This is why it is a beast. But they talk, laugh like man. . . . Christ died and was born for those who have a soul, that is who are from Adam, and not for those who are not from Adam, for they are men but have no soul. (228–229)

Paracelsus dwells with a sort of loving compassion on the destiny of those creatures in every way similar to man but innocently condemned to a purely animal life:

> And so they are man and people, die with the beasts, walk with the spirits, eat and drink with man. That is: like the beasts they die, so that nothing is left. . . . Their flesh rots like other flesh. . . . Their customs and behavior are human, as it is their way of talking, with all virtues, better or coarser, more subtle and rougher. . . . In food they are like men, eat and enjoy the product of their labor, spin and weave their own clothing. They know how to make use of things, have wisdom to govern, justice to preserve and protect. For although they are beasts, they have all reason of man, except the soul. Therefore, they have not the judgment to serve God, to walk on his path, for they have not the soul. (230)

As non-human men, the elemental spirits described by Paracelsus constitute the ideal archetype of every separation of man from himself (here too, the analogy with the Jewish people is striking). Nevertheless, specific to nymphs as opposed to other non-Adamic creatures is that they can receive a soul if they enter into sexual union with a man and generate a child with him. Here Paracelsus is connecting with another, more ancient tradition, which indissolubly tied the nymphs to amorous passion and the reign of Venus (this tradition lies at the origin of both the psychiatric term "nymphomania" and, perhaps, also of the anatomical term designating as "nymphae" the small lips of the vulva.) According to Paracelsus, indeed, many "documents" attest that the nymphs "have not only been truly seen by man, but have had sexual intercourse with him [*copulatae coiverint*] and have borne him children" (236; translation modified). If this happens, both the nymph and her offspring receive a soul and thus become truly human:

> It has been experienced in many ways that they are not eternal, but when they are bound to men, they become eternal, that is, endowed with a soul like man. . . . God has created them so much like man and so resembling him, that nothing could be more alike, and a wonder happened in that they had no soul. But when they enter into a union with man, then the union gives the soul. It is the same as with the union that man has with God. . . . If there were no such union, of what use would be the soul? Of none. . . . From this it follows that they woo man, and that they seek him assiduously and in secret. (238–239)

Paracelsus places the whole life of nymphs under the sign of Venus and of love. If he calls "Mount of Venus" the society of nymphs (*collectio et conversatio, quam Montem Veneris appellitant . . . —congregatio quaedam nympharum in antro . . .* —how can we not recognize here a topos par excellence of love poetry?), it is because, in truth, Venus herself is nothing but a nymph and an undine—even if she is the highest in rank and was once, before she died, their queen: *iam vero Venus Nympha est et undena, caeteris dignior et superior, quae longo quidem tempore regnavit sed tandem vita functa est* (here Paracelsus grapples in his own fashion with the problem of the after-life of pagan gods).

Condemned in this way to an incessant amorous search of man, nymphs lead a parallel existence on earth. Created not in the image of God but of man, they constitute his shadow or *imago*, and as such, they perpetually accompany and desire that of which they are the image—and by which they are at times themselves desired. And it is only in the encounter with man that the inanimate images acquire a soul, become truly alive:

> Just as one says: man is the image of God, that is, he has been made after his image—in the same way one can also say: these people are the image of man and made after his image. Now, man is not God although he is made like him, but only as an image. The same here: they are not men because they are made after his image, but remain the same creatures as they have been created, just as man remains the same as God has created him. (229)

The history of the ambiguous relation between men and nymphs is the history of the difficult relation between man and his images.

IX

The invention of the nymph as the preeminent love object is the work of Boccaccio. However, this is not a creation ex nihilo; rather, he is performing his habitual gesture, both mimetic and apotropaic, of transposing a Dantean and Stilnovist trope into a new realm, which we could define as "literature" in the modern sense (a term we could not apply without quotation marks to Dante and Cavalcanti). Thus secularizing essentially theological-philosophical categories, Boccaccio retroactively constitutes as esoteric the experience of the love poets (whose practice in itself is completely indifferent to the esoteric/exoteric opposition). By placing literature against an enigmatic theological background, he disrupts and at the same time preserves its legacy. At any rate, the *Ninfa fiorentina* is undoubtedly the central figure of Boccaccio's love poems and prose, at least from 1341 when he composes the *Comedia delle ninfe fiorentine*, a strange prosimetric work composed of novellas and terza rima whose title does not conceal an allusion to Dante's poem. (In 1900, by giving the title *Ninfa fiorentina* to the notebook collecting his correspondence with Jolles, Warburg discreetly evokes Boccaccio, an author especially dear to Jolles.) And once again in his *Ninfale fiesolano*, in the *Carmen bucolicum*, and in a special sense in *Corbaccio*, to love means loving a nymph.

Dante refers to the love object as nymph in few places, but they are decisive: in the third epistle, in the eclogues, and above all in *Purgatory* where she marks a sort of threshold between Eden and Heaven. Among love poets, the amorous object represents the point at which the image or phantasm communicates with the "possible intellect." The love object is therefore a limit-concept, not only between lover and beloved, between subject and object, but also between the individual living being and the "single intellect" (or thought, or language). Boccaccio makes this theological-philosophical limit-concept the locus of the specifically modern problem of the relation between life and poetry. The nymph thus becomes the literary quasi-reification of the *intentio* of medieval psychology (for this reason Boccaccio, pretending to give credit to a well-known rumor, will turn Beatrice into a Florentine maiden). The two decisive if apparently antithetical texts here are the introduction to Day 4 of the *Decameron* and the *Corbaccio*.

In the introduction, with reference to the opposition between Muses ("tarry with them always we cannot, nor they with us") and women, Boccaccio clearly takes side with the latter; he also proceeds to smooth out the separation: "The Muses are ladies, and albeit ladies are not the peers of the Muses, yet they have their outward semblance."[26] In the *Corbaccio*, however, his choice is overturned, and the ferocious criticism of women goes hand in hand with the claim of exclusive concern with the *Ninfe Castalidi*. Against the women who affirm that "all good things are female: stars, planets, and the Muses," Boccaccio opens up with brusque realism an incurable fracture between Muses and women: "It is quite true they are all females, but they don't piss."[27] With the usual short-sightedness, some scholars have tried to resolve the contradiction between the two texts by projecting it onto a chronology—that is, onto the author's biography and thus seeing it as an effect of age. The oscillation is instead internal to the question and corresponds to the essential ambiguity of Boccaccio's nymph. The gap between reality and imagination that the Dantean and Stilnovist theory of love meant to repair is here re-introduced in all of its power. If the *ninfale* is that poetical dimension in which the images (that "do not piss") should coincide with real women, then the *ninfa fiorentina* is always already in the process of dividing herself according to her opposed polarities—at once too alive and too inanimate—while the poet no longer succeeds in granting her a unified existence. The imagination, which in the love poets assured the possibility of a conjunction between the sensible world and thought, here becomes the locus of a sublime or farcical rupture into which literature inserts itself (as will, later on, the Kantian theory of the sublime). Modern literature, in this sense, is born from a scission of the medieval *imago*.

It is not surprising, then, that in Paracelsus the nymph is presented as a creature of flesh and bone, who is created in the image of man and who can only acquire a soul by uniting with him. The amorous conjunction with the image, symbol of perfect knowledge, becomes the impossible sexual union with an *imago* transformed into a creature that "eats and drinks" (how can we not recall here Boccaccio's crude characterization of the Muse-nymphs?).

X

The imagination is a discovery of medieval philosophy. It reaches its critical threshold and also its most aporetic formulation in Averroes. The central aporia in Averroism, which elicited obstinate objections from Scholastic thought, is in fact situated in the relation between the "possible intellect," separate and unique, and discrete individuals. According to Averroes, individuals unite (*copulantur*) with the "single intellect" through the phantasms located in the internal senses, in particular the imaginative faculty and memory. In this way, the imagination is assigned a decisive role: at the highest point of the individual soul, at the limit between the corporeal and incorporeal, the individual and the common, sensation and thought, the imagination is the final waste material that the combustion of individual existence abandons at the threshold of the separate and the eternal. In this formulation, it is imagination, not the intellect, that is the defining principle of the human species.

This definition is nonetheless aporetic, because—as Thomas Aquinas insistently objects in his critique, affirming that, if the Averroist thesis were allowed, then the individual man would not be able to know—it locates imagination in the void that gapes between sensation and thought, between the multiplicity of individuals and the uniqueness of the intellect. Hence—

as it usually happens when we try to grasp a threshold or a passage—the vertiginous multiplication of medieval psychological distinctions: the sensitive power, the imaginative faculty, the faculty of memory, the material or acquired intellect (*intellectus adeptus*), and so on. Imagination delineates a space in which we are not yet thinking, in which thought becomes possible only through an impossibility to think. In this impossibility the love poets place their gloss on Averroist psychology: the *copulatio* of phantasms with the "possible intellect" is an amorous experience, and love is, first and foremost, love of an *imago*, of an object in some sense unreal, exposed, as such, to the dangers of anguished doubt (called "*dottanza*" by the Stilnovists) and of failure [*mancamento*]. Images, which are the ultimate constituents of the human and the only avenues to its possible rescue, are also the locus of the incessant failure of the human to itself [*mancare a se stesso*].

Warburg's project of collecting in the *Mnemosyne Atlas* the images (the *Pathosformeln*) of Western humanity must be set against this background. Warburg's nymphs atone for this ambiguous legacy of the image, but move it onto a different historical and collective ground. In the *Monarchia* Dante had already interpreted the Averroist legacy in the sense that, if man is defined not by thought but by a possibility to think, then this possibility cannot be actuated by a single man, but only by a *multitudo* in space and time—that is to say, on the grounds of collectivity and history. To work on images means for Warburg to work at the crossroads, not only between the corporeal and incorporeal, but also and above all between the individual and the collective. The nymph is the image of the image, the cipher of the *Pathosformeln*, which is passed down from generation to generation and to which generations entrust the possibility of finding or losing themselves, of thinking or of not thinking. Therefore images are certainly a historical element; but on the basis of Benjamin's principle, according to which life is given to everything to which history is given (the principle could be reformulated as, life is given to everything to which an image is given), it follows that nymphs are, in some ways, alive. We are used to attributing life only to the biological body. Instead, a purely historical life is one that is *ninfale*. In order to be truly alive, images, like Paracelsus's elemental spirits, need a subject to unite with them. However, as in the union with the undine-nymph, this encounter hides a mortal danger. Indeed, in the course of the historical tradition, images crystallize and turn into specters, which enslave men and from which they always need to be liberated anew. Warburg's interest in astrological images has its roots in the awareness that "the observation of the sky is the grace and damnation of man," and that the celestial sphere is the place where men project their passion for images. As it is in the case of the *vir niger*—the enigmatic astrological decan that Warburg had recognized in the frescoes of palazzo Schifanoia—in the encounter with the tension-charged dynamogram, the capacity to suspend and reverse the charge and to transform destiny into fortune (*fortuna*) is essential. In this sense, the celestial constellations are the original text in which imagination reads what was never written [*ciò che non è mai stato scritto*].

In the letter to Vossler, written a few months before his death, Warburg re-formulates the project of his atlas as a "theory of the role of human image-memory" (*Theorie der Funktion des menschlichen Bildgedächtnisses*) and relates it to Giordano Bruno's thought:

> You see, here under no circumstances may I let myself be diverted until I succeed in incorporating a figure that has captivated me for forty years and that up to now still has not been properly placed anywhere, as far as I can see, in the history of ideas: Giordano Bruno.[28]

The Giordano Bruno to whom Warburg is referring here can be none other than the Bruno of the magical-mnemotechnical treatises, such as *De umbris idearum*. It is interesting that Frances Yates in *The Art of Memory* (1966) did not realize that the seals Bruno inserted in that text are shaped like natal horoscopes. This resemblance to one of his main objects of research could not have gone unnoticed by Warburg, who, in his study on divination in the age of Luther, reproduces almost identical horoscopes. The lesson Warburg draws from Bruno is that the art of mastering memory (in his case, more precisely, the attempt to comprehend the role of the human *Bildgedächtnis* through the *Atlas*) has to do with images expressing human subjection to destiny. The *Atlas* is the map that must orient man in his struggle against the schizophrenia of his imagination. The cosmos, held on the shoulders of the eponymous mythical hero (Davide Stimilli underlined the importance of this figure for Warburg), coincides with the *mundus imaginalis*.[29] The definition of the *Atlas* as "ghost stories for adults" finds here its ultimate significance. The history of humanity is always a history of phantasms and of images, because it is within the imagination that the fracture between individual and impersonal, the multiple and the unique, the sensible and the intelligible takes place. At the same time, imagination is the place of the dialectical recomposition of this fracture. The images are the remnant, the trace of what men who preceded us have wished and desired, feared and repressed. And because it is within the imagination that something like a (hi)story became possible, it is through imagination that, at every new juncture, history has to be decided.

Warburg's historiography is in this respect very close to poetry, in keeping with the indiscernibility of Clio and Melpomene suggested by Jolles in a beautiful essay written in 1925.[30] It is the tradition and the memory of images and, at the same time, humanity's attempt to free itself from them in order to open, beyond the "interval" between mythical-religious practice and the pure sign, the space for an imagination with no more images. In this sense the title *Mnemosyne* names the image-less: the farewell—and the refuge—of all images.

PART TWO

The New Media of Images
(Video, Sound, Digital)

FOUR

From Fixed to Fluid

Material-Mental Images Between Neural Synchronization and Computational Mediation

MARK B. N. HANSEN

The Heterogeneity of the Image

With the recent performance of composer Bruce Adolphe's *Self Comes to Mind* at the Museum of Natural History in New York City, it is safe to say that neuroscience has hit the aesthetic mainstream. Composed through active collaboration with neuroscientist Antonio Damasio and performed by the ever experimental Yo-Yo Ma, *Self Comes to Mind* is a musical piece in three parts that charts the emergence of selfhood and personal consciousness from more basic neural processes. The work is quite literally the product of a bidirectional transformational process, with Damasio reworking some of his material to address music more frontally and Adolphe distilling from this material "compositional techniques" that directly and consequentially implicate neural processes in the act of composing. Added to this mix of music and neuroscience is a third element assembled by Hanna Damasio, in her own right a leading contemporary neuroscientist—giant functional MRIs of a brain listening to music that are projected on a large screen during the performance of the work.

My interest in this work, quite aside from its aesthetic value, directly concerns the proliferation of images that it unleashes. This proliferation is emphatically transdisciplinary: in addition to the projected images of the brain and the aural images comprising Adolphe's composition, the work's listener-viewer is made to experience various senses of the image that are enfolded into the MRIs taken themselves as material images. These images give an "objective" static picture of the total brain state—the global distributed firing patterns of the brain's neural network—at a given moment. But they also allude to the separate quasi-autonomous neural subprocesses or mental images—patterns for color imaging, for motion imaging, for orientation imaging—that must be synchronized through some form of temporal binding if they are to generate seamless, coherent experience. Indeed, we could even say that these objectifications of global brain functioning serve as ciphers opening onto a world of microtemporal mental images that form the spectral doubles, so to speak, of the ungraspable patterns occurring in the very microtemporal thickness of the listener-viewer's present experience.

What to my mind is most striking about the transdisciplinary symphony of divergent image types implicated in Adolphe's *Self Comes to Mind* is just how poorly equipped we are to address, let alone account for, how they correlate with one another. We simply lack the conceptual terminology to bridge the divide between the role and significance of the image in neuroscience and the role and significance of the image in perceptual phenomenology. Thus, despite the recent proliferation of studies devoted to art and neuroscience, including Semir Zeki's *Inner Vision* and V. S. Ramachandran's *A Brief Tour of Human Consciousness*, we remain hard-pressed to correlate mental images and material images, images in the mind and images in the world.[1] This impasse is succinctly characterized by Michael Morgan: "The problem that has dogged the philosophy of visual perception is that seeing begins with an image—the optical image in the retina—and ends in a completely different kind of image—our perceptual image of the world outside."[2] Schematically speaking, neuroscience concerns itself with the former kind of image—mental images—while phenomenology and media studies, to mention only those areas most relevant to my aims here, focus on the latter kind of image—images of the world or material images. For the neuroscientist, moreover, images are not limited to visual sensation, but characterize patterns of different sensory types and of different sensory origin: "we refer to images based on any sensory modality—sound images, images of movement in space—rather than to visual images only," note Antonio and Hanna Damasio in their account of how subjectivity arises from the synchronization of discrete images. "Images describe both the world external to the organism as well as the world within the organism, such as visceral states, musculoskeletal structure, body movement, and so forth; and convey both nonverbal and verbal entities."[3]

When neuroscience does open itself to the comprehensive picture, as I suggest it does in its forays into art, it typically skews the results in advance by favoring a very small sample of the archive of art, namely, those art forms that correlate best with its experimental procedures. As a result, art—and with it the external world per se—becomes nothing more than a trigger for the production of mental images, and the promise of the gesture of openness goes unfulfilled. Neuroscientist Semir Zeki is forthright about this bias from the very outset of his book *Inner Vision*, whose subtitle is "An Exploration of Art and the Brain": "This is not so much a book about art," writes Zeki; "it is more a book about the brain. It arises from my conviction that, in large measure, the function of art and the function of the visual brain are one and the same, or at least that the aims of art constitute an extension of the functions of the brain . . . "[4] Thus, even a scientist like Zeki, who possesses marked proclivities toward transdisciplinarity, would seem to ratify the defining focus on internal representation that has served to demarcate psychological and neuroscientific approaches to cognition from their origin in the "imagery debates" of the 1970s. What Stephen Kosslyn says about his own focus in his seminal book, *Image and Brain: The Resolution of the Imagery Debate*, would thus seem to hold for the field as such, including its forays into art: "most interest in psychology has focused on only one facet of imagery—its role in information processing, not its phenomenology or role in emotional life. In this book, we will focus on the nature of the internal events that underlie the experience of 'seeing with the mind's eye'; we shall not consider the qualities of the experience itself. The term 'image' will refer to the internal representation that is used in information processing, not the experience itself."[5]

There is, however, one site within the cognitive sciences where this impasse between the mental and the material image would appear to be overcome. The field of cognitive archaeology focuses specifically on the "*divisive* functions of image making," and in particular on the emergence of two-dimensional images on cave walls and ceilings in the Upper Paleolithic period. For a scientist like David Lewis-Williams, it is a mistake to think that our proto-human ancestors *invented* material, two-dimensional images as a kind of image distinct from mental images. "On the contrary," states Lewis-Williams, a notion of images *and* the vocabulary of motifs *were part of their experience* before they made parietal or portable images."[6] In Lewis-Williams's account, the emergence of material, two-dimensional images on cave walls and ceilings is the correlate of the emergence of higher-order consciousness:

> Once human beings had developed higher-order consciousness, they had the ability to see mental images projected onto surfaces and to experience afterimages. Here . . . is the answer to the conundrum of two-dimensional images. People did not "invent" two-dimensional images; nor did they discover them in natural marks and "macaronis." On the contrary, their world was already invested with two-dimensional images [namely, in the form of mental images . . . projected onto surfaces "like a motion picture or slide show"]; such images were a product of the functioning of the human nervous system in altered states of consciousness and in the context of higher-order consciousness. (192–93)

Rather than representations of three-dimensional objects that are first perceived by the mind, material images are more or less direct transpositions of mental images into the world: they are, in short, originary materializations of two-dimensional mental images in a fixed, exteriorized, durable, and hence sharable form. "How then did people come to make representational images of animals and so forth out of projected mental imagery?" asks Lewis-Williams. To which he answers:

> [A]t a given time, and for social reasons, the projected images of altered states were insufficient and people needed to "fix" their visions. They reached out to their emotionally charged visions and tried to touch them, to hold them in place . . . They were not inventing images. They were merely touching *what was already there.*

From this, Lewis-Williams succinctly concludes that "the first two-dimensional images were thus not two-dimensional representations of three-dimensional things in the material world, as researchers have always assumed. Rather, they were 'fixed' mental images" (193).

Note that among other things, "fixed" here signifies *transposed into the frame of consciousness.* What this means is that, from its very origin, the interchange between mental and material images takes place *for higher-order consciousness.* The material images that fix mental images—and that stand at the beginning of a long history of material images in world culture—are images that address consciousness proper. Two points need to be made about this correlation of material image and consciousness. First, this correlation has literally defined the history of images in world culture up until our time: as the history of art and now of popular culture and media attests, images have been calibrated to resonate with the sensory ratios of human perception and conscious experience. To put this in explicitly temporal terms, material images have been synchronized on the basis of the temporality of consciousness, which is to say, as direct correlates of phenomenological experience. This is precisely the point Lewis-Williams makes when he notes that this transposition from mental to material image occurs in the wake of the advent of higher-order conscious experience. A second point relates directly to this temporal conception of the image and concerns what is left out of play by the archaeological and now media theoretical subsumption of the mental image as projected material image. What is left out is precisely the mental image as microtemporal pattern of cognitive activity.

The Microconscious Image

In a recent paper entitled "A Theory of Micro-consciousness," Semir Zeki emphasizes the functional specialization of the visual brain, which "consists of many visual areas . . . specialized to process different attributes of the visual scene."[7] Zeki notes that, notwithstanding differences concerning the extent of functional specialization in the brain, there is consensus that color and motion, if not location and orientation, each have specialized cortical centers and neural pathways and hence that each possesses a certain degree of functional autonomy. The resulting problem raised by functional specialization of the visual brain—namely, how these distinct areas "interact to provide a unified image in the brain"—is a problem that understandably occupies many of the major figures in contemporary neuroscience: in addition to Zeki, one could list Damasio, Francis Crick, Wolf Singer, and Rodolfo Llinas, to name just some of the most prominent figures.[8] The problem, as Zeki emphasizes, is not simply a spatial one, for the temporal windows characteristic of these separate areas in the visual brain differ significantly from one another. Thus, experimental results have shown that color is perceived before motion by 80 ms. and that location is perceived before color, and color before orientation. What results is a "temporal hierarchy of microconsciousnesses" leaving in its wake a distinctly temporal problem of synchronization: in virtue of what are these functionally specialized and quasi-autonomous areas of visual perception bound together in seamless, integrated macroconscious experience?

Zeki's answer to this problem, which distinguishes him from most if not all of his eminent colleagues, opens up a domain of what, with Gilles Deleuze, we can call transcendental (or infraempirical) sensibility.[9] Whereas Damasio looks for an operation that would be added to the distinct patterns of the quasi-autonomous areas of the visual brain to resolve the binding problem—he calls it a "convergence zone"—Zeki embraces the more radical possibility that binding results *from nothing other than simultaneity at the microtemporal level*, from the mere fact that distinct visual mental images *happened in the same temporal window*. Now, given the temporal hierarchy invoked previously, which is to say, the significant, though still microscalar temporal divergence of imaging processes for different attributes, Zeki's position calls on him to account for the possibility of mis-binding, the situation that arises when a color sensation attached to experience at time t coincides with a "slower" motion sensation at time $t - 1$. He accounts for mis-binding, remarkably enough, by embracing it as proof of the significant autonomy of the distinct imaging processes of the visual brain:

> Because of differences in time taken to perceive color and motion, subjects consistently mis-bind the color they perceived at time t to the motion perceived at time $t - 1$. Put more simply, they bind the (veridically) correct color perceived at time t with the (veridically) incorrect direction of motion, the direction that had been registered 100 ms. before. It follows that, over very brief time windows, the brain does not wait for each area to complete its processings; rather it simply binds what has been processed and reached a perceptual level. This in turn suggests strongly that *binding is a post-consciousness phenomenon*, and does not itself generate the conscious experience, as some have supposed.[10]

In addition to establishing that binding is a post-conscious experience, Zeki's analysis of mis-binding would seem to suggest equally strongly that the discrete processes of mental imaging involved in each of the separate areas of the visual brain are themselves "conscious," at least in some sense of the term. Specifically, the discrete perceptions of color or motion (or location or orientation) isolated experimentally by Zeki and his colleagues are conscious at a level beneath the threshold of phenomenological consciousness. They are, paradoxically, conscious *without being conscious*: conscious to the brain without being conscious to the self or subject that, following Lewis-Williams and Damasio, is the project of higher-order consciousness. Like the wavelets that, on Leibniz's account, comprise the microperceptions within the macrophenomenon of the wave—and that are cited by Deleuze as an example of transcendental sensation (sensation beyond the threshold of empirical experience)[11]—these microconsciousnesses are quasi-autonomous constituents of higher-order conscious experience that can now be isolated experimentally and modulated individually.

As important and provocative as I find this conclusion, to which I will return, I want now to take stock of the more general implications of the neuroscientific exploration of visual processing and of discrete microtemporal mental images: With regard to the general question concerning images we have been pursuing thus far, what this exploration shows is that images—whether mental or material, microtemporal or macrotemporal, proto-conscious or phenomenologically conscious—are irreducibly temporal entities or processes. It is this fundamental claim that I want to place at the very core of our efforts to understand what images are in our world today: rather than their being—and indeed as the precondition for their becoming—"fixed mental" or material, images are fundamentally temporal processes or, as I will put it below, temporalizations of "light-matter."

Dynamic Material Images

It must be said, however, that, up to this point in the history of material (or "fixed mental") images, the burden of maintaining this temporal perspective on images has been borne by the mental side of the mental-material divide. Thus, it has been those critics focused on the reception and processing of material images—critics like Arnheim, Gombrich, and the Gestalt theorists—who have inscribed the temporal dimension into our appreciation of images, while our theorization of material images themselves has tended to ossify them as static entities. This remains true, I want to argue, even in the case of cinema, where static photograms are animated in a manner that makes them temporally dynamic for a perceiving consciousness. In my account of images and framing in *New Philosophy for New Media*, I emphasized how technical images like the photograph and the cinematogram are created by machinic apparatuses that impose a pregiven, static frame on a dynamic real.[12] Whereas I was concerned there primarily with the spatial reductions involved in this imposition, what interests me in the present context are the temporal reductions of the concept of the image that result from media-specific analyses of cinematographic technics. Even Deleuze's concept of the time image, to the extent that it relies on, or at least correlates with, a certain process of spectatorship (of actualization), serves to reinforce this main point. Whether it be equated with the photogram, the juxtaposition of discrete photograms, or the sequence of photograms comprising the shot, the cinematographic image remains a static enframing of the dynamic real: whatever dynamism the time image generates comes from its ability to "shock thought," to set off a virtualization of the image (a proliferation of mental images?) in the mind of the spectator.

It is only with the invention of video that the material image becomes dynamic in itself, independently of the activity of the spectator. This is a point that has been recently brought home by philosopher Maurizio Lazzarato, who writes:

> [V]ideo technology captures movement itself: not something moving in space, but the "pure oscillations" of light . . . The video image is not an immovable still set in motion by a mechanical arrangement. Instead, it is a constantly reshaping profile painted by an electronic paintbrush. It takes its movement from the oscillations of matter—it is this oscillation itself . . . [With video, we] find ourselves in the dimension of pure oscillations, the flowing of time-matter . . . one intervenes, connects to the continual process of universal change that already existed . . . One ensconces oneself in the flow. This duration could be called "real time," a duration that is unknown to film.[13]

As a technical process, video holds forth the possibility for a fundamentally new contact between perception and the dynamic materiality of the world in becoming. Video, in short, captures the "'time-matter' from which images are made." And yet, because video simply *is* the process of generating images from electromagnetic fluxes, it frames the dynamic flux in a static or at least pre-framed form. Thus, despite the fact that there literally is no video image, that the video screen is constantly refreshing (half its scan lines being refreshed at a time, 30 times per second), what it captures remains targeted toward conscious consumption, which is to say, toward a form that is synchronous with the time of consciousness. Video artist Bill Viola perfectly captures video's deeply rooted vocation for generating images when he observes that "the camera always works; there is always an image."[14]

With the development of computational systems capable of addressing sensory fluxes at the level of their distinctive microtemporalities, we now possess the possibility to create images that would be truly dynamic. Put an-

other way, we now appear to wield the potential of simulating—and stimulating—at the level of image genesis and in the form of dynamic material
images, the very process of binding that yields what Zeki and his colleagues
call "compound" or cross-modal mental images. So far, the production of
such images has occurred predominantly, if not exclusively, in the labora-
tories of neuroscientists: for example, when Zeki and his colleagues set up
multi-object experiments designed to ascertain the relative frequencies of
imaging processes for color, motion, location, and orientation, they are in
effect creating some of the world's first internally dynamic material images.
Such images are, quite literally, visualizations of the very dynamic processes
that yield images: metapictures in the dynamic environment.[15]

What I want to ask now, and to explore in the remainder of this essay, is
whether this domain of infraempirical, temporally differentiated microsensation can be addressed by artists. Can those historically exemplary makers
of visual images somehow engage with the raw material of sensation? And,
given that such engagement by definition takes place "beneath" the threshold of phenomenological consciousness—and thus prior to the synchronization that yields material images as we have conceptualized them up to
now—can artists who work on sensation even be said to create images at all?

The Cognitive Ergonomics of the Image

Let us now turn to the work of a contemporary artist who has taken the issue of microtemporal synchronization as the basis for his art production. In
a career spanning two decades, Warren Neidich has created a body of work,
and has articulated a theory of aesthetics, predicated on the operation of
"reentry," which Neidich appropriates from neuroscientist Gerald Edelman.
The basic premise of Neidich's aesthetics is that optical inventions, which
function to deterritorialize the operation of vision from its "natural" state,
contribute to the formation of what Edelman calls the "secondary repertoire," the organization of neural elements and networks facilitated by the
context in which brains develop. Because the secondary repertoire modi-
fies the "primary repertoire," the genetically inherited microbiological brain
architecture with which we are born, it must be understood to comprise
an *agent* of culture as well as a recipient of culture's impact: themselves triggered by culture, changes in the brain feed back on culture itself. Neidich
introduces the notion of "ergonomics"—initially visual and then cognitive

ergonomics—to describe the ways in which this circuit linking cognition and culture, and more specifically visual brain and optical technologies, has become subject to "artificial" control and manipulation. By means of the technical media, we engineer "phatic images" that exert an inordinate sway over our attention:

> [T]he cinematic/virtual image is an image that by its very nature calls to the brain in a more direct way . . . Its structure and its reflexiveness attract attention in superior ways than images emerging from, for instance, nature, *because they have been engineered with the human nervous system in mind.* I will refer to these images . . . as "phatic," after Paul Virilio, and to the process of their formation as "visual ergonomics," keeping in mind that they belong to a larger process that I refer to as "cognitive ergonomics" . . . these artificially contrived images compete more effectively for neural space than their natural or organic counterparts, and build sets of neural relationships or neural networks that are in a sense artificial.[16]

Most crucial in Neidich's position is the explicitly temporal basis of his understanding of cognitive ergonomics. This means that cognitive ergonomics engages directly not only with Edelman's notion of synchronization through reentry (Neidich's focus), but also and crucially with Zeki's account of the microsensory functional specialization of the visual cortex. Indeed, what explains the efficacy of material (cinematic/virtual) images is precisely how they resonate with the differentiated, quasi-autonomous microtemporalities of visual processing. Those material images that "are more vivid, seductive," and crucially "more easily resolved by the nervous system" are the ones selected for.[17] Otherwise put: their operation and efficacy as "phatic" (attention-capturing) images occurs at a more fine-grained temporal level than that of consciousness; accordingly, by the time we experience images consciously, including images (like cinematographic images) that are synchronized to the time of consciousness, we will have always already, *nonconsciously* "experienced" those aspects that motivated their selection.

In line with the ergonomic circuit linking cognition and culture, there are two elements to this selection: first, of course, there is the affinity I have just mentioned between the temporal basis of cognition and the microtemporality of the image. But there is also what, in anticipation of my following discussion, I would like to call an "atmospheric" or "environmental" element: through their connection to "technologies . . . for their distribution and dissemination" (to which we must now add, for their creation), these images enjoy a selectional advantage due to their ubiquity in the spatial and informational environments in which we live. Indeed, as Neidich sees it, contemporary material images wage a selectional struggle of their own:

> In the world of mediated images, these images compete with each other for the mediated spaces of television, billboards, magazine covers, and recently the internet. By building relations with other phatic images, either through design compatibility or dissemination, certain such images develop stronger attracting potentials. They are thus selected for in the context of this now-transformed real/virtual interface. (140)

What Neidich's account makes clear is just how much of this selectional struggle is waged at the microtemporal level: "we" choose images (or, perhaps better: images choose "us") not because they speak to our integrated conscious selves but rather because they grab our "motion" or "color" or "orientation" microconsciousnesses. Today's images, in short, speak directly to our brains.

While Neidich makes all of this patent and indeed specifically links the problem of binding to the functioning of contemporary technical media, his emphasis on cinema—he speaks, for instance, of the "cinematic brain"—has the effect of hampering the value of his work for addressing the image culture of computation. To the extent that he channels his conception of "cognitive ergonomics" through cinema as a privileged technology of image production, Neidich remains unable to engage or even to address the production of *internally dynamic* images. Instead of embedding cognition within informational environments that facilitate, but do not prescribe, the production of asubjective, microtemporal images, Neidich continues to correlate cognition with cinematic objects that function to prescribe the form for cognitive experience. In this respect, his insight would appear to be in advance of his understanding, for the microtemporal address of today's images occurs beneath and indeed prior to the formation of the image-objects so familiar to us from photographic and cinematic culture. To this we might add the very traditional split between the visual and the discursive that continues to inform Neidich's aesthetic project, despite his attention to the neurological level of image function. This split is a direct consequence of Neidich's inability to discriminate—and hence to disjoin—the dynamic basis of imaging at the microtemporal level from the objective images that populate our macrotemporally lived world. Because he can see no way to contest the sway of the artificially engineered cinematic/virtual images that today dictate the formation of our secondary repertoires, Neidich finds himself compelled to turn away from the visual and (back) to the discursive to find a viable site for aesthetic resistance.[18] Indeed, to the extent that his own work focuses on visualizing the process through which visual and cognitive ergonomics function, we can grasp the crucial role discursive intervention plays for Neidich. What, however, gets left out in the process is precisely any investment in deploying the microtemporal structure of visual cognition toward ends other than those of "efficiency,"[19] which is to say, any possibility for contesting the sway capitalist institutions exercise over the selective struggle waged by contemporary images. Faced with this situation, we would do well to recall the quite different refrain recently intoned by philosopher Catherine Malabou: *we do not know what our brains can do*. For Malabou, the only chance for us to evade the dictates of a cognitive capitalism so deviously sophisticated that it now models itself on the very operation it would seek to control (neural networking or reentry) comes by way of an investment in the *plasticity* of our brains against their *flexibility*: we need to explore neural plasticity for itself rather than as a value serving cognitive capitalism.[20] Such an injunction, I want to emphasize, also invites us to explore the microtemporal dimensions of our sensory lives as something more than a new territory for scientifically informed capitalization.[21]

The Image as Microtemporal Convergence

Through his work and his theorizing, Neidich takes a step toward such an exploration. Despite his predominant focus on the "cinematic field"— which is to say, on a kind of phatic image that has been "constructed for the proclivities of the human nervous system"—Neidich's attention to the time frame of neural subprocesses opens the possibility for a different technification of perception that would be more directly responsive to the temporal hierarchy of the visual brain, and thus to the concrete materiality of the sensory flux. "Certain kinds of temporality," notes Neidich, "may be more efficient than others in the transfer of information. There are limits to the temporal coding patterns in the central nervous system, since certain frequencies are preferred over others." To make this point, Neidich cites the work of neuroscientist Rodolfo Llinas, whose experiments demonstrate a privilege of oscillatory activity at the 40-Hz range in the process of binding.[22] Neidich then goes on to wonder whether "certain external relations could be coded more efficiently if they came close to matching the brain's inherent temporality?" (88–89). Ultimately, this speculation is brought home in relation to—and indeed by way of an implicit contrast to—those technologies of synchronization known as cinema and video. These time-machines are now understood to operate *on top of* the more fundamental time-machine responsible for neural binding: "the special temporal qualities of cinema, its 24 images per second, and video, its 30 images per second, *superimpose* another temporal coordinate system on the 40-Hz oscillatory potential system already in place" (94, emphasis added).

If we take this superimposition to indicate the substitution of an artificial, manufactured, phatic synchronization for a more primitive, arguably more "natural" one, we can readily understand what is at stake when cinema is promoted as our preeminent neurocultural institution. Put bluntly, such a promotion—at work both in contemporary "cognitive" capitalism and in efforts, like Neidich's, to theorize and potentially to oppose it—has the effect of imposing macrotemporal binding patterns on the microtemporality of neural oscillation. While such imposition may serve covertly to introduce a microtemporal selectional factor into the domain of macrotemporal experience (since some cinematic rhythms will be more in sync with this neural oscillatory pattern than others), it still shifts focus from the open potentiality of neural oscillation to the cinematic capture of this potentiality. With this in mind, we can grasp how the cinematic capture of neural oscillation works to impose a certain model of efficiency on the microtemporal domain of sensation. And we can grasp what is necessary to oppose such an imposition: a different technification of time, a technification that disarticulates the overcoding imposed by cinema in ways that can liberate neural flexibility (or plasticity) from its all-too-seamless integration into contemporary capitalist networks of efficiency.

To get a sense for how such a liberation might work, we would, I think, be better advised to invoke artist James Coupe's recent project, *Re-Collector*, than the film it remediates—and which, not incidentally, forms the main exhibit of Neidich's essay. The film in question is Michelangelo Antonioni's *Blow-Up*, that angst-ridden exploration of photography-as-reliable-deceptive-surrogate of memory that, for Neidich, allegorizes the splitting between natural and technical vision and the ergonomic superiority of the latter:

> Thomas [the protagonist of Antonioni's film] is the product of two competitive and sometimes conflicting mnemonic codification systems. One is

a product of a kind of mimesis in which similar and synchronous origi-
nalities . . . undergo a synaptic merging; the other is a product of disparate technologies teleologized around an ergonomically driven set of
relations . . . Real inputs and the networks they form will be pushed out because . . . inputs that are more ergonomically constructed and appear more
frequently will create the most efficient neural networks. The result is a brain
that is more and more a product of artificial phatic inputs. This is the predicament of Thomas.[23]

Literally unable to bridge the gap separating his two systems of vision,
Thomas undergoes a massive bodily dissolution and complete loss of the
real: he cannot reconcile the space he occupies bodily with the space captured and ergonomically reprocessed by the photographic apparatus.

Coupe's *Re-Collector* is a public art installation that generates films using Julio Cortázar's story "Las Babas del Diablo"—the source for Antonioni's film—as a template. It makes use of the dense network of surveillance
cameras installed in Cambridge, England: a set of these cameras are programmed to recognize and capture "cinematic behaviors" that correspond
to shots from *Blow-Up*. Computer vision software analyzes the captured
footage and selectively reorganizes it into a narrative sequence, based on
matches to lines from Cortázar's story. These films are modified daily, as
new footage disturbs the narrative balance; the result is a continually mu-
tating story, one that is retold each day in a way that resonates with imperceptible behavioral changes of people in public space. Following each
daily updating, the films are projected back into the city center, offering the
public a chance to interact with and modify their behavior and perhaps to
regain control of their image.[24]

In stark contrast to Antonioni's narrative of split subjectivity, what
Coupe's work offers its viewers is a chance to join in a mode of augmented,
technically distributed vision capable of "seeing" the imperceptible, of perceiving nuances of movement at the microtemporal scale. Far from trigger-
ing a conflict between human and technical modes of vision, *Re-Collector*
feeds microsensory data back into the scene of perception; it thus functions to expand human perception beyond the time frame germane to
phenomenological consciousness. Transformed into objects of the microtemporal technical gaze, our own microtemporal movements are opened
to our perception as they function to organize the constitution of images.
That explains why this experience opens onto an asubjective mode of vision
that, notwithstanding its impossibility from the "real-time" perspective of

our "natural" capacities, belongs as much to the human as it does to the machinic.

In this sense, *Re-Collector* is an exemplary instantiation of a perceptual logic of association that differs categorically from the logic underlying the phatic image and the institutions of cinema and television that support its production and dissemination. The reason is that it assembles images based on criteria that are *shared between* the microconsciousnesses of human sensation *and* the microtemporal processes of computer vision analysis, rather than criteria that characterize higher-order temporal and perceptual processes and that would be *imposed* on sensation *from the outside*, according to the protocols of a technology (cinema) that channels microsensation into consciously perceivable events. Thus, despite the cinematic appearance of the narratives *Re-Collector* produces, what it involves—or better, what it cinematically remediates—is a direct material *coincidence* between *two* microtemporal logics of sensation and computation, respectively. What, in sum, constitutes the image in *Re-Collector* is not the cinematic frame, but the contingencies of microtemporal frames of perceptibility: broken down into such microtemporal frames, cinematic images open out onto a subterranean world of microimages that are, in effect, microtemporal binding events.

For this reason, *Re-Collector* would appear to exploit precisely that direct contact with the sensory flux that Maurizio Lazzarato, following Nam June Paik, discerns in video technology:

[A]ll images produced by electronic and digital technologies are transformations and combinations (composites) of intensities, forces, fields, taking place in the flow—the electromagnetic flow in the case of video, the optical flow in the case of the telematic, the algorhythmic flow in the case of the computer. The transition from the first to the last can be defined as an increasingly forced deterritorialization. Fibre-optic cables replace copper. Lasers and silicon cables make the control and canalization of light possible and now replace the electric shock as the vector of information bound to the net. The flow of information overcomes, again, matter, and light is just a mathematic (non-discursive) language. But in all cases, the relationship between a-significant and significant flows is the most interesting as a newly introduced paradigm—the images and sound are produced by machines with matter consisting of new materials that are being endlessly and variably modulated, and from which the flows are made.[25]

What is modulated in the case of *Re-Collector* is precisely the microconscious sensory reality of visual motion perception as it is controlled, transformed, and combined by the algorhythmic flux of computational vision analysis. Again, the key point is that the criteria for selection of images—or better, for the *modulation* of the flux of "light-matter"—is *shared between* human sensory microconsciousnesses and microtemporal computational processes, rather than imposed in a unilinear direction by one upon the other.

For this reason, as a technical modulator of the matter of sensory flux, the computer never loses contact with embodied human perception. It is also why the modulation at stake here functions in a manner fundamentally different from what Lazzarato—here closely following Deleuze—describes. For Lazzarato, as for Deleuze before him, video and digital technologies take the place of the Bergsonist body as center of indetermination within a universe of images; what results is a massive deterritorialization of perception from its allegedly constraining correlation to human embodiment and habit:

> as a relation between flows of images, between different rhythms and "durations," [natural perception] is functionally guaranteed by the body, consciousness and memory, which operate as genuine interfaces, introducing a time of indeterminacy, elaboration and choice into the streaming of flows. I want to argue that video and information technologies function according to the same principle: they cut into the streaming of flows, producing an interval that allows for the specifically machinic organization of the relation between signifying and a-signifying flows. The functional relation is guaranteed here by a technological assemblage.[26]

Operating as "machines to crystallize time," video and digital technologies increase the delay between perception and reaction; in this way, they extend our power to act beyond the well-worn contractions known as habit. Yet the key question remains whether, in so doing, they sever contact with embodied sensation.

From Media Temporal Object to Sensory Atmospherics

While I have criticized Deleuze's account of the cinema for decoupling the Bergsonist center of indetermination from its source in embodied sensation,[27] and while I would extend my criticism to Lazzarato's updating of Deleuze, this argument can now—with the assistance of neuroscientific forays into microsensation—be made in a manner that more fully respects the spirit of Deleuze's conception of transcendental sensibility. To explore the affinity of the domain of sensation explored by Deleuze—sensation "beneath" the grasp of "common sense" and "recognition"[28]—with the technically catalyzed modulation at issue here, let me now turn from Coupe's *Re-Collector* to the work of German artist Tobias Rehberger. What Rehberger's work adds—and this will prove crucial for my effort to articulate a politics of sensation—is a potential for creative engagement with technically induced sensory fluxes. In contrast to Coupe's work, which excavates the *microsensory* "ground" of cinematic images, Rehberger's environments open experience to the creativity of microsensation. Thus, while *Re-Collector* proffers a divergent and microtemporal logic of association that foregrounds Neidich's point about the 24 fps of cinema being imposed on the 40-Hz timescale of sensory consciousness, Rehberger's use of light and motion creates situations that, following Gernot Böhme, we could quality as atmospheric. As direct mediations of the microtemporal domain of sensation—what Deleuze calls transcendental sensibility—Rehberger's atmospheric situations directly solicit microtemporal sensations.[29]

In a practice spanning nearly two decades, Rehberger has sought to liberate the sensory potential of mass-media fluxes from their overcoding in the form of what Bernard Stiegler has called industrial temporal objects.[30] Whereas Stiegler's position has become increasingly bleak as he seizes ever more intently on the industrialization of consciousness that occurs through cognitive capitalism's objectification of time,[31] Rehberger strives to deobjectify media fluxes, making them available for more open and creative sensory engagement. In Rehberger's atmospheric situations, media fluxes do not comprise technical temporal objects that model the flux of time for the time-consciousness of its participants; rather these fluxes are instigations to sensory engagement that place participants into direct contact with the media environment, independently of the constitution of concrete media temporal objects. In his light installations, specifically, Rehberger operates a transformation of media-light-*objects* into sensory-light-*environments*. At stake in these works and in this theoretically inflected experiential transformation is precisely the capacity for embodied human beings to experience the very matter comprising contemporary media objects—namely, light—in a manner that does not subordinate its sensory richness to the industrialized cultural end of regulating and controlling the time of consciousness. As art historian Ina Blom puts it, Rehberger does not deploy light to illuminate

Figure 1. Tobias Rehberger. *84 Year Film*, 2002. Dimensions variable. Duration: 84 jahre. Installation view: Night Shift, Palais de Tokyo, Paris. © Tobias Rehberger, 2002. Courtesy Neugerriemschneider, Berlin. Photo: Marc Domage, Paris

objects, as the "optical and metaphysical models" of the image would have it, but treats images as temporalizations of light: "images are not a function of light, but of time [or, we might better say, of 'light-time']. Images arise only as a function of the brain's ability to contract and distribute temporal matter."[32]

The digital film *84 Year Film* (2002) comprises images of all the 2.6 million colors of which the digital video projector is capable of generating over a period of 84 years. The work begins with all pixels set to display a monochrome surface and subsequently changes each pixel to the next color in the spectrum according to an algorithmic logic. What this affords the viewer is a paradoxical experience of change *without change*, change that cannot be perceived but only sensed: thus, even as she *senses* very subtle, imperceptible changes in light output, the viewer remains unable to *perceive* any distinct change in the image (unless she leaves the room for a while and returns). (See Figure 1.)

The experience of being sensorily coupled to this microtemporal process of minimal visual change in light has the effect of rendering imperceptible larger-scale changes in the image, as if attending to the microstructure of light's flux were incompatible with grasping overcoded light-images. As a result, critic Margit Brehm has observed, "no 'film' as such actually exists, . . . rather each 'image' is created in the very instant of its appearance."[33] Despite its title, then, *84 Year Film* is not a film—nor is it a technical or industrial temporal object—but rather an environment for direct contact with the microtemporal sensory flux that, as Zeki and Lazzarato have both argued, literally comprises the materiality of our experience. In this sense, it is crucial that there is some material element present "alongside" but "beyond perception": this element is still there, even when we are not looking, and even when we don't perceive any changes in image. Perhaps we can take this to be a minimal definition of a media atmosphere: an anti-object that can't be perceived, an anti-object that coincides with its sensory microstructure, that simply *is* a duration of sensation, the duration of its own sensibility. In this sense, Rehberger's de-objectification of media experience would seem to coincide perfectly with the perspective of Lewis-Williams: rather than reified as objects that circumscribe the experience of time, material images are here brought back to their point of origin in mental processes (or mental images). The key difference between the two perspectives is, of course, that this return is made possible by digital technology—specifically, by the technical capacity of the digitally programmed video projector to operate beyond the framework of human temporal experience.

Rehberger's *Shining Shining Shining* (2002) is an even more explicitly didactic work designed to effectuate the transformation of a captured media-light flux into a deterritorialized sensory-light environment. The structure of this work is simple: it involves the projection of Stanley Kubrick's film *The Shining* on two walls behind a screen. (See Figure 2.)

Rather than viewing the projected image directly, the viewer can see only the reflection of the projection, or better, can see only the projection via the reflected light it produces. In this way, the work explicitly transforms cinematic images, which are "phatic" organizations of light, into more elemental patterns of light, color, and motion that must be assembled by our brains to generate images.

Figure 2. Tobias Rehberger. *Shining, Shining, Shining,* 2002. Wall with reflecting foil, beamer, loudspeaker, DVD-player. 390 x 1360 x 920 cm. Installation view: Night Shift, Palais de Tokyo, Paris. © Tobias Rehberger, 2002. Courtesy Neuger-riemschneider, Berlin. Photo: Marc Domage, Paris

The installations *7 Ends of the World* (2003) and *All My Last Week's Desires* (2009) deploy this deterritorializing transformation of media-light-objects to effectuate connections across space and time, respectively, and thereby to create "new" experiences. The former consists of 111 lamps ordered in 9 groups and installed within an installation space. The output of these lamps is coupled with the output of the sun: as the earth circles the sun, different lamp groups are activated, shine with increasing strength, and then fade away. (See Figure 3.)

The work thus comprises "a complex solar clock" displaying the constellation of two heavenly bodies.[34] But it is also a clock functioning to link—to make simultaneous—different places around the world, as exemplified by a group of lamps that react to the opening and closing of a bathroom door in a restaurant outside Venice. Through its various configurations, the work enables its viewers to perceive cosmic simultaneities directly, as it were, through the microstructure of fluctuations of light. As Daniel Birnbaum puts it, the viewer sees the cosmos as "luminous simultaneity" (150).

In a related gesture, *All My Last Week's Desires* channels light patterns

Figure 3. Tobias Rehberger. *7 Ends of the World,* 2003. 222 glass lamps, light bulbs, bulb fittings, computer. Dimensions variable. Installation view: Sogni e conflitti. La dittature dello spettatore, 50a Esposizione Internazionale d'Arte La Biennale di Venezia, Venice 2003. ©Tobias Rehberger, 2003. Courtesy Neugerriemschneider, Berlin. Photo: Roman Mensing

from one week past into a series of light/color columns installed within a room at the Walker Center in Minneapolis. Here the suggestion is that our direct sensory contact with the flux of the real (images in Bergson's sense) can facilitate an experience of the past that is qualitatively different—more embodied and more microtemporal—than Husserlian "recollection" and its avatars (including, I would insist, Stiegler's "tertiary memory"[35]), all of which proceed through the operations of higher-order consciousness. What Rehberger's work invites viewers to sense is nothing less than the deep continuity of time that takes place at the level of, and indeed through, microtemporal processes and that accordingly underlies and informs those selected convergences that make up memory proper.[36] By mediating multiple time scales through a repetition that can only be experienced microtemporally—via the production of microconscious images—the work attests to a fundamental Being of the sensible that imperceptibly informs conscious perception and the consumption of media temporal objects.

Toward a Comprehensive Theory of the Image

By exposing the microtemporal sensibility that comprises the matter of media temporal objects, Rehberger's installations foreground a notion of the image that resonates with the work of contemporary neuroscientists. Specifically, his works return us to a moment in the ontogenesis of images prior to the division between material and mental: in a quite literal sense, they transform material media images—including paradigmatic examples of technical temporal objects—*back into* sensory accumulations that must be microtemporally assembled into mental images (Zeki's microconsciousnesses) before they can become (macrotemporal) material images proper. Put more simply, Rehberger's atmospheric light environments compel us to generate images directly on the basis of microsensation, rather than through the mediation of frames—like the cinematic frame—that capture sensation for conscious perception. What remains for us to consider is just how this resonance of Rehberger's work with contemporary neuroscientific research into microsensation might impact our conceptualization of what an image is. How, in short, must we theorize the image in order to think the microtemporal experience that comprises its very materiality?

I began my discussion by emphasizing the need for a comprehensive theory of the image, by which I mean a theory capable of addressing the *continuum* connecting mental and material images. This led me to characterize the image as a temporal process rather than a spatial/visual figure. Now that we have opened the microtemporal dimension of the image as a process of temporal binding, it is imperative that we address this *continuum* at a level beneath the threshold of recognition imposed by phenomenological consciousness. This contemporary imperative arises in the context of the shift in marketing strategy and capitalist logic that has resulted from the neuroscientific revolution: in the wake of the cognitive ergonomics underlying contemporary images, it becomes clear that material images that appeal directly to the microtemporal processes of mental imaging acquire a distinct selectional advantage. Correlated with this shift in the logic of "image capitalism" is a *broad transformation in the mode of address* that characterizes the everyday technologies on which we have come increasingly to rely: wireless devices of all sorts, including cell phones and sensor technologies, as well as computers in general, function by constituting images that largely bypass the optical. Such images can perhaps best be described as cognitive or microcognitive events, and they function typically by giving information about how to act in a given situation or by tailoring environments to facilitate certain kinds of action.

Broadening our approach in this way allows us to appreciate that what holds mental and material images together—even as both undergo fundamental shifts in temporal scale and mode of address—is nothing other than human experience. That explains why computational technologies form a complement to neuroscientific insight into microconsciousnesses and the domain of microsensation, and also why neuroscientific research couldn't occur without the aid of computation. Indeed, this appreciation for the central role of human experience (which emphatically does not mean conscious experience) has guided my decision to correlate the neuroscientific revolution in imaging with the computational revolution in media as complementary instigators of a basic rethinking of the image as temporal process. My broad aim has been to situate and to address the image within the larger context of our co-evolution with technics (what I have elsewhere called human technogenesis[37]). At the heart of this endeavor is a conviction that today's microtemporal digital technologies do not simply impact human sensory experience from the outside, but rather materialize a potentiality that characterizes sensory experience from its very origin and at its most primitive stages.[38]

While there is much that is contingent in the development of contemporary digital technologies, including elements I would attribute to the certain autonomy that characterizes the technical history of computing, my claim is that this development actualizes a potentiality that has been there from the start. Or, to be more precise, I want to suggest that the shift to the microtemporal address characteristic of today's wireless technologies and ubiquitous computational networks exteriorizes the human power of imaging in a manner that exposes not just the microtemporal domain of sensation but also the motricity underlying (and holding primacy over) perception. In this respect, I propose to add a level of specificity to the enactive understanding of perception that has been developed by Francisco Varela and his colleagues:[39] for if sensibility is rooted in motricity, as French philosopher Gilbert Simondon has insisted and as Zeki's account of microsensation implies, then enaction does not coincide with perception, but characterizes the processing of sensation at the neural level.

What is required to conceptualize the image for our age of micro-temporal computation and neuroscientific insight is a theorization that positions the human—human imagination—as a hinge between mental processing and technical networks. In his lecture course from 1965 to 1966, *Imagination and Invention*, Gilbert Simondon provides just such a theorization. As we would expect from this philosopher of the conti-nuity of individuation from the physical to the collective, Simondon's exploration develops a comprehensive account of imaging and imagina-tion across all registers of human individuation, including its apotheosis in technics. Specifically, Simondon differentiates three developmental stages of the image: a "pure and spontaneous development" in which the image figures as an "embryo of motor and perceptive activity"; a functional development in which the image "becomes a mode of recep-tion of information coming from the milieu and a source of schemas of response to these stimulations"; and an "organization of images accord-ing to a systematic mode of linkages," rooted in "affective-emotive re-tention," that yields in the subject "*an analogue of the exterior milieu.*"[40] What is crucial in Simondon's theory is that these stages of the image ex-ist in continuity not only with one another but also with the operation of invention, in which images qua mental symbols undergo a "change of organization" and a shift to a different order of magnitude. Not only does Simondon thus present a comprehensive theory of the image, but he also correlates the image, on the basis of its intrinsic dynamics, with the operation of technical exteriorization through invention.

The crucial task of unpacking the continuity linking the image in its pri-mordial, pre-objectal functioning with the passage to invention comprises the central aim of Simondon's course, as he acknowledges from the very outset:

> This course presents a theory: the aspects of the mental image that have furnished material for previously published discussions and studies do not correspond to different species of realities, but to stages of a single unique activity undergoing a process of development . . . According to this theory of the cycle of the image, reproductive imagination and invention are nei-ther separate realities nor opposed terms, but successive phases of a single unique process of genesis . . . (3)

Viewed on the basis of this dynamic process of genesis, the image cannot be reductively identified with any of its specific forms, whether these be considered mental or material images, but must be addressed as a dynamic, temporal process that is simultaneously both local in its operation (images always address and seek to resolve cycle-specific problems) and part of a broader genesis.

The Autonomy of the Image

Simondon's dynamic, genetic perspective is anchored in two crucial, correlated, and, to my mind, counterintuitive claims about the image: first, that the image operates independently from and transversally to the organism or subject; and second, that across all three of its stages, the image always reaches beyond itself, which is to say, beyond its subjective being, thereby underscoring "the primitive exteriority of images [including mental images] in relation to the subject" (7). Together, these two claims underscore the virtual amplification through which the image, in each of its stages, can be understood to include invention:

> The tendency to exceed the individual-subject [*l'individu sujet*] that is actualized in invention is . . . virtually contained in the three anterior stages of the cycle of the image; the amplifying projection of the motor tendency, prior to the experience of the object, is an implicit hypothesis of deployment in the world; the perceptual categories [*classes perceptives*] made use of by the subjective system of reception of incidental information postulate a universal application; finally, the symbolic bond of image-memories, if it expresses in a centripetal sense the attachment of the subject to the situations that have constituted its history, also and above all makes possible the operation of reversibility that converts it into a means of access to things. At each of these three stages of its genesis, the mental image is not limited by the individual subject that contains it [*qui la porte*]. (186)

It is precisely in virtue of the autonomy of the image in relation to the subject and the constitutive metastability that connects it virtually to invention that Simondon can characterize the image as having an intermediate status: between subject and object perhaps above all, but also between abstract and concrete, local and global, ego [*moi*] and world, and ultimately, mental and material.

Indeed, it is the autonomy of the mental image in relation to the subject that catalyzes not simply the genesis of the image as such, but the *bidirectional flow between the mental and material* on which I have insisted from the outset and from which the subject emerges:

As intermediary reality between the abstract and the concrete, between the ego [*moi*] and the world, the image is not only mental: it materializes itself [*se matérialise*], becomes institution, product, resource [*richesse*], and is diffused as much by commercial networks as by the "*mass media*" that transmit information. Made of consciousness but also object, its intermediate character gives it an intense capacity for propagation. . . . The circular causality that flows from the mental to the objective real by way of social processes of cumulative causality, flow also from the objective real to the mental. Every image is susceptible of being incorporated into a process of recurrence that can be *either* materializing *or* idealizing. Inserted into fashion, art, monuments, technical objects, the image becomes a source of complex perceptions that generate movement, cognitive representation, affections and emotions. Nearly all the objects produced by humans are to some degree object-images: they carry latent meanings that are not only cognitive, but also conative and affectivo-emotive. Object-images are nearly organisms, or at the very least, germs capable of coming back to life and developing in the subject. (13)

What must be emphasized here is just how closely Simondon's description of the quasi-living object-image correlates to our earlier treatment of imaging as a process operating at the level of microsensation. Indeed, Simondon's description might be taken for an account of a "phatic" image that operates not at the level of consciousness and recognition, but at the level of the microtemporal processes that form the pre-individual basis for the emergence of this level. On Simondon's account, images, in their back-and-forth flow between the material world and the mental realm, do not so much support the experience of the subject as open a coupling of organism and world that is fundamentally independent from the one performed by consciousness.

Noting just how recent a phenomenon the attribution of images to subjectivity in fact is (he says it began in the seventeenth century), Simondon emphasizes precisely that dimension of the image's autonomy that informs my appropriation of Neidich's cognitive ergonomics: its operation at microtemporal scales beneath subjectively unified experience. Indeed, Simondon insists that "even in the best of cases [i.e., cases where the image does indeed function to facilitate conscious understanding] the act of becoming conscious [*la prise de conscience*] [hardly] exhausts all the reality of this local activity. One can suppose on the contrary," he continues, "that the conscious aspects of the local activity are nearly exceptional cases of manifestation [*affleurement*] that are linked with a continuous framework; they are linked to an infrastructure [*soubassement*] that bears them after having prepared them" (4). If we take this distinction as an effort to restore the microsensory dimension of material images, we can appreciate how it brings them into line with the operation of microtemporal mental images, which is to say, with those very images that coincide with Zeki's quasi-autonomous micro-consciousnesses and that inform the ontogenesis of consciousness and any image-objects that might have emerged as its correlate.

To his general claim for image's excess over consciousness, Simondon adds a richness of metaphoric detail that serves to emphasize the autonomy of the image: thus, he suggests, images conserve "a certain *opacity* as a *foreign* population within a well-organized state . . . they appear nearly like secondary organisms within the thinking being: *parasites* or adjuvants, they are like secondary monads that at certain moments inhabit the subject and at others leave it." Throughout this shifting coexistence with and in the subject, images—and of this Simondon leaves no doubt—comprise processes that remain autonomous from unified subjective experience: "One could assume," Simondon continues, "that this character at once objective and subjective of images in fact translates this quasi-organismic status that the image possesses insofar as it inhabits the subject and develops itself within it *with a relative independence in relation to unified and conscious activity*" (9, emphasis added). What is at stake in this independence is precisely the agency of the image: its capacity to "resist free will, to refuse to let itself be directed by the will of the subject, and to present itself according to its own proper forces, *as inhabiting consciousness like an intruder who has just upset the order of a house to which he was not invited*" (7, emphasis added).

The Politics of the Image

Whether this agency be deployed to control cognitive fluxes and bring them into line with the mandates of contemporary "cognitive" capitalism (as I think happens in "cognitive ergonomics"), or, alternatively, to open up new non-subjective, pre-conscious, microtemporal levels of cognitive agency (the promise I locate in Rehberger's transformation of fixed images into dynamic sensory atmospheres), in political terms what is crucial about the autonomy of the image is the priority it lends to (asubjective, microtemporal) sensibility as against (subjective, conscious) objectal perception. Suffice it to say here that Simondon's comprehensive, genetic theory of the image, which correlates imagination and invention as transductive operations of

embodied human beings, cuts against the grain of the modern phenomenological tradition that, from Husserl to Sartre, has defined imagination and
the image as absent or unfulfilled perception, as perception with nothing
for content.[41] Indeed, it is here that we can discern the promise of neuroscientific research for rejuvenating the project of phenomenology, since
it opens access to a domain of sensory life that was necessarily bracketed
out by phenomenological research in its classical period. More simply put,
neuroscience—as exemplified by Varela's account of the Husserlian model
of time-consciousness—opens the possibility to integrate microtemporal
sensation into the domain of what is given in experience.[42] In so doing, as
I have argued elsewhere, neuroscience converges, in an altogether remarkable development, with the insights of Husserl's final research into time in
the *C-Manuscripts* (1929–34) and with the work of such disciples as Eugen
Fink and Jan Patočka. For Simondon, whom we might number with these
key disciples, image and imagination are more primitive than perception;
indeed, it is precisely because of their constitutive microtemporality that
they form the basis, the domain of transcendental sensibility, from which
perception emerges.[43]

In line with this priority (and with the general solidarity with Bergson
that, according to Jean-Yves Chateau, it expresses[44]), Simondon's theory
holds the promise of articulating a politics of images that refuses to cede
control over the organization of the sensory to the cultural and information
industries central to contemporary cognitive capitalism. Put another way,
Simondon's investment of the pre-objectal sensibility of images against the
perception of objects opens an approach to the struggle for technical control
over the time of media that diverges fundamentally from those approaches
(from the Situationists to Stiegler, and even, in a sense, all the way up to
Neidich) that focus on media technical objects as operating autonomous
syntheses of experiential time. By defending the autonomy of the sensory,
Simondon is able to correlate the image with motricity *prior* to the advent
of perception and to maintain its independence from object perception;
this fundamental correlation of image with motricity stretches from the
primordial motricity of sensibility itself (for example, the way a one-celled
organism develops a polarity *as the expression, or enaction, of its sensibility*)
to the technically exteriorized motricity afforded by today's digital networks
and ubiquitous computational environments. Indeed, the persistence of this
independence across the distinct stages of the image attests to the priority

that motricity holds as the very operator of the entire genesis that runs from the primitive, "autocinetic" image to the organized system realized through its technical exteriorization and including living imagination "as subset." In this respect, Simondon's genetic theory of the image makes common cause with Catherine Malabou's recent plea for "plasticity" as a successor to "writing," "as a new *pure historical image*": it is plasticity and not writing," Malabou insists, that "imposes itself . . . as the most adequate and most eloquent *motor schema* for our time."[45]

Given the centrality of motricity within Simondon's theory (he argues, both in the *Imagination* course and in his lectures from the year prior on perception, that motricity is more primary than sensibility[46]), it is not in the least surprising that he should choose to conclude his course with a reminder of the plastic continuity or continuous plasticity that stretches from primitive autocinesis to technicity and that renders motricity a general figure, a *pure historical image*, for thinking the transduction of life and technics today: "At the moment of its progress toward invention, the cycle of the image perhaps appears as an elevated degree of the activity of the living being considered, even in its most primitive forms, as an autocinetic system in interaction with a milieu. The autocinetic character, which is manifested by the motor initiative in the least elevated forms, translates in forms with complex nervous systems into the spontaneity of functioning that primes, *before the encounter with the object*, the cycle of the image and that culminates in invention."[47]

In conclusion, let me underscore the singularity of Simondon's contribution to the historical correlation of sensibility and technics. As I see it, a defense of the autonomy of the sensory is necessary if we are to appreciate the experiential and evolutionary significance of the convergence between microtemporal media and microtemporal cognition that has only just begun to transform how we live today. If today's social media networks, ubiquitous computational environments, and wireless digital devices are in the process of generating a new kind of image that operates through direct transduction with the microtemporal operations of human cognition and imaging, our task as cultural theorists is to find ways of addressing and theorizing this transduction without reducing it to a higher-order exchange between consciousness and perceptual object. It is precisely toward such an end—a concept of the fluid image—that Simondon's comprehensive theory of images can lead us.

FIVE

When the Ear Dreams

Dolby Digital and the Imagination of Sound

VIVIAN SOBCHACK

> What a fine ear this poet has! And what mastery in
> directing the play of the dream devices known to us as
> seeing and hearing, the ultra-seeing and ultra-hearing,
> hearing oneself seeing . . . hear[ing] ourselves listen.
>
> —Gaston Bachelard, *The Poetics of Space*

In what follows, I want to explore the reverberations and reversals of seeing and hearing suggested by Gaston Bachelard in *The Poetics of Space*,
particularly as these might resonate in the current cinematic moment. A
phenomenological investigation of the poetic *image* as it emerges and (to
use his term) "reverberates" in literary experience and enables the reader to
inhabit various "day dreams" of felicitous space, Bachelard's study only occasionally addresses the poetics of *sound*. Here, then, although also pursuing
the "dream devices" of seeing and hearing, I propose to turn the primary
visual premise of Bachelard's poetics of image literally (or, more precisely,
sonically) on its *ear*. This should be of particular interest to our contemporary and digitized moving image culture in which general, if historical,
assumptions about the phenomenology of image-sound relationships and
"seeing" and "hearing" in the cinema have become less certain, if not completely reversed. Whereas it was once a given that vision was the dominant
and most nuanced (and hence poetic) element of cinematic experience, of
late that dominance has been challenged by shifts of emphasis and attention in both sound technology and our sensorium. Thus Don Ihde writes

in *Listening and Voice: A Phenomenology of Sound*: "Our capacities for listening are changed by technological culture. . . . We have learned to listen farther, . . . extended our range of hearing, . . . [and] made technologically produced sound pervasive."[1]

Bringing together both digital sound technology and computer graphics in new forms of "ultra-hearing" and "ultra-seeing" (I've reversed Bachelard's sensory hierarchy), the films I want to investigate are eccentric to feature-length narrative cinema, even as they ultimately tell us something significant about its contemporary configuration and aesthetic tendencies. Although eccentric, however, these films are also quite familiar to most of us, appearing regularly in movie theaters all over the United States (as well as in certain locations abroad). Specifically, these are the short theatrical "trailers" produced by Dolby Digital Sound to display—and promote—their sound systems through a purposefully poetic exploration of the relations of sound and image. Created precisely as acts and representations of "ultra-hearing" and "ultra-seeing," the trailers are particularly compelling in that they not only condense but also allegorize this exaggeration of sensory experience in the space-time of rarely more (and sometimes less) than thirty seconds each.[2] Thus the Dolby trailers are purposefully oneiric—"dream devices" that constitute both an intimate and immense poetic space in which one can wonder at, as Bachelard puts it, "hearing oneself seeing . . . hear[ing] ourselves listen" (see Figure 1).[3]

There have been, to date, nine Dolby promotional sound trailers (all of which I shall describe in some detail a bit later). The first were made in the mid-1990s and the last in 2003, this after a four-year production hiatus. Some have been digitally updated and reissued and play in theaters today; others have disappeared from theatrical view; and six have now become available on DVD for testing—and celebrating—the sound systems of an ever-increasing number of "home theaters." Dolby's promotional literature and ancillary reviews tell us that the trailers "combine stunning computer graphics with state-of-the-art soundtracks," "show off the multi-channel format," "keep everything [sonic] clean and unmuddied," "help exhibitors take full promotional advantage of the name most widely associated by audiences with high-quality film sound," and, perhaps most interesting from both a rhetorical and poetic perspective, "open people's ears in a new way."[4]

We might say that what is projected in the literature—and in the theater—is a felicitous and constitutive space for, as Bachelard puts it, "an ear that knows how to dream."[5] Thus, the Dolby trailers should be of special

Figure 1. Dolby's "Train"

interest to those of us who want to focus on the poetics of sound-image /
image-sound relations in the contemporary cinematic experience. Made to
foreground sound (as well as to corporately shape it), the trailers exist as
an extreme and contemporary distillation of (to paraphrase Bachelard) "the
sonority of [cinematic] being" (xii). That is, they offer a kind of historically
and culturally qualified phenomenological reduction or "thematization" of
sound not only as it is realized in actual cinematic practice, but also as it is
conceived in contemporary digitized cinematic culture.[6] Furthermore, insofar as these trailers need to fill the screen with images as they fill the theater
with sound, they do so abstracted from the auditory constraints and acoustic conventions of feature-length narrative.

Taken together as a group, the trailers thus offer up an "audio-vision" (to
use Michel Chion's terminology) not only of how sound phenomenologically is given to and is perceived in contemporary cinematic experience but
also, and more interestingly, how that "acousmatic" perception (in which
cinematic sound is heard without its originating cause being seen on-screen)
is rendered graphically as a visible appearance.[7] Indeed, the desire to mark

sound as visible rather than the *visible as sounding* provides the main impetus for and function of the Dolby trailers. In all but the most recent of them, sound originates, dominates, and shapes the image rather than the image dominating and grounding (or anchoring) the sound. This phenomenological—and cinematic—"turn to the *auditory dimension*," as Ihde writes, is

> potentially more than a simple changing of [the relations among] variables. It begins as a deliberate decentering of a dominant tradition in order to discover what may be missing as a result of the traditional double reduction of vision as the main variable and metaphor.[8]

Furthermore, he not only points out that within a "visualist tradition" it is extremely difficult to attend to listening but also emphasizes that, indeed, "*It is to the invisible that listening may attend*" (14). The paradox of the Dolby trailers is that—as *cinema*—they must promote an attention to listening not only by sounding the invisible but also by visualizing it. In this regard, the invisible (and off-screen) "acousmatic imagination" of the Dolby trailers provides a compelling and compressed on-screen visual glossary of what are acoustically perceived to be sound shapes, sound aspects, and sound effects. (Indeed, as I first watched them, I distinctly remember wondering: "How does sound look?")

But let us, for the moment, put sound "out of the picture"—and, since this is cinema we are exploring, let us begin (as we have from the beginning) with the concrete image of a train slowly chugging its diagonal way across the screen before us. This cinematic train, however, is *not* the legendary one that arrived at the Paris Grand Café on the night of December 5, 1895, to cause its audience apocryphal panic and also trouble Maxim Gorky into writing of the event:

> It is terrifying to see, but it is the movement of shadows, only of shadows. . . . Suddenly something clicks, everything vanishes and a train appears on the screen. It speeds straight at you—watch out! It seems as though it will plunge into the darkness in which you sit, turning you into a rippled sack full of lacerated flesh and splintered bones, and crushing into dust and into broken fragments this hall and this building. . . . But this, too, is a train of shadows.[9]

While also a "train of shadows," the cinematic train I want to foreground here is a more contemporary vehicle, for all its nostalgic and old-fashioned look, and appears in one of the first and most memorable of the Dolby Dig-

Figure 2. The ghostly train dissolves.

ital promotional trailers (see Figure 2). Its appearance on the screen is, like Lumière's train, extremely brief and discrete, and constitutes the entirety of the film—however, despite similarities to its earlier forebear, this train purposefully chugs its way across the screen in a dynamic movement that runs quite literally *counter* (both in cinematic direction and function) to that of Lumière's awesome engine.

For one thing, Lumière's train was perceptibly silent. As an image, it could only be *visually* reverberant for its audience, its chuffing and chugging only *virtually* resonant—the image the source of the sound that resonated not in the theater but in the acoustic imagination of its viewers. Certainly, as we know full well from our rich sensory experience of silent cinema, this imaginative evocation of "sonorous being" is no small accomplishment by the image. Thus, when Bachelard asks, in particular relation to the poetic image, "Then how shall we see without hearing?" he responds that we cannot do so—and points to the synaesthetic experience that phenomenologically informs visuality with something more than mere visibility: "There exist complicated forms which, even when they are at rest, make a noise.

Twisted things continue to make creaking contortions."[10] Here, *the objective eye subjectively imagines sound.*

Dolby's "Train" is of another sort than Lumière's, however. It emerges not as an objectively silent image that generates sound only in the subjective imagination but, rather, as a subjectively resonant image generated by, and from, objective sound. Here, *the objective ear subjectively imagines the image.* That is, Dolby's "train of shadows" (often called "Ghost Train") comes into visible being on the screen in a temporalized, reverberant, and echoed response to an inaugural sounding-out that calls the image forth in the formal vagueness of something much like a dream or memory. Thus, while this train, like Lumière's, has an extraordinary and poetic intensity of "presence," it is less visually generated than sonically generated. Indeed, visually, this train is even more "shadowy" than Lumière's: it never quite resolves into a coherent image, a clear image, a fulsome image, or a fixed image. Rather, it exists visibly as something of an irresolute "abstraction"—without as much visible "body" as the Lumière train, without a comparable station, without passengers, and without any trace of a surrounding and contextualizing world. And thus abstracted, it figures against, and almost blends into (as Ihde describes the visual field of our imagination and memory), a "background of almost indiscernible color and extension," one that is vague, indefinite, and visibly latent or "implicit."[11]

As well, unlike Lumière's train, this ghostly engine's strained but powerful trajectory accelerates (if one can even call it that) not toward us in a threatened plunge into the darkened space in which we sit, but away from us—its great and effortful wheels chugging off into an irresolute space where it slowly dissolves into the semblance of film grain and amorphous grayish smoke from which it seemed to emerge. Furthermore, given its mythology, as it was phenomenologically perceived to "suddenly" bear down on and threaten its viewers, Lumière's train not only arrived at the station "on time" but also arrived "too soon"—whereas the Dolby train seems always to have arrived on-screen "too late," a visual echo delayed in its visible being as the trailing and fleeting "after-image" of the distant, thin, and evocative sounding of a stationmaster's timpani announcing the very departure that called it into existence. Indeed, half hidden in the shadowy grain of the image, there are a series of faint superimpositions—visual echoes—as if the great wheels were trying to temporally "catch up" with themselves and their sounding before they completely dissipated.[12]

Let us return to that sounding—and to the attentive listening it provokes. Throughout, and always in temporal motion and dynamic modulation, is the "sonorous being" of this irresolute and nostalgic train—massive to the ear and in screen size but visibly weightless, fading away and away from us as an image even as it comes into imaginative realization. As an imaginative figment—or figure—that image first emerges from the aforementioned thinnest of dream sounds unattached to the dark screen before us: a high-frequency and faint "tin-tin-tin" that, in its rhythm and pitch, gives us the merest suggestion of historically imagined departure soundings in old train stations. Then, for the briefest moment, there is a silence born of expectation—followed by the hiss of what sounds like steam and the almost simultaneous grinding of metal against metal, both sonically resolving into the heightened and intense acoustic presence of the "starting up" of an imagined steam engine. It is only then that the image emerges inaugurally from the darkness and amorphous and grayish forms that hint at—but do not become—smoke. Rather, these forms tentatively resolve into a discernible but "grainy" train engine—this in response to the sounds that audibly gather in texture and palpability to become a sonorous, highly amplified, and invisible admixture of steam, clanging metal, and sonic whines sensible as the resistances of great mass and weight. These soundings are then temporalized in an effortful chugging—their increasing acceleration and sonic mass also the very onset of their extensible fading away into a reverberant last note.

Here, what Bachelard writes of the poetic image, we might apply to this poetic sounding. From those first distant and tinny notes (for they are notes as much as they are noises):

> Murmur and clangor go hand in hand. We are taught the ontology of presentiment. In this tense state of fore-hearing, we are asked to become aware of the slightest indications, and . . . things are indications before they are phenomena; the weaker the indication, the greater the significance, since it indicates an origin.[13]

With our contemporary train, what we have is first its "fore-hearing"—and, in that brief moment of expectant silence and presentiment before the image emerges, we are indeed "asked to become aware of the slightest indications" that foretell its visibility. Indeed, as a figure emergent from and within the film's intensified soundings but never fully resolved, the train exists throughout tenuously—more as an "indication" of a train than as a phenomenal "thing." However, as Bachelard suggests, this very *lack* of resolution—the phenomenal "weakness" of the visible image—lends it greater poetic significance and points to an "origin." That origin, however, is elsewhere—neither on the screen nor in the image. Finally, then, the only material presence, however insubstantial, that actually—and palpably—enters and fills the space of the theater audience is not the imaged train but the resolution, realization, and amplified resonance of its imagined sound. A "vibrating sonorous world" emerges—and, as Bachelard suggests,

> Here to "fill up" and "plenitude" [have] a completely different sense. It is not a material object which fills another by espousing the form that the other imposes. No, it is the dynamism of sonorous life itself which . . . fills the . . . space, or better, the . . . world it assigns itself by its movement, making it reverberate, breathing into it its own life. (xiii)

It bears emphasis that these sonic reverberations neither "animate" nor "thicken" the image *as it has already been formed and given* but, instead, *cause* the image—calling it forth into visible, if tenuous, temporal being. Thus, in this context, we might quarrel with Bachelard when he writes: "Very often, it is in the opposite of causality, that is, in reverberation, . . . that I think we find the real measure of the being of a poetic image. In this reverberation, the poetic image will have a sonority of being" (xii). Indeed, Bachelard's opposition between causality and reverberation seems undone in "Train," in which the sonority of being is a priori and causes, takes precedence over, and serves as the "measure" of the visible poetic image. Less undone, however, than sensually reversed, the motivating "poetic image" here is not an image at all; it is the temporalized and reverberant "poetic sound." "Sonority of being," in this instance, emerges from the "reverberations" of an objective sounding—paradoxically inviting us, as Bachelard suggests, "to go beyond the auditory threshold, to hear with our imagination," yet this in a way very different from that solicited by Lumière's silent train (166). Seated in the audience, we find our listening activated not merely by our own imaginations but also—and acousmatically—by the auditory imagination of an "other": by an unseen "ear that knows how to dream" (166).[14] What that ear dreams is the visible image—and, as Bachelard notes, "What a fine ear this poet has! And what mastery in directing the play of the dream devices known to us as seeing and hearing" (181). Thus, "Train" ends with the self-promotion of its "fine ear," of its sensory "mastery." Indeed, once the train dissolves into grain, and the grain into the faintest trace of smoke against the dark screen,

Figure 3. *Dolby* emerges from the fog of its "Train."

the company logo emerges into visibility, shimmering first as if reflecting the gray smoke and then resolving into what became the trailers' typical shimmering gold graphic: opposing and doubled *D*s, next to the boxed text *Dolby*, both set above the word *Digital*. (See Figure 3.)

Resounding with the earliest and most silent of films while promoting the latest and loudest, "Train" may be the most cinematically—and poetically—reverberant of the Dolby trailers. Nonetheless, it is not unique, and shares visual characteristics and auditory effects found in nearly all of them. Thus, at this point, I want to indicate what can be only "traces" of the other trailers—beginning, because of its anomalous status, with the last one made, titled "Stomp" in reference to the dance troupe that appears in it. "Stomp" is the only Dolby trailer that is not computer-graphically rendered (if computer-graphically enhanced). In this regard, however sonically energetic and acoustically engaging, "Stomp" constitutes sound-image relations that are quite different from its forebears'. First, using atypical live-action cinematography, the trailer anchors sound to the image much more conventionally, emphasizing their "syncretism"—that "spontaneous and irresistible" relationship of audio-visual simultaneity that Chion sees as a gestalt "weld" of sound and image.[15] Second, "Stomp" has a much higher proportion of "sync points" ("salient" and "prominent" moments of audio-

visual synchrony) than do the earlier trailers, so that sounds (such as metallic banging and clanging) are firmly attached in a logically causal—and
conventionally "realistic"—relation to the image's specificity (such as showing dancers banging garbage can lids together) (58). Thus, although sound
is certainly foregrounded in "Stomp" (particularly percussive sound), it is
not as acousmatically imaginative and generative as it is in the other trailers;
rather, it appears generated from the physical action of the dancers seen on
the screen instead of being their inaugural and driving force.[16]

In addition to "Train" and "Stomp," the trailers are all titled by Dolby
in the most general terms: "Egypt," which sinuously and slowly moves to
music through the dark and columned interior of a vaguely ancient, empty,
and Orientalized building toward a sunlit aperture on a far wall (see Figure
4); "Rain" (sometimes called "Digital Rain"), which gives us abstract variations of water droplets and puddles accompanied by sounds that convey
crystal glass and are produced by an instrument called the "waterphone"
(see Figure 5); "City" (also called "Broadway"), which, to the sound of ro-
tor blades and heavy bass, has a helicopter diving and zooming in close-up
through a neon-lit, chiaroscuro urban setting that features a movie theater
(see Figures 6 and 7); "Temple," which slowly moves inward and upward
along the steps and toward the columns of an ersatz Greco-Roman ruin to
sounds meant to echo the empty space; "Aurora," which presents a wavy
and multi-colored curtain of light to swelling choral music (see Figure 8);
"Canyon," which, to syncopated rhythms, faint animal cries, and the sound
of wind, moves us fast and low through dark rock formations and then rises
toward a rim of blue sky (see Figure 9); and "Game," which, to mechanical
noises of revved-up vehicles, gives us computer-graphic grids and digital
game figures chasing and zapping each other in game cycles and helicopters
(see Figures 10 and 11).

Given this quick gloss, how might we begin to describe more phenomenologically the Dolby trailers as a group—particularly insofar as the reverberations of their "sonority of being" are heard and seen to imaginatively
cause or produce their visible images? I emphasize here the "imaginative"
production of images because (with the exception of "Stomp") the three
most apparent features of the trailers are, first, that sound calls the images
into being rather than emanates from them and then continues to lead
them throughout; second, that the images are in constant movement and
visible "fluctuation"; and third, that in concert with their digitized sound,

Figure 4. "Egypt"

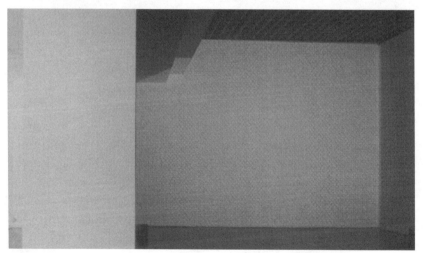

Figure 5. "Rain"

Figure 6. "City/Broadway"

Figure 7. "City/Broadway"

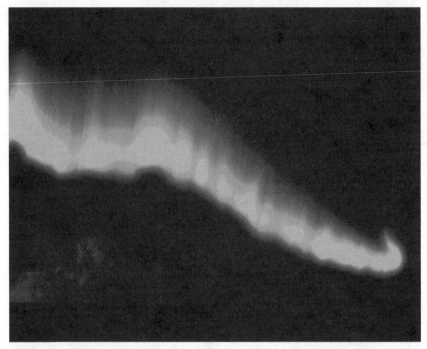

Figure 8. "Aurora"

Figure 9. "Canyon"

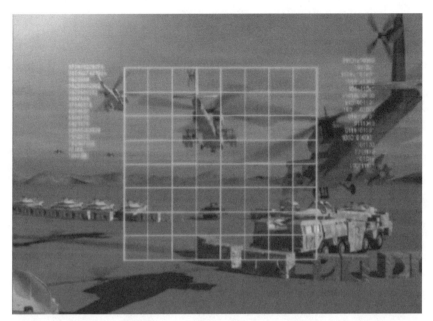

Figure 10. "Game"

Figure 11. "Game"

the images are computer-graphically "rendered" rather than photographically "reproduced."

In this regard, Bachelard points to "poets [who] often introduce us into a world of *impossible* sounds," and tells us that "it would be quite superfluous for such images to be true. They exist. They possess . . . absoluteness."[17] In the trailers, this imaginative "absoluteness" emerges not only from the paradox of hearing sounds that are impossible but also from the trailers' general *abstraction* and visual *virtuality*—both these qualities generating the phenomenological sense that despite their detail (or perhaps because of it) and constant kinetic movement (or perhaps because of it), *they do not exist in space as such*. That is, the trailers appear as "pure" image and seem to have no weight, no existential thickness, no "world." Indeed, their visible reverberations visually *echo*—neither "in sync" with nor having the palpable force of—the very qualities of the sound that inaugurates and sustains them, the sound in the theater (rather than on the screen) that, by contrast, seems more materialized, more concrete, and more present to our experience than what we see.

We might suggest that these images, however visually compelling in the moment, affirm themselves as "rendered" by sound—not only computer-graphically but also in the sense of Chion's distinction between sound "reproduced" and "rendered," this latter defined against realism as sonically conveying or expressing the feelings or effects associated affectively with the situation on-screen.[18] Here the affective "situation" is off-screen, its sonorous feelings conveyed as the *visual effects* of its sounding (and not the reverse). In this regard, it is worth noting that taken solely as the kinetic display of computer-graphic imagery, the trailers are hardly groundbreaking. We've all seen the light shows, the zooming, humanly impossible, ersatz camera movements, the quasi-atmospheric yet sharp-edged chiaroscuro many times before. Thus, the trailers are exciting to watch and often applauded by audiences less for their computer-graphic bravura than for their primary function of visibly articulating sound—and, more important, of visibly imagining and articulating *sound as such*. (See Figure 12.)

But before we look at these visible articulations of "sound as such" (and what such a phrasing might mean), we need to hear and describe the acousmatic sounds and soundings that inform them. Except again for "Stomp," in which the emergence of both sound and image is highly synchronized, all the trailers begin only with sound and a darkened screen. All are significantly amplified and acoustically "unmuddied" and bear only metaphoric

Figure 12. Dolby writes itself into the walls of the canyon.

relation to sound as we normatively engage it in daily life—(at least when we are unattached to contemporary devices such as the Walkman and iPod). In most of the trailers, music and sound effects are combined and synthesized so that it is difficult to tell them apart-yet, equally often, "special" sound effects are heard as particularly discrete and isolated so as to show off the multi-channel format that uses all of the six speakers placed around the theater. (In "Canyon," for example, a sound almost like wings fluttering is foregrounded before, during, and after an "almost image" of something flying that flits too rapidly across the screen to be clearly "figured out," and the sound of "wind" is particularly exaggerated at the trailer's end.) Furthermore, all the trailers (including "Stomp") create ongoing contrasts between deep thrumming bass and tinkling high-frequency sounds. Music and sound effects also tend to be syncopated, with dramatic percussive background notes emphasized: drums, cymbals, bells, tuned crystal glass, and, in the high-frequency range, violins. In some of the trailers—such as "Egypt" and "Canyon"—the music's rhythms mark it as exotically non-Western. Yet mechanical noises and "electronic" sound effects are prominent and discrete even in these more "lyrical" trailers, where they prominently stand in for "natural" sounds such as water, wind, and bird or animal calls. These mechanical and electronic sounds are particularly foregrounded and fill the soundscape not only in "Train" but also in both "City" and "Game," in which we hear the sonic "rendering" of helicopter blades and the simulated whizzing and zapping of computer-graphic vehicles. Also, in almost all of the trailers, there are frequent "tinkling" sounds in the high register, and the majority end with an "upswelling" of sound that then "fades away"— indeed, this sound dynamic constitutes the entirety of the early "Aurora" trailer (recently enhanced and re-released for theatrical exhibition).

Throughout, emphasis is on sound emergent, moving, swelling, and fading, on sounds separated, spatialized, and amplified to create an intensified sense of acoustical presence and sonic immersion. Nonetheless, from a phenomenological perspective, "immersion" needs to be qualified here. Despite the emergence, swelling, and fading, and despite what can only be called the frequent "simulation" of echoes and reverberation, this is not the phenomenological sound of the concert hall that one feels is palpably filled with—and inhabited by—the plenitude of a sound gestalt in which one is immersed with others. With the trailers, sound certainly seems palpable— this, very much a function of amplification.[19] At the same time, however, it also seems *contained*, indeed *framed*.[20] That is, while the amplified swelling sounds fill what seems like a vast space, that space seems nonetheless discrete and doesn't precisely coincide with—even as it intersects with—the actual space of the theater in which we sit. The space of the sounding, particularly in its discrete elements, seems "deep" with a depth that has no discernible parameters, and yet its breadth seems to have sharply defined edges and seems absolutely bounded in its clarity, its lack of sonic "leakage." Furthermore, foregrounded in their clarity, the more isolated sounds and effects move from place to place (and speaker to speaker) around the listener and the theater but don't so much "fill up" the space continuously as "describe" it in a kind of discontinuous "mapping."

In *Audio-Vision*, Chion considers the sound qualities of these promotional trailers—albeit very generally and briefly, and with specific reference to THX and its "quality control"–driven "regulation" of theatrical sound delivery.[21] In terms of their promotional trailers, however (albeit their different kinds of visual imagination), THX and Dolby have similar sound qualities—both creating, as Chion puts it, "a *superfield*, a general spatial continuum," in which the screen is only one element in a much broader spatial field.[22] After describing THX's trademark upswelling "Deep Note"—thirty seconds of "a bunch of glissandi falling toward the low bass register, spiraling spatially across the room from speaker to speaker, ending triumphantly on an enormous chord" (100)—Chion goes on to note that, along with their "overwhelming volume," two characteristics of such trailers "typify current taste":

First, the bass sound that the glissando ends on is *clean of all distortion and secondary vibrations.* . . . What the demo short is doing . . . is showing off the technical capacity to *isolate* and *purify* the sound ingredients. Second, one feels *no trace . . . of the reverberation* that normally accompanies . . . loud sounds in an enclosed space. . . . The sound event remains as *clear* and *distinct* as if we heard it on . . . a compact home stereo. . . . The real size of the auditorium is immaterial, *amplification no longer has a true scale of reference.* (100–101; emphasis added)[23]

Chion is not kind to today's digitized theatrical sound systems, and certainly would seem to challenge my emphasis here on the Dolby trailers' poetic "reverberation"—indeed, on digital reverberation of any kind.[24] His descriptions are damning—if, from an objective acoustical perspective, accurate. Initially summarizing the characteristics of Dolby and THX, he points to their "stable sound, extremely well defined in high frequencies, powerful in volume, with superb dynamic contrasts, and also, despite its strength and the probably large theater space, a sound that does not seem reverberant at all." But then he continues:

New movie houses . . . have indeed mercilessly vanquished reverb. . . . The result is that the sound feels *very present* and *very neutral* and suddenly one no longer has the feeling of the real dimensions of the room, no matter how big it is. So what results is the *enlargement, without any modification in tone,* of a good home stereo system. (100; emphasis added)

Ultimately, Chion feels, we no longer hear and are part of what once was the "*collective* sound" heard in the movie theater; instead, we're provided with "inflated *personal* stereo sound" (101; emphasis added).

Certainly, Chion is not wrong in his acoustical descriptions. Indeed, in various ways, the trailer images and their "scenarios" affirm his sense that we have moved from the space-filling and plenitudinous reverberations that provided the collective sound of previous theatrical experience to a paradoxical state in which cinematic sound, on the one hand, inscribes a larger, more amplified, and encompassing "superfield" and yet, on the other, is reduced to the dimensions of an extremely personalized and privatized phenomenon.[25] In regard to this paradox, however, we might conceive of how "reverberation" can mean something quite other than Chion's objective acoustic description would allow. If we follow Bachelard poetics instead, qualities of spatial expansion, amplification, vastness, and immensity are not phenomenologically incompatible with "intimate" space—and, indeed, they may provide the large and often "cosmic" or "elemental" dimensions that allow for a site of less objective reverberation and resonance than the architectural theater: that is, the "intimately immense" space that allows for the internal reverberations of *reverie*. The Dolby trailers' abstracted imagery; their movement, which, however kinetic, is generally linked to no visible body-subject and has no fixed object; and their frequent visible evocation of an elongated but fragile temporality are particularly telling here—these characteristics figure most prominently in the "empty" architectonic ruins of "Egypt" and "Temple" and the "timeless" rock formations of "Canyon," but are also present in the "cosmic" imagery of "Aurora," the irresolute "ghostliness" of "Train," and the heightened "slow motion" of "Rain." Thus, in concert with the privatization, intensification, and amplification of digitized sound, the digitized imagery renders not only the immensity, intimacy, and heightened detail of reverie but also the surrounding vagueness of its internalized and hermetic space. Here, as if in the computer game of "Myst," one is *alone* in the sounding world—encountering and meditating (even if only for thirty seconds) on traces of time emergent and time past, on temporality sounding itself out.

There is also, however, another kind of internalization—and privatization—of sound at work in the trailers. Perhaps best exemplified by "City" and "Game," but present in all, this is a sound internalized as a sounding not only within the space of the theater, but also within the space of the listener's *body*. This is a most compelling—and subjective—form of objective reverberation. As Ihde tells us: "As an exercise in focal attention, the auditory dimension from the outset begins to display itself as a pervasive characteristic of bodily experience. Phenomenologically, I do not merely hear with my *ears*. I hear with my whole body. My ears are at best the *focal* organs of hearing."[26] And Sean Cubitt, in *Digital Aesthetics*, elaborates:

> We do not, and it is impossible to, distinguish between the vibration of the air, the vibration of the eardrum and the bones (the feet, after the ears, are our most sensitive receptors, especially of bass notes; the collarbone and the chest respond to more airborne sounds). . . . Sound events create a space with no respect for the sacrosanctity of the epidermis. . . . At the same time, sound source and sound perception are physically connected by air, proximity, and hearing. . . . The phenomenological interpretation of object and subject is far more difficult to undo in aural than in visual arts.[27]

The thunderous and abrupt sounds of "Game" and particularly of "City" with its crashing percussive and, dare I pun, "cymbalic" pronouncement echoed on the theater marquee as "The Sound of the Future"; the deep and constantly modulating bass of imagined helicopter rotors moving down and inward and around and up in acoustical and visual space; the sheer noise thundering from the speakers to cover up the gap between them all reverberate in an amplified and substantial existence that would seem to run counter to Chion's description of digital sound as non-reverberant. The reverberation here, however, is of another kind. That is, it is not objectively inscribed in the sound but, rather, comes into existence subjectively—locating and amplifying its sonorous being in the listener's whole body.[28]

In these thunderous percussive trailers, as contrasted with others, reverie is not a phenomenological option. Temporality is not perceived as elongated or cosmic—although it is certainly elemental in its extraordinarily amplified immediacy and presence. Indeed, its presence and "present-ness" are felt in the *doubling* of its "here-ness"—sound resounding through and amplified both outside and inside our being. We thus reverberate with an *accelerated temporality* and, more specifically, in an *accelerated present*, in a sounding that quite literally quickens our blood and the very internal tempi of our physical—not meditative—existence.

In both their elongated and accelerated modalities, then, the trailers reverberate with and intensify sound as an embodiment of the sense of time. But, however hermetic, this is not time in the abstract. As Cubitt suggests: "Sound as an art of distance, of space and time, is an art of *movement*."[29] Indeed, in the auditory dimension, sound *is* movement and time. And Ihde tells us that sound is "a gestalt . . . experienced as a succession within the span of duration."[30] Describing this temporal gestalt as essential to even the most ordinary auditory experience, he writes:

> When I listen to auditory events there seems to be no way in which I can escape the sense of a "coming into being" and a "passing from being" in the modulated motions of sound. Here temporality is not a matter of "subjectivity" but a matter of the way the phenomena presents itself. I cannot "fix" the note nor make it "come to stand" before me, and there is an *objectivelike* recalcitrance to its "motion." (94)

In the Dolby trailers, we can *see*, then, how sound *hears* and then *imagines* itself temporally sounding. We are in the audible presence of a vision that is constantly moving, "coming into [visible] being" and "passing from [visible] being." Thus, as sound theorist Philip Brophy notes, "Time is not only a sequence of events but also a state of transition [and] morphological development."[31] Here, in the trailers, motion itself is intensified, and no "thing" can be made to "stand" fixed before us because of the constant movement. In all but "Stomp" (where the cinematographic camera is also always in motion, panning right across the moving dancers in an uncharacteristic horizontal movement), the trailers' virtual camera moves sinuously through, abruptly up and down and inward—but it never stops (at least until we see the Dolby logo). Furthermore, it is important to emphasize (because it is something we take for granted and never think about) that the movement as such, while experienced as overwhelmingly present and kinetically powerful, is—like sound itself—*immaterial*. Thus Steven Connor writes:

> I say that certain kinds of sound belong not to the order of ostension which dominates the image—in which everything is à voir, to be had by and made clear to the eye—but to an order of mutative commixture, characterized by the encounter and transformation of imaginary substances. . . . Sound is the realm of metamorphosis.[32]

In this regard, the sonorous being of the trailers' inaugural sounds always dreams its own visible realization in relation to movement, modulation, morphological transformation, and flux. Chion also touches on this entailment of temporality and movement when he speaks of "*visual microrhythms*," and points to "rapid movements on the image's surface caused by things such as curls of smoke, rain, snowflakes, undulations of the rippled surface of a lake, dunes, and so forth—*even the swarming movement of photographic grain itself*, when visible." (Here, we are brought back again to "Train" and its computer-graphic simulation and dynamics of photographic grain.) As if describing the visual microrhythms of Dolby's "Aurora" or "Rain" or some of the very early and abstract THX trailers, Chion continues: "These phenomena create rapid and fluid rhythmic values, instilling a vibrating, trembling temporality in the image itself. . . . It is as if this technique affirms a kind of *time proper* to sound cinema as a recording of *the microstructure of the present*."[33] Elsewhere, he speaks of certain filmmakers who are "visualists of the ear," and who make "light flutter, vibrate, murmur, twinkle on all kinds of occasions." From all this tremulous movement, he suggests, "we get the feeling that this visual volubility, this luminous patterning is a transposition of *sonic velocity* into the order of the visible" (134; emphasis added). Here, in terms of the trailers and this "sonic velocity" transformed into light and "the order of the visible," we might refer to

"City" with its abrupt and thunderous flashes and light-saber helicopter blades as exemplary, but Chion goes on to suggest that this "sonic velocity" drives contemporary "action" films. "In these movies," he writes, "matter—glass, fire, metal, water, tar—resists, surges, lives, explodes in infinite variations, with an eloquence in which we can recognize the invigorating influence of sound on the over-all vocabulary of modern-day film language" (155). Thus, we might well understand the contemporary primacy of action films and their often criticized lack of narrative or character complexity as more sonically inaugurated and driven than previous narratives, "sonic velocity" the equivalent of—and equivalent in importance to—visible "spectacle."

Untethered to narrative, however, unanchored to the sonic gravity of specific sounds anchored firmly to things fixed in the phenomenal world, the Dolby trailers abstract and intensify the sonic velocity and visualizations that usually only punctuate narrative films and serve as their spectacular moments of auditory and visual synchrony and synchresis. Indeed, these primarily "punctual moments" (that serve as the "punctum" of a less spectacular narrative "studium") *are* the Dolby trailers. In them, light vibrates and, in chiaroscuro, comes and goes; and gases, smoke, water, and particles of atmospheric dust visually echo and double the insubstantial yet intense *presence* of sound, movement, and morphological development in their most essential temporal and visual forms. (See Figure 13.) In this, we might well see the Dolby trailers as both an example and an allegory of what Brophy, writing about sound and animated film, calls the "illusion" of "the proto-molecular dissolution of two communicative modes into a single technological phenomenon."[34] Thus, despite a certain lack of reverberation and polyphonic synthesis in the objective digitized sounds Chion decries, we have instead a polyphony of sound as it subjectively imagines and "figures" itself out in the image. Here, then, in the relationship between sound and image in the trailers, there is indeed a blurring of communicative modalities that, as Brophy says of music, "are not only juxtaposed, sequenced or related to one another but are also able to *be evoked within and from one another* via the practice of polyphony, transposition, and modulation" (81).

In sum, in relation to the way in which sound dreams its own reverberant image in the Dolby trailers, I would suggest it functions poetically as more akin to allegory and to certain tropological forms than to mere illustration. The images we see in flux on the screen *parallel* sound qualities in a form of hierarchical *simile* ("this is *like* that") that does not collapse into the syn-

Figure 13. On-screen speakers emerge as part of the "Game."

chronic substitution of *metaphor* ("this *is* that"). The images also *extend* and *elaborate* sound qualities, hyperbolizing and generalizing them into *allegorical* significance. (In "Egypt," "Temple," and "Canyon," for example, restless movements through a "timeless" and "elemental" architectural space evoke, as Brophy says in a related context, "a feeling of imminence, of the suspense of something on the verge of happening, of the erotics of *eventfulness*" [86; emphasis added].) Finally (and quite significantly), the trailers' images *fill in* and *substitute* not for another figural form but for a *lack* in certain qualities of their digitized sound—but they do so *in a different modality*. Hence they function as a form of *catachresis*, sometimes called false and improper metaphor. Used when no proper, or literal, term is available, catachresis is differentiated from metaphor insofar as it forces us to confront, as Paul Ricoeur puts it in *The Rule of Metaphor*, the "failure of proper words, and the need, the necessity to *supplement* their deficiency and failure."[35]

Imagined and inaugurated by sound, the Dolby trailers come into being not only to promote the wonder, power, and difference that marks digital sound, but also to supplement its "lack" and "failure." Indeed, they present us with audio-vision both objectively testing and subjectively dreaming its own possibilities and suspecting its own limits. In this regard, they are exceptional texts, for they dream these possibilities and test these limits within a *digital horizon*. And it is here that they not only assert their presence but also their prescience. If, as announced on the theater marquee in "City," this is "The Sound of the Future," we should listen to and look at it closely, for it tells us much about the contemporary trajectory and dynamics of what we have come to call the "cinema." Thus, as Connor suggests: "The new sound films perhaps look beyond their condition of film: look forward to or begin to sound out the more complex and turbulently convoluted worlds of matter and information, meaning and noise in the emerging sensory orders that may be coming to life."[36]

In his prescient essay "The Animation of Sound," Brophy points to film looking beyond its condition of film to something else. Distinguishing significant modal differences between live-action and animated film, he contrasts the "cinematic apparatus" with what he calls the "animatic apparatus": "a means for constructing film (for and by both maker and audience) . . . based on an understanding of the *processes of animation* rather than the *principles of animism*."[37] That is, "the animatic apparatus is a machine derived not from animism but from the perceptual model of dynamism" (69). Dormant since the early 1900s, the animatic apparatus reemerged in the 1980s with the advent of both the spatial liberation afforded by Steadicam and the gravity-defying dynamism of computer animation. Unlike the cinematic apparatus, bent on constituting sequences and scenes from fragmented shots, the animatic apparatus is "interested in frames, images, cuts and parts more as events and occurrences than elements or components." It is also "attuned more to the speed and tempo of fragmentation than the formal sequencing or structural organization of fragments" and is concerned with film "more as a transition than a process" (68). Such a visual "animatics" thus "dissolves" the discretion of image and sound—if not at the surface, then certainly at the "proto-molecular level" (74).

This emphasis on the image as an event of sound and the advent of sound as an occurrence of image, this attunement to the speed and tempo of "dissolution," and this concern with transition and the "proto-molecular" also inform the poetic and allegorical work of the Dolby trailers. With the exception of "Stomp," which, however spectacularly, remands us to the photographic and profilmic temporality and soundings of the real (even if the "real" of a Gap clothing advertisement), the Dolby trailers emerge not from the cinematic apparatus but from the animatic apparatus. With the digital limitation as well as the digital imagination of their sounding, they transubstantiate their soundings into figuration that visually reverberates when and where the digitized sound cannot, to create a poetic "sonority of being." In so doing, they resonate not only with the dreams of a digitized ear but also with the reality of contemporary cinema.

SIX

Imaging Sound in New Media Art

Asia Acoustics, Distributed

TIMOTHY MURRAY

> We also have sound-houses, where we practice and
> demonstrate all sounds, and their generation. We have
> harmonies which you have not, of quarter-sounds, and
> lesser slides of sounds. Diverse instruments of music
> likewise to you unknown, some sweeter than any you
> have; together with bells and rings that are dainty and
> sweet. We represent small sounds as great and deep;
> likewise great sounds extenuate and sharp; we make
> diverse tremblings and warblings of sounds, which in
> their original are entire. We represent and imitate all ar-
> ticulate sounds and letters, and the voices and notes of
> beasts and birds. We have certain helps which set to the
> ear do further the hearing greatly. We have also diverse
> strange and artificial echoes, reflecting the voice many
> times, and as it were tossing it: and some that give
> back the voice louder than it came; some shriller, and
> some deeper; yea, some rendering the voice differing in
> the letters or articulate sounds in trunks and pipes, in
> strange lines and distances.
>
> —Paul D. Miller (a.k.a. DJ Spooky), "Algorithms:
> Erasures and the Art of Memory"[1]

Imaging sound? On its own terms, sound might seem incongruous with image, if not with the activity of imaging. Put simply, sound is something heard while image is something seen. Sound can permeate the body as if from within, minus the geometric ordering of image. Sound occurs whether from near or far, inside or outside. And we can easily build sound-houses where the naturally recorded sound, say, of wind and waves can reverberate from within as if surrounding the listener without the distracting mediations of visual representation. Here the force of wind or the crash of wave might seem to happen naturally without the addition or supplement of imaging that is required in order to achieve the visual representation of sound or its effects.

Yet, the very artistic sound-houses described in the epigraph by DJ Spooky, "where we practice and demonstrate all sounds, and their generation," are necessarily multimedia environments. Such soundings happen within the confines or surrounds of built spaces. The reception of sound is contingent not only on the architectonics of space but also on the very same procedures of representation that bring mediation to the fore when imaging enters the picture. "We represent and imitate all articulate sounds and letters," says the DJ, in a way that muddies the purity or clarity of sound thought as natural. Indeed, the sound-house itself lends pitch and echo to voices and notes in a way that can "give back the voice louder than it came." The representation or articulation of sound lends to the acoustic field the textures of rhetoric and hermeneutics through which the voice differs in letters and articulated sounds.

Put similarly by Jean-Luc Nancy, who philosophizes on the shared space of sound and meaning, the latter, meaning, "is made of a totality of referrals: from a sign to a thing, from a state of things to a quality, from a subject to another subject or to itself, all simultaneously. Sound is also made of referrals: it spreads in space, where it resounds while still resounding 'in me.'"[2] Nancy's writings on both imaging and listening may be helpful in positioning sound as central to any consideration of the philosophy of the image. In two successive volumes, *À l'écoute* (2002) and *Au fond des images* (2003), he foregrounds resonance, resounding, and the correlative distension of form as philosophical events that conjoin the visual and the audible in the "function of the image." As the carrier of both "intimate force" and "intensity," the image, even when musical, choreographic, or cinematic, does not so much "represent" as "activate" and "intensify" representation and its "touch."[3] It is this "immaterial" force that lends the image its "impalpable nature" and that constitutes that which it "images." To image sound, in this context, would necessitate activating the intransitive verb favored by Nancy, "to image" neither "to illustrate" nor "to imagine" but "faire l'image," to lend touch, intensity, and force to what is by definition incorporeal, to what lies solely neither in material nor in its materialization (126–27).

One reason for approaching the philosophy of the image via the contact zone of "imaging sound" is to reflect on the important legacy of immateriality and its variations at the core of experimentations in art. This is particularly true in the last fifty years of multimedia projects whose aim is to stretch and distend the limits of the audio-visual. For Nancy, the promise of the immaterial lies in the artistic experimentation with the oscillation between sound and image, cinema and video, image and text that occludes the distinction between "the emission of sense and the reception of form" (137). Understood by Nancy to range in form from painting to poetry and from theater to video, immaterality allows for "the expansion of sensation" at the expense of signification every time a poem or a video "images forcefully" in sonorous and visual matter (133–34).

Of course, Nancy is not the first French thinker to champion immateriality as the foundation of a new linkage of philosophy and the audio-visual. In 1985, Jean-François Lyotard staged his exhibition *Les Immatériaux* at the Centre Pompidou in Paris as a collaborative celebration of the productive "technological stain" of immaterial emanations from the early free software movement, video installation, the Minitel, and poststructural philosophy. Highlighting conceptual and electronic artworks of an almost virtual kind, from sound to work created on early home computing devices, Lyotard's curatorial initiative derived from the philosophical imperative of embracing artistic "immaterials" that challenge modern philosophical confidence in the subject's analytical control over objects in time and space. And well before that, literally fifty-one years to the date of this writing, 3 June 1959, Yves Klein presented his lecture *The Evolution of Art Toward the Immaterial* to the Sorbonne in which he positioned "immateriality" as what he had in common with multimedia artist Jean Tinguely. Klein's goal was "to create an ambience, a pictorial climate that is invisible but present in the spirit of what Delacroix in his journal called 'the indefinable'" or what Klein termed in his essay "the force of attraction."[4] Interestingly, Klein's featured example was from his monotone symphony of forty minutes of electronic sound, whose length was scripted "to show [*faire voir*] the desire to overcome time" (135). Nancy takes this linkage of electric sound to temporality one step further by locating "sonorous time" as the very immaterial stuff of expansion and resounding as "a present in waves on a swell, not in a point on a line."[5]

Asia Acoustics

While Nancy stops with video in his consideration of new media platforms of imaging, I propose that consideration of recent acoustic experiments in the new media environment might provide an immaterial realization of these very "waves on a swell," as they both perform time and embody the digital condition of imaging sound itself. Consider the interesting intervention on imaging acoustics made by the installation *Life: fluid, invisible, inaudible*, which was installed in 2007 at the InterCommunication Center (ICC) in Tokyo. This tremendously ambitious and fascinating interface of the visual arts and sound was the result of a collaboration between the electronic musician Ryuichi Sakamoto, a founder of Yellow Magic Orchestra, and the video artist Shiro Takatani, who was one of the original members of the celebrated artistic collective Dumbtype. In this innovative installation, which so successfully solicits participants "to-be-with-it" for extended periods of concentration, participants enter something of a sound-house in which nine acrylic water tanks, three feet by three feet and approximately nine inches thick, hang suspended from the ceiling. The thin surface of water inside the tanks pulsates with varying thicknesses of fog and undulations catalyzed by ultrasonic waves generated by pumps installed in the corners of the tanks. Here the sound of water's motion itself constitutes the fabric of the visual field because these foggy water boxes function as screen surfaces for varying silent video sequences that are projected from above each one and that are accompanied by electronic sound and narrative tracks mixed by Takatani. Both the video and sound mixes are generated, somewhat randomly, from a server linked to all of the projectors. Almost as if following the leads of DJ Spooky and Yves Klein, this installation seems to articulate the widest variety of sounds and letters, not to mention the voices and notes of beasts and birds. Adding to the mix is the mechanics of the environment that requires participants to lie with their backs on the floor in order to view the screens suspended above them. That *Life*'s diverse, strange, and artificial echoes give resonance to cross-cultural footage foregrounding the fraught histories of Eastern and Western exchanges in science, art, letters, and war thus lends to this installation a pitch much shriller and deeper than those found in the sound-houses of the opening epigraph. *Life*'s image-sound montages vary from medical scans and shots of everyday Japanese culture to Western file footage from World War II and clips from weighty films such as *Hiroshima mon amour* that reference the Holocaust. It is characteristic of *Life* that its sonorous time stretches the boundaries of linear history in a multimedia sound swell of a montage of the force of attraction, both past and present.

The cross-cultural mélange of *Life*'s mixed-media montages, whose sound images surround the visitor in a swell of East/West intensities, couldn't be more different from the cultural context of the Spooky sound-house. The opening epigraph was not written but only cited by Paul D. Miller, the bearer of the pseudonym DJ Spooky, from a text composed by a cultural ancestor from 1627, Francis Bacon, who described the sound-house in his utopian treatise *The New Atlantis*. I wish to call attention to the contestatory framework of Bacon's sound-house, which is situated as but one ideal environment in the Society of Solomon's House, "the noblest foundation . . . that ever was upon the earth."[6] Framing the description of the sound-house is Bacon's written portrait of the king Solamona, who founded the Society in keeping with the empathy of his laws, such as those pertaining to harboring strangers, which stand in contrast to those of its cultural other, China, whose application of a "like law against the admission of strangers without license" is, writes Bacon, "a poor thing; and hath made them a curious, ignorant, fearful, foolish nation" (244). While China serves as the template for Solamona's rules, it provides the ignoble contrast to inscrutable good. The irony of Bacon's sound-house, when considered from the global context of our multimedia aesthetic, is that it is situated in a utopic land that remains free of the cultural pitchiness of something peculiar to China and its neighbors.

While this scapegoating of Asia is fascinating and very much worth keeping in mind for its historical resonance, it fortunately failed to carry over into more contemporary discourses on sound and its experimental extensions in the visual field. On the contrary, I wish to suggest that the experimental importance of Asia Acoustics lies at the heart of any philosophical consideration of developments in imaging sound and its multimedia installation. In Klein's lecture to the Sorbonne, for instance, he prefaces his passage through the dematerialization of sound with an analogy of how "the Orientals" have for years transformed hierarchic rituals of *métier* (such as painting or martial arts) into "effective dynamic reality."[7] While the Asian influence on his acoustic practice is more procedural than practical, he follows a long line of performers, from Artaud to Debussy to Glass, whose formal experimentation derives from their interface with Asian cultural practice. As noted by Susan McClary, who is recognized as a founding proponent of the "New Musicology,"

> Debussy was just the first of a distinguished line of Western composers drawn not only to Asian music practices, but also to the philosophies and theologies that sustain them. . . . [and who] featured gamelan-inspired textures or foregrounded the recitation of Hindu mantras in their work. The list would also include a virtual *Who's Who* of 1960s minimalism: La Monte Young, Terry Riley, Pauline Oliveros, Laurie Anderson and Philip Glass. Thus, a colonialist enterprise that set off to impose European values on the rest of the globe also produced the reverse effect, as an increasing number of the West's most creative artists—weary of what they perceived as the cul-de-sac of the European tradition and its attendant ideologies—jumped ship. Several of these went far beyond the simple imitation of alien musical styles: compelled first by the non-violent and non-linear cyclic sound-patterns they heard, they eventually converted to Buddhism.[8]

While perhaps not a convert, John Cage also frequently turned to Buddhism to help present his experimental relation to sound and his beloved silence. When sound approximates the emptiness of silence, he writes, "then things—sounds, that is—would come into being of themselves. Why is this so necessary that sounds should be just sounds? There are many ways of saying why. One is this: In order that each sound may become the Buddha."[9] More recently, this cultural resounding of Buddhism has gone both ways, as made particularly evident by Yehlin Lee, one of the winners of Taiwan's 2005 Yageo Sound Art Prize, who describes his sound piece, *Countless Count*, as inspired by the Avantamsak Sutra in an attempt "to escape from the linear perspective of earthly experience by freezing the moment of the sound life when appearance turns to annihilation, or by stretching that moment into an endless flow . . . like the tides and waves in the boundless ocean."[10]

Although probably not sharing the worldview that gave rise to the "waves on a swell" that figure Nancy's "sonorous time," it is precisely such a formulation of what McClary calls the "cyclic repetition" of Asian music that may appear to constitute the global flow of global sound art and installation. This celebration of cyclic repetition, which aims to fuse nature with its sound and image, tends to be the focus of two varying strategies of exhibition in more recent installations in which abstraction joins with realism to extend the participatory boundaries of natural repetition. In a group installation featured in the 2007 exhibit on Water at 21_21 Design Site in

Tokyo, censors captured the movement of visitors to enhance the audio-visual environment of the sound of waves. As the room ebbed and flowed with the passage of visitors who moved or stood in different locations, an abstract visual stream grew and morphed the geometric lines appearing on one wall of the room in a way that mapped the flow of visitors through the sonic field of waves. The more motionless the user remained in contemplation of the surround sound (we could imagine the resounding of "meditation" here), the quieter the visual noise on the wall, as if a performance of the immobility constitutive, for Nancy, of the image and its "distension of a present of intensity."[11] A contrary strategy is employed by the Taiwanese artist Yi-Chieh Chen for his video *La Mer*, whose projected single-track image of waves morphs from realism to depictions of sound waves, while remaining grounded in the abstract sounds of a synthetic track. The digital video's opening sequence of geometrically balanced waves arriving on land becomes increasingly pixilated and broken up through the exposures of the digital data field underlying the illusion of realistic video grabs of nature. The repetition of synthetic sound within the ocular field of the diversity of visual tremblings and warblings mimes the rhythm of the artist's sound waves in this digital video while also seeming to contribute to the increasing entropy of the figural waves whose abstraction mounts in consort with the complexity of sound. In the case of both of these pieces, however, whether reflecting analogue or digital practice, the play between realism and abstraction, analogue and digital, sound and image could be said, as Chen suggests, to pick up the promise of cyclic repetition and its associations with the mantric viewing practices of Eastern mysticism, one that stretches the moment of time into an endless flow.

A much more interesting and complex instantiation of digital intervention on naturalized space and sound is made by Ryoichi Kurokawa in the video *A Few Walks*. This is a more subversive piece that lures the spectator into a somewhat touristic journey through a clearly demarcated European village. As the projected video cruises at ground level through ancient European streets, a viral animation of vinelike graffiti quickly inhabits the facades of the buildings and cobblestones. Vines rapidly climb buildings, encircle window casings, and shoot across the cobblestones of an unpopulated village. The quick linear rhythm of this touristic journey is tempered by the non-linear cyclic sound-patterns associated with the beat of the mystical gong or the synthesized echo of new music's repetitive refrain. Yet this sound becomes complexified through digital extension and interference as the visual journey proceeds, just as rhizomatic patterns of flora and fauna seem to clutter the architectonic structures of medieval village life. Nevertheless, the rhythmic sound of the gong persists, much like the allusions to scenic naturalism and the simplicity of earlier Western times. Sound here combines with animation to pick up the cyclic repetition of the Asia Acoustic in a way that stretches the video moment, as Yehlin Lee would say, "into an endless flow."[12]

It well could be that my earlier example of the audio-visual installation aptly entitled *Life* also reflects, through its watery emphasis on fluidity, invisibility, and inaudibility, a similar mantric fusion of rapidly montaged imagery and repetitious synthetic surround sound. Yet only the most practiced of yogi could be lulled into focused concentration while lying uncomfortably on the hard gallery floor of the ICC to view *Life*'s many contrasting image-sounds from upside down, or while avoiding the nudge of one's prostrate neighbor, or while jostling for a better position with the crowds of already well-positioned viewers while relocating one's aching body under each different screen. There is something else going on here, perhaps concerning less the mantric comforts of environmental sound and cyclic art, through which sound and image could become fused into "one," than the artistic manifestations of the struggle itself, from struggle with the viewing environment to the aural clashes of Takatani's environmental noise and the out-of-sync figurations of war ghosting the vaporous screens. The artistic intervention of *Life* delivers a different or even differential relation to Asia Acoustics in which immaterial intensity confounds the calm of mantric fusion.

Noises of Ambiguity

Mary Russo and Daniel Warner have suggested that such a differential constitutes the fundamental characteristic of audio culture, one they attribute not to the cyclic repetitions of sound and its spiritual matchings in image but to the continuous variations of noise.

> Noise, as we have described it, is a differential. There is no absolute state of noise, nor is there foreseeably (pace Habermas) a noise-free state of music, of communication and information, of life. Noise is not that which escapes or is prior, but is the mark of entry. Noise is ambiguity: it is not meaningless or without social contents and hierarchies (the band). Noise is cruel. Noise is

not, as information theorists would have it, a signal that *we* do not want to hear. It is signal that *someone* does not want to hear. Noise is pain.[13]

While the authors' emphasis on ambiguity as the cruel framework of noise brings to mind Cage's anti-Western emphasis on atonality as "the maintenance of an ambiguous tonal state of affairs,"[14] their text alludes much more forcefully to the Italian futurist Luigi Russolo. It was Russolo, the author of the incomparable futurist manifesto *The Art of Noises*, who insisted on the artistic potential of modern culture's machinic noise, from the brutal sounds of combat during World War I to the numbing drone of industrial machinery and urban life.[15] At the heart of Russolo's aesthetics lies a deep dissatisfaction with the mimetic correlation, be it of sound and image or sound and meaning. "Although the characteristic of noise may well remind us brutally of life," writes Russolo, "the art of noises should not limit itself to an imitative reproduction. It will achieve its greatest emotional power in acoustical enjoyment itself, which the inspiration of the artist will know how to draw from the combining of noises."[16]

Rather than soothing the ear with the grain of Buddhist Sutras that envelop the site of meditational mandalas, this edgy tradition of noise art and its assertive ambiguities, what the German's call *Klangkunst,* has provided the point of departure for the most ambitious Asian endeavors in the promotion of sound art, including those that have featured many of the sound and video works we have just considered. Indeed, the complex appropriation of the tradition of noise art lends to the Asian Acoustic a tone very different from the mantric calming sought by early sound artists whose inspiration moved from West to East. One of the most impressive initiatives on this horizon has been undertaken by the Taipei collective Et@t, which has sponsored the innovative biennial of international sound art, b!as, since 2003. Its first curators, Jun-Jieh Wang and Fujui Wang, both acknowledge their debt to the legacy of Russolo's manifesto. Their curatorial projects have featured many works that exemplify Russolo's insistence that "we must break out of this limited circle of sounds and conquer the infinite variety of noise-sounds" (11). As if retracing Ryoichi Kurokawa's contemporary graffiti interventions in the video of the classical European village, Russolo argues,

> To be convinced of the surprising variety of noises, one need only think of the rumbling of thunder, the whistling of the wind, the roaring of a waterfall, the gurgling of a brook, the rustling of leaves, the trotting of a horse

into the distance, the rattling jolt of a cart on the road, and of the full, solemn, and white breath of a city at night. . . . Let us cross a large modern capital with our ears more sensitive than our eyes. . . . We will amuse ourselves by orchestrating together in our imagination the din of rolling shop shutters, the varied hubbub of train stations, iron works, thread mills, printing presses, electrical plants, and subways. (12)

It is not surprising that one of the prize winners of the 2005 Sound Art Biennial performs this very sound imaging of the urban ear.

To create the award winner, *Asylumatad*, the Taiwanese artist Li Wei Chiang combined sounds from the machinic environment of the contemporary workplace, such as typewriters, electric currents, and copy machines. After listening repeatedly to the varying processes of each sound source, the artist "modulated them to compose new tunes in a quasi-extemporaneous way."[17] Of additional interest here is how the artist relied on sonorous repetition as a structural feature of the creative process itself in order to foreground the differentials of modulated noise within the piece. It is almost as if Chiang were applying the dictum of Russolo that "we want to give pitch to these diverse noises, regulating them harmonically and rhythmically. Giving pitch to noises does not mean depriving them of all irregular movements and vibrations of time and intensity but rather assigning a degree of pitch to the strongest and most prominent of these vibrations."[18]

This somewhat contradictory emphasis on foregrounding the strength and intensity of particular features of differential noise (an important aspect of the paradoxes of Italian futurism) hasn't gone unnoticed in the curatorial corridors of the Asian Acoustic. What I find interesting in the Taipei biennial endeavor, which has developed into one of the most significant international exhibitions of sound art, is how its curators have expressed ambivalence about the same interfaces of sound and figure that lend differential richness to the many video pieces I have already discussed. A central premise of Jun-Jieh Wang's 2005 curatorial essay, *Alternative Frequencies: Perspectives on Sound Art*, is that

[b]y the end of the 20th century, the concept of "intermedia" seemed to have become universally accepted in contemporary art. But while the distinction between different artistic disciplines is no longer an issue in the digital age, we are now flooded with an overabundance of "images," so that sound must once again be liberated.[19]

Were we to wonder just what it might mean to so liberate sound from image, I suspect we would have been taken back to the disturbance of mimesis through which "images" might so easily have stood in for "sounds." Most significant would be the renewed insistence on an aesthetics of ambiguity, whether in the Cagean sense of "the denial of harmony as a structural means,"[20] or in the sense of the cruel enigma, to return to the thoughts of Russo and Warner, of an informational signal that someone does not want to hear. This is the paradox of the liberationist discourse of the avant-gardist futurist manifesto that disrupts the smooth harmony of sound and image. The result is a heightening of the cruelty of noisy ambiguity that summons the sonorous present of listening.

The ambiguities of acoustic intensity, its uncanniness and its force, bring to mind psycho-philosophical reflections that extend the horizon of sound image to the horizons of sensation and psyche. Parallel to the notion of an aesthetics of ambiguity are Jean Laplanche's theorizations of sound as a traumatic carrier of the "enigmatic signifier." Here sound lies at the heart of the cruel ambiguity of trauma in the very intensity of its imaging. As an enigmatic signifier (à), it may "lose what it signifies, without thereby losing its power to signify *to*."[21] Just such a sensitivity to the unwilled force of sound could well lie at the heart of Nancy's text, À *l'écoute*. Such ambivalent attraction to (à) something heard even against one's will, may well have influenced the b!as(ed) jury process that awarded the 2005 Exclusive Prize to the Taiwanese artist Punkcan for his sound piece *Isolated Illusion* (the artist won First Prize in the 2003 B!as Festival). For *Isolated Illusion*, Punkcan developed the "pink noise" on which the artist relies to cancel out sound that might be exterior to the processes of his own work. The effect, however, is something other than mere blockage or disavowal of everyday sounds. The jury's statement foregrounds the ambiguous contradictions that result: "From the humming noise he vaguely sensed a certain intangible existence. It is like trying to trace someone's voice, but then a sudden downpour of randomly generated sounds drown the few clues you think you have."[22] The manipulation of pink noise here functions not so much as an act of the disavowal of everyday sounds, but rather, as something of a "meta-operation." This is Brandon LaBelle's term for the way noise "directs a certain understanding onto the field of the symbolic, onto the territory of code, without putting into practice that very code. . . . Here, a theory of noise is defined by its ability to remain an operation rather than a sign, to always remain a pure drive away from heralding anything."[23]

While turning us in the direction of the meta-operational, I don't want to lose track of the emphasis placed by Punkcan's curator, Jun-Jieh Wang, on his salvationist distinction between image and sound, which seems to have led us to distinguish between operation and sign. Interestingly, he turns to a different philosophical source to clarify his distinction, one that could lead us away from the idealistic appropriation of Buddhism by Western sound artists. The philosophical text to which Wang points to expand the theoretical implications of the liberation of sound is Jacques Derrida's essay on Husserl, *Speech and Phenomenon*. What seems to intrigue Wang about this text is its emphasis on wholeness and being, something perhaps akin to the aura of Buddhism so compelling to Western sound artists. Wang appears to be drawn to Derrida's analysis of voice in Husserl through which "the phenomenological power of voice," freed of the mimetic anchorage of image, involves "the unity of sound and voice, which allows the voice to be produced in the world as pure auto-affection [and] is the sole case to escape the distinction between what is worldly and what is transcendental."[24] Yet, Derrida adds that such a distinction is based on disavowal itself, disavowal of the very operationality that positions sound in space and, thus, in time. Even the kind of operation that makes uncanny the code underlying itself requires the very temporalization and spatialization of the code itself. Even if enigmatic and traumatic, "the temporalization of sense [think here of the very operation of the sound track]," Derrida insists, "is, from the outset, a 'spacing'" (86). The moment that we admit "spacing" as both interval (or difference) and as openness to the outside, the possibility of an absolute inside, let's call it voice or sound without image, is nullified.

New Media Folds, or Digital Distribution

It is along these lines that something like Nancy's space-time of the sonorous present becomes reinscribed in the sound aesthetics of ambiguity. This could lead us to follow the lead of a long list of artists and theoreticians who describe sound as fundamentally spatial, well outside the specifically architectonic frameworks of the multimedia installations discussed earlier. I noted at the outset that Nancy reflects on how the referral of sound spreads itself "in space, where it resounds while still resounding 'in me.'"[25] Somewhat similarly, Edgard Varèse promotes acoustical arrangements that "would permit the delimitation of what I call 'zones of intensities' . . . differentiated by various timbres or colors or different loudnesses. Through such a physical process these zones would appear of different colors and of different magnitude, in different perspectives for our perception."[26] And, in writing on the refrains of noise, Gilles Deleuze and Félix Guattari turn to Debussy, Varèse, and Cage to ponder a "wave without harmonics" by which "the forces of folding" and "what is necessary to make sound travel, and to travel around sound" consists of "nonvisual forces that nevertheless have been rendered visible."[27]

It is this latter philosophical path, one reflecting precisely on the folds of twentieth-century intermedia, that might have provided Wang with a different appreciation of the imagined isolation of sound from image and the interrelated mappings of sound in the new media environment of Asia Acoustics. A variable tack would have brought the Taiwanese curator into contact with Derrida's philosophical compatriot, Deleuze, who reflects in *Cinema 2: The Time-Image* on what he calls the "pure sound images" or "sonsigns" of postwar cinema (whose "direct presentation of time" was foreseen Asia Acoustically, so Deleuze argues, by none other than the Japanese impresario of prewar film, Yasujiro Ozu). For Deleuze, the sonsign constitutes that aspect of modern cinema in which synchronized sound and image peel off from one another, while also separating the cinema of action and description from the habitation of time and space central to experimental cinematic practices from Godard and Resnais to Akerman and Duras: "the calling into question of action, the necessity of seeing and hearing, the proliferation of empty, disconnected, abandoned spaces."[28] Instead of filling space or standing in as the referential supplement of action, the sonsign provides a "direct presentation of time" and the sonorous horizon for the thought of time. While the more conventional movement-image, which is synchronized with sound, stands "in a relationship only with an indirect image *of* time (dependent on montage), the pure optical and sound image, its opsigns and sonsigns, are directly connected to a time-image, which has subordinated movement . . . movement is the perspective of time" (22). Rather than insisting that the sonsign be liberated from the image, Deleuze suggests that the cinematic sonsign is juxtaposed or enfolded via irrational cuts with the pure optical sign that serves a corollary function of imaging intensity. A pure optical and sound image "makes us grasp, it is supposed to make us grasp, something intolerable and unbearable.. . . . It is a matter of something too powerful, or too unjust, but sometimes also too beautiful, and which henceforth outstrips our sensory-motor capacities" (19).

So instead of needing to liberate sound from image in the intermedia environment, we could take the lead from Deleuze to dwell on the folding of image into sound, as the aural horizon of intensity itself. Indeed, the irrational interstice, that is, the irrational cut between two images, the visual and the sonorous, actually reinforces what Deleuze calls "the victory of the audio-visual" (253). Crucial to the irrational relation of the two dissymmetrical trajectories of the visual and the sonorous, however, is Deleuze's insistence that "the audio-visual image is not a whole, it is 'a *fusion* of the tear'" (268).

This remains a delicate business in relation to the role of sound in new media, however, since we're no longer talking simply about what we observe or hear on the screen, that is, what Deleuze would call a "sound situation" in which the listener on the screen (or the seer in the case of the opsign) has replaced the agent of action in cinema. For the new media environment could be said to embody the very folding of soundings into the mechanics of listening, where the computing machine itself is the actor, where digital acoustics is the mise-en-scène of information itself, and where their automation is not so much represented on the screen as envelops the artistic event itself.

This necessitates a shift in how we think sound and its imaging. As I argue in *Digital Baroque*, at stake is a willed forgetting of the hegemony of the mechanics of perspective, in form and idea, to give rise to a more fluid dynamic of the "fold" of image into sound, or vice versa.[29] In contrast to the Cartesian legacy of projection as the culmination or end point of reason (grounding later phenomenological notions of self-presence and perspectival vision), the fold appears to Deleuze as a continuous labyrinth determined by its "consistent and conspiring surroundings."[30] This temporal fold, much like cinema's irrational cut, positions the spatialization of sound as ongoing event, rather than as penultimate image.

Deleuze comes close to articulating this when referring to the "media-effect" of Syberberg's work, in which "the disjunction, the division of the visual and the sound, will be specifically entrusted with experiencing the complexity of informational space."[31] But I think that we need to return to the space of new media per se in order to appreciate fully the sound imaging of informational aesthetics. Perhaps a good place to start would be with works from another Asia Acoustic collaborative sound project, this time the *OpenMind* CD, a collection of sound art pieces curated by Yukiko Shikata in pre-celebration of the 2003 opening of the Mori Art Museum in the Mori Tower in Tokyo.[32] Shikata's curatorial initiative aimed to provide a platform for the latest wave of sound, noise, and digital media by artists living in Japan and Asia. Consider, for instance, the sound track of Ryoji Ikeda's 2005 ICC installation, *db*. Installed in an anechoic chamber, *db* was designed, as Ikeda puts it, "to quite physically explode the senses." Built with the highest and lowest frequencies that human ears can bear, *db* is described by the artist as "a hyper-dense composition of sine waves, white noise and other elements, which blurs the lines between noise and music, thought and matter."[33] This is what I mean by the fold as the sonsign of the digital environment in which the digital composite of sine waves provides the spatial surround of thought and matter.

It is interesting to note that Kim Cascone, the composer who formed the Anechoic Media label in 2000, identifies Ikeda with precisely the "serene quality of spirituality" that typifies contributions to the emergent field of "glitch" sound through which the digital tools here "break new ground in the delicate use of high frequencies and short sounds that stab at listeners' ears."[34] But I'm not sure I would go this route while still joining with Cascone to identify Ikeda with what the latter describes as "The Aesthetics of Failure." This happens when the artist seizes upon computer "glitches, bugs, application errors, system crashes, clipping, aliasing, distortion, quantization noise" as the raw data of sound (393). The tools themselves become both the instruments and conspiring surroundings of sound, thus realizing something like those "strange lines and distances" of Francis Bacon's (anti-Asian) sound-house, where the lines are further blurred between thought and matter. The result of Ikeda's *db* doesn't seem to me any more "spiritual" than the sonorous architectonics provided by Keichiro Shibuya's *er* in the same collection. This is a piece whose entire form entails the formlessness of error. "Never resorting to deliberate randomizing or random structures," the artist insists, "a system incorporating errors will never revert to a loop. Think about a model," he adds, "a model in which errors generate alternative independent structures, which themselves include errors . . . generated inside the computer."[35] How such an aesthetics of failure might then function in a multimedia environment has been realized by Ikeda's 2007 Beijing installation, *Data.tron*, in which sound and data join to provide a combination of pure mathematics and sound along with a figuration of the "vast sea of data present in the world." Projected onto a large screen in the Beijing exhibition, *Beautiful New Worlds: Contemporary Visual Culture from Japan*, sound and image were enfolded in the darkened viewing space of *Data.tron*. As Ikeda understands the project, it heightens and intensifies "the viewer's perception and total immersion within the work." If there is anything like total immersion, however, this would have to involve less the viewer's perception or alignment of sensory-motor capacities, both of which are rendered asunder by audio-visual intensity, than interconnection within the data world. Rather than solicit the cinematic codes of spectatorial recognition or sensory-motor synchronization, this installation engages in the energetic event of data encounter. This is how the rise of new media art necessitates a deeply significant archeological shift from visual projection to temporal fold that is emphasized, if not wholly embodied, by the digital condition. Ikeda's *Data.tron* enacts just such a shift away from the remnants of humanistic visions of subjectivity and cinematic "projection" toward a rhizomatic model of the "folds" of intersubjective knowledge and cross-cultural archives. Much like the sound fields of the aesthetics of ambivalence and failure, the passage of sound is here enfolded in the matter of code and the complexities of data accumulated through the overlapping passage of spectators, space, and time.

To understand even better how this vibrant field of Asia Acoustics might be theorized in relation to the history of the sonic fold, I would recommend that we look beyond Deleuze's cinematic notion of the sonsign and audio-visual image to his earlier conceptual work on fields of distribution in *Difference and Repetition*. It would have been difficult for him to have imagined in 1968 the flow of data that now maps all participants in the new media sound installation not only with the error machines of production but also with the noise of receptive immersion in the flow of the internet. In his chapter "Difference in Itself," Deleuze articulates the philosophical groundwork of the very noisy differentials that Russo and Warner attribute to the digital soundscape. He contrasts two practices of distribution. First are the "fixed and proportional determinations which may be assimilated to 'properties' or limited territories within representation. . . . Even among the gods, each has his domain, his category, his attributes, and all distribute limits and lots to mortals in accordance to destiny."[36] This we can understand in relation to the distributions of aesthetics in which we distinguish along with Russolo between the strongest and most prominent of vibrations, or along with Bacon between the Occidental purity of the sound-house that "poor thing" of China, which made it "a curious, ignorant, fearful, foolish nation." In contrast, Deleuze might point to the contemporary curiosity of the data flow as made manifest across the field of Asia Acoustics. This would involve what he describes as

[a] completely other distribution which must be called nomadic, a nomad nomos, without property, enclosure or measure. Here, there is not longer a division of that which is distributed but rather a division among those who distribute themselves in an open space—a space [could we add a "data space"] which is unlimited, or at least without precise limits. Nothing pertains or belongs to any person, but all persons are arrayed here and there in such a manner as to cover the largest possible space. Even when it concerns the serious business of life, it is more like a space of play, or a rule of play, by contrast with the sedentary space and nomos. To fill a space, to be distributed within it, is very different from distributing the space. It is an errant and even "delirious" distribution in which things are deployed across the entire extensity of a univocal and undistributed Being. (36–37)

Didn't we initially begin by discussing just such a delirious distribution of the serious business of life in Sakamoto and Takatani's *Life: fluid, invisible, inaudible*? Arrayed here and there across a vast space of fluid screens, which hang almost weightlessly in the surround of sound, the participants in *Life* experiment with the conventions of audio-visual play while finding themselves distributed within a complex network of synthesized sound, historical video, and computerized imagery. Such errant, if not also delirious, distribution also constitutes the ground and conceit of Ikeda's *Data. tron*. By disrupting the sedentary space and nomos of the gallery, *Data.tron* redistributes motion, sound, and the accumulating plastic stuff of artistic deployment. Indeed, isn't the deployment of errancy of its electronic folds what conjoins the artistic projects of sound and figure in the most acoustic of Asian new media installations, those that are produced by the play of the data field instead of reproducing the spirituality of the limited territories of the projection of image and sound?

What better way to conclude than by reflecting on the distributional differentials of networked art as it conjoins the motion fields of sound, image, and space considered throughout this essay. With this in mind, we could easily contrast the distributional representation of "water" in the video of waves of Chen's *La Mer* with Norimichi Hirakawa's redistribution of waves in his 2007 ICC installation, *Driftnet*. You will recall that *La Mer* relies on the frame of single-track projection to present a video of waves that morphs from realism to abstract lines and pixels, which are enveloped in the sound waves of a synthetic track. The video's opening sequence of waves becomes increasingly pixilated and diffused through exposure of the digital data field underlying the allusion of realistic waves. Chen suggests that the play between realism and abstraction, analogue and digital, sound and image plays on the promise of cyclic repetition that stretches the moment into an endless flow. This envelope of the endless flow could be said to lend to *La Mer* a representational reference to Buddhism and its cross-cultural embrace.

Much like Chen's *La Mer*, *Driftnet* opens with a shot of ocean waves, but only for what seems like a fleeting second before it even more quickly morphs into abstract imaging. But here the moving image displays not the disintegration of realism in the service of the representation of something larger on a mystical scale; rather, its viewers are confronted by an errant and even delirious distribution of data sets to the beats of shrill and loud synthetic sound. Appearing as something like an animated scan of the room's synthetic sound field, *Driftnet*'s visual field consists of three-dimensional sequences of rapid redistributions of lines and loops that bounce off the three walls. Key here is the artist's appropriation of data waves for the figuration of the global economic system as distributed virtually from the vantage point of the island-nation Japan. The ocean here functions not as the pictorial alibi of realism but, instead, as a stand-in for the internet, just as the pixilated data of the representational distribution of the internet's data of commerce, pleasure, and art is synonymous with the representational pixilation of errancy itself.

By virtue of their motion through artistic space, the visitors literally enter into, if not become, this multimedia event. When the participants move within the space, "as if crawling through the waves of information generated from internet data," their motion is captured by sensors to activate internet links emerging between the waves. Additional movement brings with it new visual waves and aural assaults that seem to envelop the participants and expand the visual/aural boundaries of the installation. Thus abandoned is the stability of projection and its passive spectatorial reception through the installation's refoldings of data transfer and data becoming, a process dependent on the continuous variations of performative participation, networked data, and computerized sound.

What takes place is a sort of digital body surfing in which virtual and physical play merge in the surge of data. The interactive play is here much noisier, indeed far more immersive, than with, say, Ikeda's *db*. For the movement of the participants maps onto and is mapped by the data flow of *Driftnet* to the extent that the imaging of immaterial data becomes the play of corporeal errancy. The continuous variations of such ongoing redistributions lie at the heart of the sound-image as it is thought within the new media folds of Asia Acoustics. Returning to Nancy, we can now say that sound here images in full intensity, in the sense of redistributing viewing and listening across the network of immaterial wiring. As for the digital distributions of these installations, couldn't these be said to enact the event of Nancy's "sonorous time," as the ongoing distribution of "a present in waves on a swell, not in a point on a line"?

SEVEN

Three Theses on the Life-Image (Deleuze, Cinema, Bio-politics)

CESARE CASARINO

I. The life-image is what the time-image becomes under a fully realized regime of bio-political production.

In his two-volume study of the cinema, Gilles Deleuze produces what is at once a synchronic and a diachronic account of cinema. Such an account is synchronic to the extent to which it consists of "a taxonomy, an attempt at a classification of images and signs."[1] It is diachronic to the extent to which—Deleuze's protestations to the contrary notwithstanding—it also consists of a bipartite periodization of the history of cinema, which pivots around the break of the Second World War. These two aspects of Deleuze's account share and interfere with one another in what constitutes the principal argument of this study: the cinema developed from an indirect representation of time in the movement-image and its varieties, in the period before the Second World War, to a direct time-image and its varieties, that is, to a direct insertion of time in the cinematic image, in the period after the Second World War. Whereas the movement-image subordinated time to movement, the time-image liberated time from the harness of movement and expressed time in its pure state, time as such—that is, time as the eternal, immobile, and unchanging form of all that passes, moves, and changes. Deleuze thus is able, on the one hand, to declare in the first sentence of his two-volume study, "This study is not a history of the cinema," and, on the other hand, to follow this declaration immediately with a series of historical periodizations (xiv). There is no contradiction here: the point is that the prime object of Deleuze's historicization is not cinema per se but the condition of possibility of all historicization and, indeed, of historicity itself, namely, time. Deleuze's study constitutes an attempt to think a momentous event in the historical experience of time through the cinema: Deleuze's study is a history of time that needs the cinema in order to think a radical transformation in the way in which time is produced, embodied, and lived in historical forms. This is a transformation that Deleuze identifies in the paradigmatic shift from the movement-image to the time-image, from the indirect representation of time to the direct expression of time in the cinematic image.[2]

It is the claim of this essay that the radical transformation in time, which in the cinema is materialized as the shift from the movement-image to the time-image, constitutes the most important—if not the most obvious—index of a regime of bio-political production. It is the further claim of this essay that the life-image emerges from within the time-image—without, however, ever leaving it behind, and, on the contrary, by incorporating it—at the moment in which such a regime of bio-political production comes to its full fruition and realization.

This is not the place to retrace the complex intellectual genealogies of the term as well as of the concept of "bio-politics"—a term that was coined famously by Michel Foucault in 1974 and a concept whose origins arguably hark back to the early-modern era.[3] For my purposes, what I find most compelling is the critical re-elaboration of the concept of bio-politics that has been undertaken during the past two decades by a group of thinkers—such as Michael Hardt, Antonio Negri, Judith Revel, and Paolo Virno—who in effect have brought to the foreground as well as pushed to its logical conclusions an insight that had remained largely implicit and latent in Foucault. This insight concerns the necessary and symbiotic relations between, on the one hand, bio-politics understood as a complex assemblage of modern technologies of power for the direct management, organization, and domination of life in all of its forms, and, on the other hand, capitalism understood as a complex assemblage of modern technologies of production for the management, organization, and exploitation of labor-power in all of its modalities. Virno expresses such an insight in a powerful thesis that I take as axiomatic for my present project: "[B]io-politics is merely an effect, a reverberation, or, in fact, one articulation of that primary fact—both historical and philosophical—which consists of the commerce of potential as potential."[4] Such a "commerce of potential as potential," of course, is the defining feature of the exchange between capitalist and worker inasmuch as what is exchanged there is labor-power, what Karl Marx identified in *Capital* as that aggregate of all mental and physical potentials that is inseparable from the living body of the worker.[5] Looking at the concept of bio-politics through the filter of the Marxian concept of labor-power, thus, Virno asserts:

> Capitalists are interested in the life of the worker, in the body of the worker, only for an indirect reason: this life, this body, are what contains the faculty, the potential, the *dynamis* . . . Life lies at the center of politics when the prize to be won is immaterial (and in itself non-present) labor-power. For this reason, and this reason alone, it is legitimate to talk about "bio-politics."[6] (Virno 82–83)

All other differences notwithstanding, what brings the aforementioned group of thinkers together is that they posit—either explicitly or implicitly—the type of argument exemplified here by Virno as the necessary premise from which to draw the following conclusions: bio-politics comes to its full fruition with that shift in the capitalist mode of production that goes by the name of post-Fordism and that is to be understood primarily as a reaction to the revolutions of the 1960s and to the new forms of subjectivity forged in the heat of those struggles; or—to put it differently—post-Fordism is another name for a fully realized regime of bio-political production. It is Negri who best captures the co-extensive, symbiotic, and synonymic natures of post-Fordism and of bio-politics when he states:

> In the world of immateriality in which we live, reproduction—which is the first possible definition of biopolitics—and production can no longer be distinguished from each other. Biopolitics becomes fully realized precisely when production and reproduction are one and the same, that is, when production is conducted primarily and directly through language and social exchange.[7]

Such is the paradox of bio-politics: it realizes itself by dispersing itself completely throughout the myriad and ubiquitous networks of production; it finds its best determination in the absolute indetermination of the limits separating it from production; it is most discernible when it is not discernible from production—and when both reign omnipresent. In this paradox, Negri describes the completion of a process whose origins and presuppositions were articulated earlier by Virno: if bio-politics fulfills its philosophical nature as well as its historical mission at the moment in which it can no longer be distinguished from post-Fordist capitalism as such, that is so precisely because capitalist exchange relations—the "commerce of potential as potential"—constituted the condition of possibility of bio-politics in the first place.[8]

In my reading, the line of argumentation articulated by this group of thinkers has the following crucial implication. An unprecedented event is enabled to take place within that zone of indistinction between bio-politics and production that characterizes post-Fordist capitalism: namely, for the first time in history *all* those potentials that make up labor-power are in principle exploitable and directly productive. In a process of production that is fueled crucially by the communication of thought, language, and affect (and hence also of knowledge) in all their myriad forms, we are all exploitable and increasingly exploited to the full extent of our potential to produce (albeit, of course, not all of us in the same way or with the same pay).[9] Undoubtedly, isolated and periodic instances of this exploitation of labor-power as such—in its heterogeneous yet isomorphic entirety—can be found throughout the history of production. It is only with the emergence of a fully realized regime of bio-political production, however, that such a form of exploitation turns into a definitional and dominant norm. Such a regime, in other words, marks that moment in history when potential qua potential is hunted down in all the most recondite burrows of being, brought out to the light of day, and turned into a spectacle for all to see—in all of its absolute splendor and infinite misery. It is precisely because all the potentials constituting labor-power are now subsumed by capital that potential qua potential is all the more visible in its invisibility, perceptible in its imperceptibility, corporeal in its incorporeality, material in its immateriality, present in its non-presence—in short, all the more powerful and expressive as non-present cause immanent in its own effects. And this is that moment in history too—after the revolutions of the 1960s and during a ruthless process of reaction—when the time-image increasingly gives rise to the life-image.

The concept of the life-image, thus, constitutes an attempt to answer the following question: how can we identify and articulate the relation between, on the one hand, the complete indistinction of bio-politics and production that characterizes post-Fordist capitalism, and, on the other hand, the complete realization of the cinema as medium of expression of time qua time? Put differently, how can we think the relation between a fully realized regime of bio-political production and a fully realized cinema of the time-image?[10] The life-image is posited here as a paradigmatic and defining product of this relation—or, at the very least, as a heuristic device for thinking such a relation.[11]

II. The life-image expresses labor-power.

In this context, life needs to be understood as the diachronic, corporeal, material, present term corresponding to synchronic, incorporeal, immaterial, and non-present labor-power. Life and labor-power are one and the same thing conceived from two different standpoints: they are the two inseparable sides of the same coin. The life-image, thus, is the image of an era in which life and labor-power are torn apart irreparably from each other, an era in which life is turned into the fetish par excellence while labor-power is at once foreclosed and exploited like never before. From the lethal discourses of the "pro-life" political-religious movements to the no less deadly consumer-culture discourses around anodyne notions of "lifestyle," nowadays we are confronted incessantly by a life whose increasing ubiquity is directly proportional to its elusiveness, whose increasing inflatedness is directly proportional to its vacuity. If a stand-up bicycle in a gym can be called a "life-cycle," you can rest assured that the more garrulously life speaks today the dumber it has become, and that what you are riding, as you pedal away eagerly while going absolutely nowhere, is no longer a bicycle of any sort but a bio-political joke of world-historical proportions—which is to say, of course, that in our era the world-historical can no longer be distinguished from the trivial and the inane as such. Such a spectacular fetishization of life is closely related to the fact that the secret of production that is hidden away in life and its forms can be squeezed now for all it is worth: if invocations of life nowadays sound like so many empty clichés, that is so because for the first time life has been emptied out completely of its only possible content, namely, labor-power. Today, life and labor-power more than ever stand apart from each other—separated by that limit that is capitalism.

Lest I begin to sound as cranky as a latter-day Adorno, however, let me add that the life-image at once is born out of this state of affairs and yet does not belong to it. The life-image does not represent life, or, more precisely, does not limit itself to representation. An image that limits itself to representing life must also turn it into a fetish, into a cliché, into a commodity—in short, into dead labor. In the life-image, rather, the representation of life rests upon and points to the expression of labor-power—and by "expression" here I mean that non-representational kind of knowledge and mode of communication that Deleuze finds embedded in Baruch Spinoza's ontology.[12] The point is that labor-power cannot be represented: it is invisible, incorporeal, immaterial, non-present—by definition. Labor-power can only be expressed. If the image that limits itself to representing life inevitably ends up turning life into dead labor, that is so because such an image forecloses rather than expresses that which brought the image to life in the first place, namely, labor-power. Representation without expression can only reify. The life-image, however, represents life and expresses labor-power at one and the same time; or, more precisely, expresses labor-power in representing life—thereby presenting them as immanent to one another, and positing both as what Giorgio Agamben might call an indivisible, dynamic, pulsating form-of-life.[13] This means also that the life-image is a form of biopolitical resistance, that is, at once a form of resistance against bio-politics as well as a form of resistance that is itself bio-political—in short, a form of resistance that uses and turns bio-politics against itself.

III. The life-image finds an exemplary instance within and against the spectacle of AIDS.

Rarely have more fetishistic and reified images of life proliferated at such a prodigious speed and in such a voluminous quantity than during that historical conjuncture that saw the spectacle of AIDS at its zenith, approximately from the early 1980s to the very end of the last century—a period and a spectacle with which we have yet fully to come to terms. Many are those who have told us already the story of the spectacle of AIDS.[14] One way of telling this same story from the standpoint of my present investigation would be to point out that some of the most reifying forms of representation were rapidly enlisted in the service of a pernicious construal of AIDS as the deserved product of the possibilities opened up by the political critiques of the 1960s—including not only the gay and lesbian liberation movements but also the critique and subversion of those very forms of representation. I have written elsewhere about the relation between, on the one hand, a certain critique of representation that was articulated around 1968, and, on the other hand, the spectacle of AIDS that unfolded in the 1980s and 1990s: suffice to say here that the AIDS pandemic occasioned a revengeful recrudescence of the deployment of representation that thinkers such as Deleuze and Guy Debord—among others—had critiqued in very different yet significantly congruent works that appeared between 1967 and 1969.[15] (I am referring to Debord's *Society of the Spectacle* and to Deleuze's more implicit yet no less powerful critiques, such as his related attempts to produce a concept of "simulacrum" as radically different from "copy" in the first appendix to *The Logic of Sense*, as well as to produce a concept of "expression" as distinct yet indiscernible from "representation" in his landmark study of Spinoza, *Expressionism in Philosophy*.)[16] The AIDS pandemic provided the spectacle with the perfect opportunity to discredit and humiliate the political energies of that historical moment when the spectacle had come most intensely under attack, and hence also with the perfect opportunity to act increasingly unrestrained. This is to say that the spectacle of AIDS was at once attendant and constitutive of an exponential leap in the spectacularization of everything everywhere, and especially of the most macroscopic and microscopic life processes, namely, of those two poles in the exercise of power over life that Foucault had identified as the anatomo-politics of the human body and the bio-politics of the population, and that the AIDS pandemic has made virtually indistinguishable from each other. The spectacle of AIDS emerged as an intensification of spectacular logic: it marked the bio-political turn of the spectacle. But if the spectacle of AIDS could mark such an exponential leap in the representational logic of the spectacle, that was so not only because the AIDS pandemic was seized as the perfect chance for a vicious backlash against the 1960s but also because the AIDS pandemic was immediately understood as posing a dangerous threat in its own right to such a representational logic. Another and complementary way of telling the story of the spectacle of AIDS, in fact, would be to point out that the spectacle spectacularizes that which has the most potential to undermine its representational logic, or, which is to say the same thing, that which harbors the most potential for the emergence of the life-image. AIDS and its suffering had to be spectacularized at all costs because the threats it posed to dominant forms of representation—and not least of all to scientific and medical representation—were bound to generate new images that might challenge and evade the logic of the spectacle altogether.

In this sense, the spectacle of AIDS needs to be understood not only as a reactionary backlash against past and present critiques of representation but also as a preemptive strike against the life-image and its future possibilities.

It is deep from within the spectacle of AIDS that a number of filmmakers, video artists, photographers, painters, novelists, and poets attempted to extract the life-image from the viciously stereotyped—that is, utterly reified—images of life that have been saturating our sensorium since the very beginning of the AIDS pandemic. Throughout the 1980s and 1990s, the likes of Derek Jarman, David Wojnarowicz, Hervé Guibert, Aaron Shurin, Gregg Araki, John Greyson, Cyril Collard, Marlon Riggs, Rosa von Praunheim, Keith Haring, Peter Friedman, and Tom Joslin, as well as many others, produced works that constitute sustained experimentations with what I have been calling the life-image. I will end this essay with a snapshot of such experimentations.

In the 1993 documentary *Silverlake Life: The View from Here*, Tom Joslin pitilessly records the devastating impact of AIDS-related conditions on his life up until and including the instant immediately following his own death—when his naked, emaciated, ravaged body is exposed to the impassive gaze of the camera in a stunning and paradoxical display of what Foucault might have called care of the self. Here, I am concerned with one specific sequence, which takes place toward the end of the documentary, lasts approximately two minutes and six seconds, and consists of thirteen shots. The sequence unfolds according to a seemingly random or not immediately apparent logic: the shots follow one another in no apparent order; they appear and disappear with no self-evident relation either to the preceding ones or to the succeeding ones. It is only well into the sequence that one may infer that the thin thread holding the shots together visually is the Silver Lake neighborhood in Los Angeles as viewed from the terrace of Joslin's apartment. (The retroactive realization that the Silver Lake neighborhood functions as the cement of the whole sequence—and hence as its unwitting yet undisputed protagonist—is crucially enabled by the strategic inclusion of street signs, revealing that the scene takes place on Silver Lake Boulevard, in the second, fifth, and tenth shots.) Rarely has a camera been at once so distracted and so focused, so scattered and so keen: shot after shot, one is presented with now one view, now another, now one more facet, now yet another, of the area surrounding the terrace from which the camera is zooming in onto the familiar world of the neighborhood, at once taking it apart and putting it back together into a series of discrete yet irreparably inseparable images. Or—to put it differently—each of these shots has nothing or very little to do with any of the others, but they all partake of that most aleatory yet most poignant of signifiers: *Silverlake Life*—whose reverberations are most intensely felt perhaps in the voice-over. The scopic and epistemological aimlessness of the images, in fact, is echoed in the aural and ontological aimlessness of Joslin's words: as one watches such a singular patchwork of Silver Lake slowly take shape in front of one's eyes, Joslin speaks in a tone of voice that is at times exhausted, at times halting, at times suddenly re-animated, vital, and clear—and at times trailing off into the sonic shadow-land of whispers. This is what he tells us:

> What is this that passes before my eyes every day? I spend most of my time looking, seeing. Just watching . . . this strange thing pass in front of me. I am not much of a participant in life any more. I am a distant viewer. Just watching it all pass by, knowing that . . . I am not going to have that much longer to keep . . . my eye on the . . . on the prize. Do you hear that industrial sound in the background? Another big dumpster is being pulled up, someone re-building a house, more trash going to some dump that doesn't have room for it, on a freeway that's full of cars. This civilization is so strange. I've never felt much a part of it. I think being gay separates you a little. Certainly having AIDS and . . . [almost laughing] being a walking dead!—if you will—separates one from the everyday world. [Singing to the tune of *Mister Rogers' Neighborhood*'s theme song:] It's a beautiful day in the neighborhood![17] It really *is* a beautiful day, by the way: wonderful sun, not too hot, not too cold, new breeze. I don't know what anybody could ask for more.[18]

To put it quickly and all at once: in this complex sequence, we witness the time-image giving rise to the life-image.

Let us now retrace our steps through Silver Lake in slow motion. The first ten of the thirteen shots of this sequence are steeped in the world of the time-image, as they exhibit five of its most crucial and defining features.

1. In each of these shots, on the one hand, there is some—often minimal—movement within the frame (such as a sparrow fluttering over a stoplight, a car speeding by, a tarpaulin agitated by the wind), and, on the other hand, the hand-held video camera is almost always completely still (or at times wavering almost imperceptibly, as if swaying under that very wind that we see blowing in the shots themselves). These shots, in other words, bear a close family resemblance to those cinematic still lifes that Deleuze identifies as the primal scene of the time-image. It is in the films of Yasujiro

Ozu that Deleuze finds some of the first and paradigmatic examples of such still lifes, which—much like Joslin's panoramic snapshots of the familiar neighborhood—always portray the quotidian, the "ordinary," the "banal." Deleuze writes:

> The still life is time, for everything that changes is in time, but time does not itself change, it could itself change only in another time, indefinitely . . . Ozu's still lifes endure, have a duration, over ten seconds of [a] vase: this duration of the vase is precisely the representation of that which endures, through the succession of changing states.[19]

Joslin's time-images, however, do more than this: in them, that which endures is not merely a trash bin, a lamppost, a street sign, a building, a fragmented cityscape. As the voice-over reveals to us, what endures against all odds here is above all a life—Joslin's own life, which indeed "endures . . . through the succession of changing states." Here, thus, one may catch already a glimpse of what is to follow the first ten shots, as the life-image is heard buried alive and latent at the very heart of the time-image.

2. Throughout this sequence, sound and image are radically disjoined from one another: each refers to the other in syncopation, elliptically and indirectly, if at all. Consider, for example, a particularly multilayered shot, the eighth shot. As the image is saturated in its entirety by the nearly abstract, silvery, shimmering, undulating expanse of the lake, the voice-over asks: "Do you hear that industrial sound in the background?" And, indeed, simultaneous with the question, one does hear the sound of a revving engine, which the voice-over proceeds immediately to identify as the sound of a dumpster truck: "Another big dumpster is being pulled up, someone re-building a house." Whereas one does hear the sound of the dumpster truck, however, the truck itself does not enter the frame and hence the field of vision, and, in fact, will remain forever in the out-of-field. Moreover, one does not see the house that is being rebuilt—nor, for that matter, does one hear the presumably ongoing construction work—there from where the dumpster is being pulled up. It is only later, in the tenth shot, that one does see a building under construction: by then, however, the dumpster truck has departed, and the voice-over has gone on to relating and indexing other matters. For Deleuze, such complex disjunctions between sound and image constitute one of the fundamental characteristics of the time-image.[20]

3. Strip malls, construction sites, run-down buildings, busy freeways, empty street after empty street, the beautiful desolation of metropolitan

structures . . . What unravels throughout this sequence is what Deleuze refers to as *espace-quelconque*, "whatever-space": a certain type of post-war urban space—either fragmented and disconnected or vacuolized and deserted, as well as always disorienting—which was captured most iconically by the cinema of Italian Neorealism, and which enables, among other things, the direct insertion of time in the image.[21]

4. Possibly the most conspicuous absence in these images is the human form: there are no people here. One supposes that somebody must be driving all these cars, but we don't really see them clearly, as they whiz by rapidly in and out of the frame. For Deleuze, whereas the primary political import of pre-war cinema consisted in the presence of the people—from Sergei Eisenstein to Frank Capra—the political import of post-war cinema lies precisely in drawing attention to the conspicuous absence of the people, in knowing how to show that the people are that which is missing.[22] In this sense, the political vocation of the cinema of the time-image for Deleuze consists "not . . . of addressing a people, which is presupposed already there, but of contributing to the invention of a people" to come. Such words resonate all the more urgently here: in the context of the AIDS pandemic, in fact, to show that the people are missing cannot but also refer mournfully to the myriads of untimely and avoidable deaths as well as envision the coming community of a world without AIDS.

5. Deleuze remarks repeatedly on the fact that the cinema of the time-image corresponds to and records the emergence of a new form of subjectivity. The manifold processes of modernization—including the increasing mechanization of everyday life, automatization of industrial production, saturation of lived environment by the image, mediation of experience through myriad forms of telecommunication—result in the problematization, or, at times, even in the breakdown, of the sensory-motor link, namely, of the relation between perception and action: the subject no longer knows what perceptions have triggered its actions, and hence no longer even experiences such actions as its own, that is, the subject acts without knowing why; or, conversely, the subject no longer knows how to act on the basis of what it perceives, no longer knows how to react to a given situation. This explains why for Deleuze the cinema of the time-image is a cinema of entranced seers, observers, sleepwalkers: a cinema populated by subjects who largely watch, stare, and bear witness to damaged life, to events so unbearable as to be paralyzing.[23] And this is precisely what Joslin's voice tells us during these first ten shots: he no lon-

ger acts—rather, he sits, stares, and records; he no longer participates in life—he only looks at it from afar.

To recapitulate: Still life as representation of that which endures, disjunction of sound and image, whatever-space, the missing people, the subject as witness of life rather than as agent in life: such are at once the palpable traces that time leaves on the image, as well as the features of an image that draws attention to the passing of time, that indexes the emergence of time in the shot itself, that makes time visible as such. After the first ten shots of this sequence have unraveled under the sign of the time-image, however, a singular event takes place: in the eleventh and twelfth shots—each of which is significantly longer than all the preceding ones—we see the shadow of the recording apparatus, which consists of an indivisible assemblage of Joslin's body and his prosthetic video camera: in the shadow, they are one; there can be no distinction between the two. After having expressed time in image after image, the recording apparatus has nothing else left to record but its own power to record; it has nothing left to do but to enfold over itself, to turn onto itself, or, more precisely, to turn to its incorporeal, immaterial, non-present existence—that is, to its negative, to its shadow. Such is the life-image: it does not merely represent body, matter, life per se; it expresses, rather, a pure potential to be, to act, to record, to produce as the body's ubiquitous shadow-image. If—as Deleuze claims—the time-image expresses time as the absolute by activating an infinite relay between the virtual and the actual, the life-image emerges from the time-image by expressing the power of the absolute, or, rather, its two distinct yet indiscernible powers or potentials: the potential to think or to know, and the potential to be or to act.[24] Here, the first potential corresponds to the eleventh shot, in which the recording apparatus records its power to know by recording its own shadow: here, in other words, the recording apparatus records the trace of its own recording, records the negative of itself in the process of knowing. The second potential corresponds to the twelfth shot, in which the recording apparatus records its power to act by recording its own moving hand and its own singing voice. In this last singular shadow, we see a body on the verge of disappearance, a life on the brink of death, asking itself what more it can do. What this body can do is to turn a silly song and a campy wave of the hand seamlessly into an arresting gesture of joyous valediction: index finger raised pointing to an absolute out-of-field, waving good-bye to the world and to life itself, this body basks content in the bright light of a beautiful day, and expresses its power to be to the very end.

PART THREE

Past and Future Itineraries of the Image-Concept

EIGHT

On Producing the Concept of the Image-Concept

KENNETH SURIN

One of the great divisions in the reflection on culture undertaken by the Western tradition has been the one between the *image* (seen by this tradition as belonging to the realm of experience) and the *concept* (seen as being in the realm of the understanding or reason). This problematic dichotomy reached its culminating point in Immanuel Kant, who assigned its respective terms to two completely different faculties (though to be precise Kant did not use the term "image," preferring instead to use the term "object of experience")—Kant located the *concept* in the domain of judgment (his first *Critique*), while the image was placed in the domain of taste or opinion (his third *Critique*).

My essay has three parts. The first outlines the theory of conceptual production employed in this essay, and it will soon be clear that this theory is indebted to the writings of Gilles Deleuze. The second traces the history of this dichotomy, going back to Plato and up to contemporary Anglo-American philosophy, where the *image* continues to be identified with the particular, and the *concept* with the universal (witness the protracted debates on the issue of denotation [image-object] versus connotation [concept] in the tradition that extends from Frege via Russell to Quine). This dichotomy also has a profound resonance in popular culture, instanced in the commonplace distinction, typically to be encountered on television shows with a "pop psychology" component such as Oprah or Dr. Phil, between someone's "body image" (basically to do with entirely subjective self-perception, as when I say "I'm really fat" or "My baldness makes me unattractive") and the "bodily concept" (what the consensus of experts such as dieticians and doctors tells us, "objectively," about the body—if your body mass index is X, then you are "normal" or "obese" or "morbidly obese," etc.). The third part deals with one very significant attempt to cut the Gordian knot with regard to this dichotomy, namely, the notion of the *image-concept* in the work of Gilles Deleuze. The aspects of Deleuze's position to be considered here include his treatment of the notion of involuntary memory (Bergson and Proust influenced this area of Deleuze's work), which seems to be neither fully image nor fully concept. Also pertinent here is Deleuze's notion of the cinematic image, which like involuntary memory, seems to be both image and concept and yet not fully either at the same time.

Conceptual Production

But first, by way of some initial footwork, the question of producing a concept needs to be broached.[1] Deleuze and Guattari are explicit about relating the genesis of a concept to the *event* of its production. To quote at some length a relevant passage from their *What Is Philosophy?*:

> The philosopher is the concept's friend; he is the potentiality of the concept. That is, philosophy is not the simple art of forming, inventing, or fabricating concepts, because concepts are not necessarily forms, discoveries, or products. More rigorously, philosophy is the discipline that involves *creating* concepts. . . . The object of philosophy is to create concepts that are always new. . . . Concepts are not waiting for us ready-made, like heavenly bodies. There is no heaven for concepts. They must be invented, fabricated, or rather created. . . . Nietzsche laid down the task of philosophy when he wrote, "[Philosophers] must no longer accept concepts as a gift, nor merely purify and polish them, but first *make* and *create* them, present them and make them convincing. Hitherto one has generally trusted one's concepts as if they were a wonderful dowry from some sort of wonderland," but trust must be replaced by distrust, and philosophers must distrust most those concepts they did not create themselves.[2]

If we proceed in accordance with this Deleuzean prescription, we will need to distinguish adequately between the concepts of a *theory* of X (X could be culture or cinema or religion or whatever), the concepts *intrinsic* to X (i.e., a particular culture or cinema or religion, etc.), and that culture or cinema or religion in its barest empirical or material *conditions*.[3] A theory of X is something that is produced or created no less than its putative object X. It is a practice, just as cultures and cinemas are multilinear ensembles of practices. A theory, to be more precise, is a practice of concepts. A theory of culture or cinema is not "about" culture or cinema, but about the concepts that cultures or cinemas happen to generate, concepts that are themselves related in more or less complex ways to other practices, and so on. A theory, in short, operates on the concepts integral to the practical expression of this or that culture or cinema.

A *theory* of culture does not therefore impinge directly on the sheerly empirical phenomena constituting culture, but on the concepts of culture, which, however, are no less practical, actual, or effective than culture itself. (This is simply another way of registering in a way that is as unavoidable as it is problematic that scarcely deniable affectivity of "thought" with which the "idealist" philosophical traditions have always been impressed, but which their materialist counterparts have found embarrassing or not susceptible to adequate description and analysis, or else reducible in principle to something more fundamental and compelling, namely, "matter.") Culture's concepts are not given in the assemblages of practices that constitute it, yet they are culture's concepts, not theories about culture. Every culture or cinema generates for itself its own "thinkability" (and concomitantly its own "unthinkability" as the obverse of this very "thinkability"), and its concepts are constitutive of that "thinkability." Another way of making this point would be to say that a culture or cinema has to secrete its myriad expressivities precisely in order to be able to be what it is and that its concepts—in ways that are inevitably selective, limiting, and even arbitrary—are the thematizations or representations of these expressivities. Or, more generally, the concepts of a culture (or a cinema) are its expressivities rendered in the form of that culture's (or that cinema's) "thinkability."

Theories of culture (or cinema), by contrast, are theories produced by reflection on the natures, functions, and so forth of these expressivities. They operate on a culture's (or a cinema's) "thinkability." It is fine and salutary to ask the question "What is culture?" but there is another kind of question to be asked as well, in this case "What is (a) theory of (culture)?" Culture itself is an immensely varied and complex practice of signs and images, whose theory philosophers of culture and others must produce, but produce precisely as conceptual practice. No theoretical determination, no matter how subtle or thorough, can on its own constitute the concepts of culture. As indicated, these concepts are expressed in advance and independently of theoretical practice. Theorists, qua theorists, can only traffic in theories of culture (or religion or cinema).

The concepts that theorists deal with can function in more than one field of thought, and even in a single domain it is always possible for a concept to fulfill more than one function. For example, depending on the context, the concept "video image" can function in fields as diverse as cultural studies, forensic criminology, electronics, information science, digital art, advertising theory, and so on. Each variable of thought is of course defined by its own internal variables, variables that have a complex relation to their external counterparts (such as historical periods, political and social conditions and forces, even the sheer physical state of things). (It is tempting here to understand this complexity in terms that are akin to Althusser's sense of the "overdetermined" relation between formations.) It follows that a concept comes into being or ceases to be effective only when there is a change of function and/or field. Functions for concepts must be created or abolished for them to be generated or eliminated, and new fields must be brought into being in order for concepts to be rendered irrelevant or invalid.

All the above seems like a long drawn-out clearing of the throat, but I'm not saying anything really new here—Foucault's *Les mots et les choses* contains a now famous depiction of visibility that conforms in outline to my somewhat perfunctory accounts of function and field. There Foucault discredits the age-old conception of visibility as something that has its origins in a general/generative source of light that casts itself upon and thereby "illuminates" pre-existing objects. For Foucault, visibility is determined by an apparatus (*dispositif*) that has its own particular way of structuring light, determining the way in which it falls, spreads, and obscures; an apparatus that demarcates the visible from the invisible, in this way bringing into being entire arrays of objects with this or that mode of visibility as their condition of possibility; a scopic apparatus or regime that also causes objects to be wholly or partially effaced, hidden. Hence even something so taken for granted and innocuous as the very visibility of things is created by an apparatus or regime, in this case a scopic regime, which provides "rules" that govern the very existence and operating conditions of visibility. (And these conditions, as Foucault himself never tired of pointing out, are always "political.") It seems obvious that the concept of the *image-concept* likewise conforms to such "rules" for the generation and perpetuation of concepts.[4]

A Preceding Intellectual History

The intellectual-historical conditions for the production of the (Deleuzean) image-concept are to be found at the heart of the previous philosophical tradition. According to this tradition, the being of a particular, qua particular, can only be received passively through human intuition—I can have a grasp of singular being only by having an actual experience of the particular in question. Concepts, however, can be employed independently of any actual experience, and do not depend on the passive sensible receptivity of an empirical "given" for their use—in Kant's words, concepts are marked by a productive "spontaneity," in contrast to the non-creative "passivity" of sensible intuitions.[5] Deleuze is certainly not the first philosopher who sought to dismantle this dichotomy between concept and intuition, and it is now something of a commonplace to say that Heidegger is the contemporary philosopher who more than any other elevated this dismantling into the quintessential philosophical "project." But Heidegger's basis for this dismantling is still placed within the confines of a phenomenological ontology, that is, he sought to answer the question "how is receptivity possible?" by resorting to the notion of the pre-givenness of being, and in the process could not account for the productive processes that underlie sensibility itself. For Deleuze, by contrast, the central task of philosophy is precisely the creation of a metaphysics capable of accounting for these productive processes.

The problem with this separation between concept and intuition, or *noesis* and *aisthesis*, is one that has permeated the very core of the philosophical tradition. The age-old distinctions between epistemology and aesthetics, (true) judgment and (mere) taste, all have their basis in this separation. And just as venerable are the attempts to overcome this disconnection, an attempt nowhere more apparent than in Kant's realization that he needed to write a *Critique of Judgment* (to wit, aesthetic judgment) to "complete" the project that began with his *Critique of Pure Reason* (dealing of course with judgment in the domain of truth governed by reason). For Deleuze, the attempts to overcome the dichotomy between (general) concept and (particular) sensible intuition are bound to fail, and this because the principles devised in this philosophical "overcoming" succumb to unavoidable metaphysical illusions. The most common of these illusions involves the use of abstract concepts to group together isolated particulars. These abstract concepts—Being, Unity, Thought, Matter, and so forth—are then inevitably bestowed an a priori ontological superiority denied to the metaphysically inferior particulars, and this because notions like Being and Unity and so on are simply not "given" in immediate experience, and thus must be positioned as a pure exteriority transcending the contents of immediate experience.[6] There is no way round or out of this predicament as long as the distinction between (transcendent) *noesis* and (transcended) *aisthesis* is retained, and Deleuze opts instead to cut the Gordian knot by assigning to the concept a totally different function and status.

The Image-Concept

Rather than give the abstract concept the policing or custodial role accorded it by the previous philosophical tradition, Deleuze prefers to abandon the tradition's static view of the concept as purely designative, denominative, or descriptive, and instead views the concept as active and creative. A concept for Deleuze (and Guattari) has three intertwined components: a "possible world, existing face, and real language or speech."[7] A field of experience in their view is always related to a simple "there is." Hence, if I experience fear now that the swine flu has reached my hometown of Blacksburg, Virginia, then it is a condition of having this experience that there is such a thing as the swine flu, that there is a place (Blacksburg) that happens to be my hometown, and so forth. But this world, the world that *is*, is always in a position to be interrupted and transformed—someone who gazes at it with a look of fear opens up the possibility of a frightening world, a look of fascination opens up the possibility of a fascinating world, a look of bewilderment opens up the possibility of a bewildering world, and so on. Thus the frightening world in which the swine flu comes to Blacksburg can be transformed into a world of hope when I find out that there is an ample supply of flu vaccine at the local hospital, that the known cases of swine flu in Blacksburg and the surrounding towns have been quarantined, and so on, so that I now gaze on the world with a look of hope. Likewise, Tibet is a possible world (it also happens of course to be a part of the actual world), one that becomes real when Tibetan is spoken or Tibet is mentioned within a given realm of experience (a high school geography lesson, a speech by the Dalai Lama, etc.). A possible world is expressed by a face that gazes on a situation (with a look of fear, or fascination, hope, or bewilderment, or whatever), and it takes shape in a language that makes it real (in the way that "Tibet" is made real by those who speak Tibetan or when it is spoken about in a given domain of experience).

A concept also has a relationship to other concepts by virtue of the shared problems addressed by the concepts in question—hence the concepts "hunger" and "poverty" are related to each other in a "problematics" constituted by the need to alleviate famine in a poor country, but have no such connection in a domain of experience where a Wall Street investment banker says "I'm really hungry" as he opens the door to a Michelin three-star restaurant in New York City, where the cheapest entrée costs seventy dollars (in this latter situation there would be a completely different "problematic," namely, "I'm feeling hungry, but I'm looking forward to a splendid feast prepared by one of the world's most renowned chefs," as opposed to the speech-forms inherent in the former "problematics," whose typical mode of expression would be "I'm starving, but there's not even a bowl of gruel to be had"). Concepts also relate to each other by having similar components:

> Concepts, which have only consistency or intensive ordinates outside of any coordinates, freely enter into relationships of nondiscursive resonance—either because the components of one become components with other heterogeneous components or because there is no difference of scale between them at any level. Concepts are centers of vibrations, each in itself and every one in relation to all the others. This is why they all resonate rather than cohere or correspond with each other.[8]

For example, the concepts "being a sumo wrestler" and "being a whale" could have the element or component "being gargantuan" in common, though of course "being a sumo wrestler" and "being a whale" may have little else in common (since as far as we know, whales don't wrestle and sumo wrestlers unaided by oxygen tanks aren't able to spend several hours underwater without surfacing for air). There is thus no logically ordained relation between concepts. Hence, while "this is a square circle" expresses a contradiction, this particular contradiction is manifested only when "square" and "circle" come to be related to each other in the same proposition, whereas the proposition "in Kandinsky's painting *Bright Lucidity* a square is painted next to a circle" is certainly not contradictory. There is nothing intrinsic to "square" and "circle" as concepts that requires them to resonate, or that prevents them from resonating, with each other, as they do in the case of

Kandinsky's *Bright Lucidity*. For this reason Deleuze insists that relationships between concepts are constitutively "agrammatical."

The claim that concepts relate to each other, or that this or that component of a concept relates to the components of other concepts, exclusively
in terms of their intensive vibrations and not at the level of logical or grammatical connectivity, is precisely what enables Deleuze to identify the concept with the image. Identifying a situation, typically to be seen in the films
of Sergei Eisenstein, where there is a movement from image to concept and
concept to image, Deleuze says there is a third case, one in which there is an
identity of concept and image:

> The concept is in itself in the image, and the image is for itself in the con-
> cept. This is no longer organic and pathetic but dramatic, pragmatic, praxis,
> or action-thought. This action-thought indicates *the relation between man
> and the world*, between man and nature, the sensory-motor unity, but by
> raising it to a supreme power ("monism"). Cinema seems to have a real vo-
> cation in this respect. . . . Hitchcock's cinema . . . goes beyond the action-
> image towards the "mental relations" which frame it and constitute its link-
> age, but at the same time returns to the image in accordance with "natural
> relations" which make up a framework. From the image to the relation, and
> from the relation to the image: all the functions of thought are included in
> this circuit. . . . This is definitely not a dialectic; it is a logic of relations.[9]

Deleuze gives an example of how this circuit between "mental relations,"
"natural relations," and the image works—violence, he says, is "of the image and its vibrations" (164), and not "that of the represented" (164), and
a concept such as "grandeur" can only be expressed by "composition" and
not "a pure and simple inflation of the represented," since in the latter instance "there is no cerebral stimulation or birth of thought" (165). The project embarked upon here by Deleuze is ambitious but not altogether novel
(Deleuze clearly views Artaud as a precursor in this enterprise), namely, "a
possibility of thinking in cinema through cinema" (165):

> Artaud . . . says specifically that cinema must avoid two pitfalls, abstract
> experimental cinema, which was developing at the time, and commercial
> figurative cinema, which Hollywood was imposing. He says that cinema is a
> matter of neuro-physiological vibrations, and that the image must produce
> a shock, a nerve-wave which gives rise to thought, "for thought is a matron
> which has not always existed." Thought has no other reason to function than
> its own birth, always the repetition of its own birth, secret and profound. He
> says that *the image thus has as object the functioning of thought, and that the*

functioning of thought is also the real subject which brings us back to the images. (165, emphasis mine)

While the object of the image is the functioning of thought, in this Artaudian account followed closely by Deleuze, it has to be noted that the thought in question here is not a "thought of the whole," but rather of a "figure of nothingness," a "hole in appearance" (167). Cinema, in this view, is concerned "not with the power of returning to images, and linking them according to the demands of an internal monologue and the rhythm of metaphors, but of 'un-linking' them, according to multiple voices, internal dialogues, always a voice in another voice" (167). This (cinematic) thought "can only think one thing, *the fact that we are not yet thinking*, the powerlessness to think the whole and to think oneself, thought which is always fossilized, dislocated, collapsed" (167, Deleuze's emphasis). Drawing on the work of Maurice Blanchot, Deleuze poses the question of how the movement from this "I-am-not-yet-thinking-is-all-I-can-think" to the "I-am-forced to-think (and will attempt [real] thought because I'm forced to think)" is possible. His answer accords with Blanchot's, namely, our ability to think hinges decisively "on the one hand [on] the presence of an unthinkable in thought, which would be both its source and barrier; on the other hand [on] the presence to infinity of another thinker in the thinker, who shatters every monologue of a thinking self" (168). In cinema (as in philosophy and literature—Deleuze is explicit about this), thought, which is inseparable from the image, "as soon as it takes on its aberration of movement, carries out a *suspension of the world* or affects the visible with a *disturbance*, which, far from making thought visible . . . are on the contrary directed to what does not let itself be thought in thought, and equally to what does not let itself be seen in vision" (168, Deleuze's emphasis).[10]

The metaphysical context for these declarations take us well beyond cinema. In an astonishing paragraph, with its echoes of Nietzsche and the Adorno of *Minima Moralia*, Deleuze dramatizes this contemporary metaphysical condition:

The modern fact is that we no longer believe in this world. We do not even believe in the events which happen to us, love, death, as if they only half concerned us. It is not we who make cinema; it is the world which looks to us like a bad film. . . . The link between man and the world is broken. Henceforth, this link must become an object of belief: it is the impossible which can only be restored within a faith. Belief is no longer addressed to a different or transformed world. Man is in the world as if in a pure optical and sound situation. The reaction of which man has been dispossessed can be replaced only by belief. Only belief in the world can reconnect man to what he sees and hears. The cinema must film, not the world, but belief in this world, our only link. . . . Whether we are Christians or atheists, in our universal schizophrenia, *we need reasons to believe in this world.* It is a whole transformation of belief. It was already a great turning-point in philosophy, from Pascal to Nietzsche: to replace the model of knowledge with belief. But belief replaces knowledge only when it becomes belief in this world, as it is. (172, Deleuze's emphasis)

The function of the image-concept is thus to restore this now-lost link between us and the world. The claim that we are "in the world as if in a pure optical and sound situation" has undeniable resonances with the work of Baudrillard after the Gulf War, or the worlds of some of Borges's fables, but for Deleuze there can be no (restored but transformed) linkage with the world if we had no alternative but to dwell in a world consisting exclusively of optical or auditory intuitions or experiences (i.e., pure images)—this world would be little different from a purely hallucinatory universe. What the image-concept accomplishes, in its ability to disturb or suspend this purely optical and auditory world, is precisely to reconnect that which we see and hear with its exteriority, its "excess," an "excess" that is immanent to that which we see and hear, but that at the same time is capable of taking us to the level of belief (i.e., the concept). It should be made clear that Deleuze accepts that there are many types of images and concepts of a kind that do not require or presuppose any linkage with each other. But what Deleuze does, in his delineation of the image-concept, is to provide an elaborate metaphysical circuitry for establishing this connection between belief and world on an entirely new basis, but also in the process, to dismantle the age-old separation between *noesis* and *aisthesis*, concept and sensible intuition. Cutting this Gordian knot is no small philosophical accomplishment, even if some of us may cavil at some of the metaphysical principles adverted to by Deleuze in this undertaking.[11]

NINE

The Romantic Image of the Intentional Structure

FOREST PYLE

> We are only beginning to understand how this oscil-
> lation in the status of the image is linked to the crisis
> that leaves the poetry of today under a steady threat
> of extinction, although, on the other hand, it remains
> the depository of hopes that no other activity of mind
> seems able to offer.
>
> —Paul de Man, "Intentional Structure of the
> Romantic Image"

1. The Romantic Image

I have taken as my epigraph the enigmatic closing sentence of the essay by Paul de Man invoked in my title. By way of the "oscillation in the status of the image" in a few decisive texts of Romantic and post-Romantic poetry and criticism, I hope to show how we might still only be at the "beginnings" of the understanding to which de Man alludes in the conclusion of that essay first published in French in 1960. The date of publication is worth noting because this is old work: old, not simply because de Man's essay appeared fifty years ago but because its topic, the function and status of the image in Romantic poetry, seems itself to be a thing of the past. But given the rich and exciting work presently being done on the production and circulation of the visual image, it might be worth revisiting some older accounts of the Romantic image in order to see whether their story of the image or, even the Romanti-cism from which it is derived, is in fact over. Some important contemporary French developments in philosophy and aesthetics suggest that it is not. The recent work of Jacques Rancière, for instance, is premised on reiterating the Romantic advent of "the aesthetic regime of the image": for Rancière "the future of the image" and its radically liberatory potential is a principal legacy of a Romanticism that is far from exhausted.[1] For Alain Badiou, on the other hand, the urgent task is precisely the opposite: "can we be delivered," he asks, "*finally* delivered, from our subjection to Romanticism?"[2] For Badiou, moreover, Romanticism is just another name for "the aura of the poem" and our "captation" by poetic "rhythm and image."[3] What, then, is this Romantic image that still seems to have the capacity to imprison or to liberate us?

Though the original venue of its publication may have been *Revue internationale de philosophe* and though its protocols are thoroughly comparativist in nature (the principal frame of reference is Mallarmé, and the textual example from Wordsworth is "juxtaposed" with passages from Rousseau and Hölderlin), de Man's essay has most often been read against the institutional backdrop of an Anglo-American New Criticism: Cleanth Brooks, William K. Wimsatt, Ruben Brower, William Empson, Frank Kermode. Perhaps this is the case because so many readers first encountered the essay in its English translation and in one of the most indispensable and decisive critical anthologies ever published in the field: Harold Bloom's *Romanticism and Consciousness* (1970), where it is included in the first section of essays under the rubric "Nature and Consciousness," a group of essays that Bloom characterizes as "the advanced criticism of Romanticism."[4] Bloom pairs de Man's essay with William Wimsatt's "The Structure of Romantic Nature Imagery": these two essays, writes Bloom, "move the discussion to the imagistic edge of consciousness" in order to "illuminate the structure of Romantic imagery" (*RC*, 1–2).

I would like to begin by pairing de Man's essay with another text from this constellation of New Critics, Kermode's *The Romantic Image*, published in 1957. Given the acrimony that characterized their professional relationship in subsequent decades, it is difficult now to fathom the relative proximity of their positions in the late 1950s as two critics pursuing work "at the imagistic edge of consciousness." If Kermode would endorse de Man's assertion that "as in all Romantic poetry, the most revealing stylistic unit will be the image," there is very little agreement between them on what that stylistic unit actually reveals.[5] Unruffled by potential complexities, Kermode's position is remarkable now only for the confidence of its declarations: the Romantic image is "a radiant truth out of space and time," which, "standing free of intention" and "affective considerations," "provides its own vigour."[6] Kermode understands the image to be both the embodiment and the product of "organicist modes of thinking about art" (*RI*, 53). And, decisively, for Kermode the image is the medium of reconciliation.

To be sure, these are not the positions or conclusions we are ever likely to ascribe to the author of "Intentional Structure of the Romantic Image." And yet there is considerable agreement about what we might call the trajectory and terrain of the image. We could, for instance, ascribe to de Man what Kermode says of Romanticism's prolonged historical reach: the term "Romantic," writes Kermode, is "applicable to the literature of one epoch, beginning in the late years of the eighteenth century and not yet finished" (*RI*, 52). Moreover, for Kermode as for de Man, *Yeats* is the decisive poet, the one who deployed and exploited the Romantic image and then interrogated it to its limits and undid it. This means that for both critics Modernism remains very much at stake in the critical interpretation of Romanticism. In fact, one could argue that from this perspective the Modernist discourse of the image is an event—something on the order of a fold—*within* Romanticism. De Man's own critical attention to the image is, to the best of my knowledge, limited to the essay I am invoking with my title and to the chapter he devoted to Yeats in his dissertation. That chapter, "Image and Emblem in Yeats"—written in 1960 and reprinted twenty-four years later in *The Rhetoric of Romanticism*—explicitly takes up Kermode's interpretation of Yeats "as the successful seeker for 'the reconciling image'" and makes visible the full extent of their interpretive differences.

Kermode claims that what he says about Yeats is "the very heart" of his account of the Romantic image; and what the critic has to say about "Among Schoolchildren" is "the very heart" of his interpretation of Yeats as the poet who not only identifies but achieves the ambitions of the reconciling image. "'Among Schoolchildren,'" writes Kermode, "might well be treated as the central statement of the whole complex position of [artistic] isolation and the Image" (*RI*, 103). In what Kermode calls the "magnificent concluding stanza" of that poem, we are presented with the "Dancer-image," the presence of an image that has effaced the difference between dancer and dance, physical body and aesthetic object.

> O chestnut-tree, great-rooted blossomer,
> Are you the leaf, the blossom, or the bole?
> O body swayed to music, O brightening glance,
> How can we know the dancer from the dance?

The triumph of this reconciling image is achieved once Yeats's poetry abandons the image that is nothing more than "picture" or "dramatization" of "abstractions"—"*mere* images"—and begins to forge "a poetic image which will resemble . . . living beauty" (*RI*, 101, 102). Independent of what Kermode terms "separable intellectual content," the image of the dancer as immediately and forever indiscernible from the dance delivers us to a poetry "where art means wholly what it is" (*RI*, 102).

"It might seem far-fetched or even perverse," writes de Man of these same iconic lines, "to find here anything but a splendid statement glorifying organic, natural form, its sensuous experience and fundamental unity" (*RR*, 197). Yet, in what stands as the best-known counter-reading of these lines, de Man "finds" just that: *anything but* such a splendid statement. De Man demonstrates that Kermode's "reconciling" interpretation of the lines rests on the assumption that they take the form of "rhetorical questions that express unity and state the impossibility of distinguishing the part from the whole, the action from the actor, or the form from its creator" (*RR*, 200). But it is only as the result of what we could call the ideology of the image (as linguistic medium of reconciliation and unity) that a critic *decides* to identify the question as rhetorical. "The question," insists de Man, "could just as well express the bewilderment of someone who, faced with two different possibilities, does not know what choice to make. In that case, the question would not be rhetorical at all, but urgently addressed to the 'presences' in the hope of receiving an answer" (*RR*, 200). The final, condensed—and certainly most famous—version of de Man's reading is presented in "Semiology and Rhetoric," where it is identified as one of three exemplary instances of deconstruction as "undecidability": "two entirely coherent but entirely incompatible readings can be made to hinge on one line, whose grammatical structure is devoid of ambiguity, but whose rhetorical mode turns the mood as well as the mode of the poem upside down."[7] But in the earlier version of the argument as it appears in "Image and Emblem in Yeats," de Man seems, as Ian Balfour puts it, "unambiguous . . . that the true reading of the line is the 'negative' one, the one that stresses the difficulty of knowing rather than celebrates the inseparability of dancer and dance."[8] And on this point at this moment in his career de Man is indeed unambiguous: "the final line is not a rhetorical statement of reconciliation but an anguished question" (*RR*, 202).

De Man comes to this conclusion because the image of the dancer and the dance—for Kermode the epitome of the Romantic image—is not in fact an image at all but what Yeats called an *emblem*. De Man's treatment of the relationship between emblem and image "corresponds roughly," as

Balfour puts it, "to the distinction between allegory and symbol" proposed in the "Rhetoric of Temporality" (*LPdM*, 54). "The ways of the image and the emblem are distinct and opposed," asserts de Man: if the image promises the reconciliation of dancer and dance in the glorious production of what Kermode calls "a radiant truth out of space and time," for de Man the emblem "states the inadequacy and the downfall of precisely that type of natural image" (*RR*, 197).[9] According to de Man, Yeats "often treats the dance as if it were the dancer, that is, he presents emblems *disguised* as natural images" (*RR*, 203). But "what appears as a synthesis" or a "reconciliation" is in the example of the closing lines of "Among Schoolchildren" "one more veiled statement of the absolute superiority of the emblem over the image" (*RR*, 201). Or, to adopt the idiom of "Semiology and Rhetoric," the claims for the image are "undermined, or deconstructed" by the workings of the emblem.

What is at stake in the "deconstruction" of image by emblem—"a recurrent strategy in Yeats's mature work" (*RR*, 195)—are the claims and the seductions of the visual. What de Man calls the "emblematic reading" demanded by Yeats's poetry not only "defeats" the "natural image" but also "destroys" the "wonderful picture" the image projects: "the very discomfort one experiences in thus destroying a wonderful picture is an essential part of Yeats's statement" (*RR*, 195). Does it go without saying that this is also an "essential part" of *de Man's* own project, both the critical violence and the affective discomfort that results?[10] It seems inevitable that in one form or another the poetic image conjures the visual, posits language's picture-effect. A thousand shades of subtlety might separate phenomenological and post-phenomenological accounts of the literary image from C. Day Lewis's succinct definition—"the image is a picture made out of words"—but pictoriality is never entirely banished. However much one might acknowledge that the visual aspect of the literary image is a linguistic effect, a rhetorical sleight of hand, the status of the image as mere sensation persists if only in the form of a ghostly residue. Even when the image is not mimetic, as when an image is understood to be the visual manifestation of an idea or concept, it commits itself to the vicissitudes and seductions of perception, as when we are made to imagine we might actually *see* meaning.

Though de Man's critical vocabulary develops considerably and his philosophical points of reference are substantially amplified, versions of the "destruction" of "wonderful pictures" remain an "essential part" of his work throughout his career and constitute, in both the technical and the figurative sense, his iconoclasm. Of course, de Man never takes credit for this destruction: even in "Emblem and Image" the critic merely reveals the violence Yeats's poems perform on their own. But the disarticulation between phenomenality and materiality that is crystallized here in the oscillation of the image is arguably the principal topic—the "through line"—of de Man's critical project. In the late essays devoted to the problem of the aesthetic, for instance, de Man demonstrates how the *Third Critique* reveals the disjunction of phenomenality from cognition and perception from language. In one of his most compelling formulations, de Man argues that this "deep, perhaps fatal, break or discontinuity" in Kant "marks the undoing of the aesthetic as a valid category," for "the bottom line [in the *Third Critique*] is the prosaic materiality of the letter and no degree of obfuscation or ideology can transform this materiality into the phenomenal cognition of aesthetic judgment."[11]

If in the earlier scholarship the "bottom line" in Yeats is ultimately the "materiality" of the emblem, de Man's reading of the poet demonstrates how the oscillation between phenomenality and materiality is the principal pivot to the development of Yeats's poetics: the merely "decorative" image of the earliest poems—"hardly more than picturesque detail" and "devoid of metaphorical or emblematic depth"—is supplanted "with an image which belongs to a much more complicated species" (*RR*, 152):

> The movement of the image, which started in perception, then fused the perceived object and the perceiving consciousness into one by means of a verbal transfer, now returns to the original perception, making the object itself into the perceiver. From purely perceptual, then metaphorical (or symbolic), the image has become one of self-reflection, using the material properties of the object . . . as a means to allow a self-referential consciousness to originate. (*RR*, 154)

This is indeed "a much more complicated species" of image, one in which "by means of a verbal transfer" the original object of sensory perception is itself *made* "into the perceiver." The means of this oscillation are linguistic or, more precisely, rhetorical; and its effects are specular: "a self-referential consciousness" *originates* by way of the *images'* properties of self-reflection.[12]

Though de Man is describing here the specific operations of an image from *The Wanderings of Oisin*, the reading summarizes his understanding of the trajectory of Yeats's poetry as it leaves behind the "purely decorative" or "merely descriptive" image for one that is fully "self-reflective," one that "is able to cross the gap between subject and object without apparent effort, and to unite them" (*RR*, 153). Though Kermode never devotes this kind of sustained attention to the rhetorical properties of this process, the outcome is precisely what he identifies as "the Romantic image."

As de Man sees it, the decisive moment for Yeats's poetics, the "conflicted" event that "determines the subsequent development of his poetry" (*RR*, 170), is the turn from the image to the emblem, from the sensory perception of an object to the intralinguistic relationship between divine (or literary) "voices" and human expression, from a horizontal relationship with the potential for reconciliation to a fundamentally discrepant vertical relationship between humans and the gods. According to de Man, Yeats's turn to the emblem "represents a radical departure from one of the main tenets of the Western poetic tradition. This tradition conceives of the *logos* as incarnate and locates divine essence in the object" (*RR*, 168). Yeats's "claims for the emblem," which "go far beyond anything dreamed of by his predecessors," are realized in his desire "to write divine voices into existence" (*RR*, 169). But, in de Man's estimation, "Yeats's 'conversion' to an emblematic conception of language is never complete" (*RR*, 170), and Yeats's achievement is measured in his poetry by the failures of the natural image and not by the success of the emblem. In a sense, Yeats's "conversion" to the emblem is imposed upon him as a result of the accumulation of failures of the natural image. Moreover, and more disturbingly, the course of Yeats's mature poetry is marked by a series of progressively powerful failures: the "downfall" of the image and the inability of the emblem to fulfill the profound "hopes Yeats had invested" in them: "There is no return," writes de Man, "out of his exploded paradise of emblems back to a wasted earth" (*RR*, 238). As de Man understands it, the trajectory of Yeats's poetry is one of sheer and successive negations, from the merely pictorial or decorative images of the Pre-Raphaelites through the perceptual complexity of the "vital" images that are part of the legacy of Romanticism to the emblematic language of the sacred word. In so doing Yeats reaches an absolute impasse because "the failure of the emblem amounts to total nihilism" and there is no way back to the image for Yeats or, by the same token, for de Man, who here takes his own leave of the image as well as the emblem that would succeed it.

2. Of the Intentional Structure

If, as de Man asserts at the very beginning of "Intentional Structure," "the importance of the image as a dimension of poetic language does not remain constant," the faculty most associated with the image—the imagination—"steadily grows in importance and complexity in the critical as well as in the poetic texts of the period" (*RR*, 1). Perhaps by virtue of its role in Kant's critical philosophy, the concept of the imagination escapes the fate suffered by the image. If, for de Man, the *poetic* discourse of the image courts, at worst, "mere pictorialism" and, at best, the spurious claims of symbolic reconciliation, the *philosophical* discourse of the imagination in, for instance, Kant's analytic of the sublime, is the very site at which we experience the destruction not only of "wonderful pictures," but of phenomenality itself. "The faculty of *imagination* is itself beyond images," writes de Man in "Kant's Materialism"; "*Einbildungskraft* is *bildlos*, and the absurdity of its own name records its failure" (*AI*, 122). Thus is the imagination understood to take leave of the image. The account of this leave-taking is by no means restricted to de Man. The parting of image from imagination is, in fact, a legacy of Romanticism, one that always seems to attract the attention of its best readers, regardless of theoretical orientation. It functions as what de Man describes as the repetition of an "epiphany": "the rediscovery of a permanent presence which has chosen to hide itself from us" (*RR*, 5).

Earl Wasserman, for instance, discerns a similar trajectory in Romanticism's most philosophically ambitious poems. In his still unsurpassed reading of Shelley's "Mont Blanc," Wasserman describes the "transfiguration" of "imaging" (sensory representations that function at a phenomenal level) into what Shelley calls "imaginings" ("transcendent intuitings in the successive suppositions of the simile, the trance, and the dream").[13] Wasserman's reading demonstrates that in Shelley's poetics of the sublime, "imaginings" indeed begin where images leave off and nowhere more powerfully than in the poem's famous closing lines addressed to the mountain: "And what were thou, and earth, and stars, and sea, / If to the human mind's imaginings / Silence and solitude were vacancy?" (ll. 142–144).[14] The *bildlos* dimension of "silence" and "solitude"—in which the prospect of a final "vacancy" is posed as an unanswered question—arises when the "gleam" of the image is extinguished from the poem.[15]

But this parting goes both ways. If the imagination can take leave of the image, this also means that images can circulate without the imprimatur or authorization of the imagination. So, what happens to the disposition of this relationship between the imagination and the image when, by what Kant calls "a certain subreption," the faculty of the imagination becomes a poetic image, when the ostensible cause (or necessary condition) is rendered an effect? What happens, in other words, when the imagination—which de Man identifies alongside "will" as one of the two "main faculties of a conscious mind"—is reduced to an image? And, finally, what happens when that imagination "lifts up itself" in the form of an image and does so without any will or any intention on the part of a "conscious mind"? These are some questions posed by the iconic passage from Book VI of *The Prelude* that de Man refers to in order to illustrate the eruption of the autonomous "power" of imagination:

> Imagination!—lifting up itself
> Before the eye and progress of my song
> Like an unfathered vapour, . . .
> . . . In such strength
> Of usurpation, in such visitings
> Of awful promise, when the light of sense
> Goes out in flashes that have shewn to us
> The invisible world . . . (VI. ll. 525–538)

As de Man sees it, the imagination makes its appearance through the very extinguishing of the senses: Wordsworth "insists that the imagination can only come into full play when 'the light of sense / Goes out'" (*RR*, 16). Thus, at the moment of its greatest *productive* power, "in such visitings / Of awful promise," *Einbildungskraft* is indeed *bildlos*. De Man's interpretation corresponds to the narrative trajectory of Book VI in which Wordsworth arrives at this experience after the earlier disappointment when "the summit of Mont Blanc," that emblem of sublimity, is "unveiled" and "first beheld." The poet and his traveling companion "grieved / To have a soulless image on the eye / That had usurped upon a living thought / That never more could be" (VI. ll. 525, 524, 525–528). This is how I chart that circuit of images: "Soulless image" "usurps" "living thoughts," which are, in turn themselves "usurped" by the non-phenomenological eruption of the imagination as a power whose "strength" is measured in part by its very liquidation of sensory images.

All that de Man says of the manifestation of this imagination is that "we know very little about the kind of images that such an imagination could produce, except that they would have little in common with what we have come to expect from familiar metaphorical figures" (*RR*, 16). There is certainly nothing "familiar" and nothing "metaphorical" about the image produced in this passage of the poem, a passage iconic enough to function as an image of Romanticism itself. In the 1850 version of the passage, the "light of sense" has already been eclipsed when the "awful Power" called "Imagination" materializes, "rising up from the mind's abyss / Like an unfathered vapour" not as something to be beheld but as a rhetorical dimension of language, a catachresis: "the Power so called / Through sad incompetence of human speech" (VI. ll. 592–595). But in the version of the passage de Man chooses for the purposes of his demonstration, the figures of visuality have not been liquidated: "Imagination" of its own accord "lifts up itself" and presents itself *as an image* "before the eye" of the poet's song. For the Wordsworth of 1805, in other words, the imagination flashes up as a *sight to behold*, originless, vaporous but an image nonetheless. This "imaging" of the imagination threatens to arrest the "progress" of the poem and thus the destiny of this faculty to "put into question in the language of poetry, the ontological priority of the sensory object" (*RR*, 16).

At issue here is not merely the persistence of the visual in *The Prelude*; after all, the sensory residue in this passage is effectively erased in the poem's final version. What is of particular interest both for our understanding of the Romantic image and for our continuing assessment of the legacy of de Man's critical project is the way in which the image as the flickering play of the presence and absence of visuality converges with what de Man, in his lecture on Walter Benjamin, later identifies as "the fundamental non-human character of language": "the play of linguistic tensions, linguistic events that occur, possibilities which are inherent in language—independently of any intent or any drive or any wish or any desire we might have" (*RT*, 96). If the image and its seductive appeal to the senses serve as the very epitome of what de Man would come to call "the aesthetic ideology," it also bears within itself the form of an agency that de Man will understand to be a property of language. It is, in other words, not merely a matter of what images *are* but *how* they originate as poetic words.

"This requires," says the younger de Man, "that we begin by forgetting all we have previously known about 'words'" (*RR*, 3). "In everyday use words are exchanged and put to a variety of tasks": they are "used as established signs to confirm that something is recognized as being the same as before" (*RR*, 3). Only as fully conventional signs can words be relied upon to accomplish what we intend of them. And this includes their ability to provide likeness with that which occurs to the senses. But, continues de Man, "in poetic language"—and here he is referring to brief examples from Hölderlin, Mallarmé, and George—"words are not used as signs":

> The fundamental intent of the poetic word is to originate in the same manner as . . . "flowers." . . . The image is essentially a kinetic process . . . It originates with the statement, in the manner suggested by the flower image, and its way of being is determined by the manner in which it originates. (*RR*, 3)

Words and flowers come together in the Romantic image not on the basis of any resemblance but by virtue of their mode of origination. If "the word originates like a flower," "how do flowers originate?" The answer: "they rise out of the earth without the assistance of imitation or analogy" (*RR*, 4). The Romantic image presents us with "the fundamental intent of the poetic word," a linguistic agency that manifests itself as an *event*, a singular occurrence that, to anticipate Shelley, makes all that we seemed to know about words "appear as if it had been not." Suffice it to say that we are a long way from Frank Kermode.

What is also "suggested by the flower image," of course, is the organicism conventionally associated with Romanticism, an organicism that can cause readers and critics to mistake this event of origination for the resemblance to natural objects. But Romantic poetry is also replete with images that, "like an unfathered vapour," rise up without any analogy to botanical modes of production or any likeness to the processes or products of the natural world. Indeed, the text of and notes to Coleridge's "Kubla Khan: Or, A Vision in a Dream. A Fragment" offer in every sense an allegory of "the romantic image of the intentional structure." In the finest reading of the poem I have encountered, Timothy Bahti entertains seriously the "temptation" to take the "poem's constituents as the exemplary representation of romantic poetry as a whole."[16] I might rephrase Bahti's "temptation" this way: are we to regard "Kubla Khan" as the *very image* of Romanticism given the full range of "exemplary" "Romantic" elements on display there, which include its motifs of specularity, ideas of the sublime, Orientalized setting, fragmented form, quasi-sacred tone, visionary rhetoric, as well as its specific images and its story of origination? In the anxious note affixed to the text on its first publication in 1816, Coleridge explains the poem's existence as the result of the unintended appearance of a series or sequence of images. "In consequence of a slight indisposition," "the Author" had taken a "prescribed" "anodyne"—opium, most likely—and reading *Purchas's Pilgrimmage,* fell asleep in his chair . . . The Author continued for about three hours in a profound sleep, at least of the external senses, during which time he has the most vivid confidence that he could not have composed less than two to three hundred lines; if that indeed can be called composition in which all the images rose up before him as *things*, with a parallel production of the correspondent expressions, without any sensation or consciousness of effort.[17]

Whether celebration or excuse, this is the dream—or nightmare—of sheer origination, for it is only *without* an "intentional structure," only "without any sensation or consciousness of effort" that "images" *can* "rise up" as *things* and give rise to something like "Kubla Khan."

Coleridge's prefatory note is the first entry in Wimsatt and Beardsley's benchmark essay of critical ascesis, "The Intentional Fallacy": they classify the preface as "the classic 'anodyne' story," in which Coleridge "tells us what he can about the genesis of a poem which he calls a 'psychological curiosity,' but his definitions of poetry and of the poetic quality 'imagination' are to be found elsewhere and in quite other terms."[18] Wimsatt and Beardsley's project, of course, is to distinguish rigorously between the stories of a poem's genesis, fanciful or otherwise, and the imaginative product in and of itself, the nature of the poem as a "verbal icon." Though they will declare that "it is not so much a historical statement as a definition that the intentional fallacy is a romantic one" (*VI*, 6), the real target of their criticism, however, is not "Kubla Khan" but *The Road to Xanadu*, J. L. Lowes's groundbreaking if now ignored—and if ignored, in no small part as a result of the New Criticism—account of the poem from the perspective of its many literary sources and cultural and scriptural allusions. Wimsatt and Beardsley scarcely contain their contempt for "the whole glittering parade" of Lowes's book, which they invoke solely to exemplify the two principal forms of the intentional fallacy. "In certain flourishes," write Wimsatt and Beardsley, "and in chapter headings like 'The Shaping Spirit,' 'The Magical Synthesis,' 'Imagination Creatrix,' it may be that Professor Lowes pretends to say more about the actual poems than he does" (*VI*, 11). Instead, they claim, one finds only "more and more sources, more and more about 'the streamy nature of associations'" (*VI*, 12). And yet it is ironic that in fixing their attention on the mode of Lowes's criticism, the authors of "The Intentional Fallacy" overlook the radical implications posed by Coleridge's preface to "Kubla Khan": the image of a poem, a genuine "verbal icon," as an unintended object.

But even if we were to agree to the critical injunction to excise Coleridge's "classic 'anodyne' story" from our interpretation of the poem, even if we do employ what Wimsatt and Beardsley describe as "the action of the mind which cuts off roots, melts away context" (*VI*, 12), we will not solve the problem of origination in "Kubla Khan," for that is the problem *of* the poem "*itself.*" There is, of course, the poem's opening or originating image: the declaration of the "decree" by which Kubla Khan—and "Kubla Khan"—calls the "pleasure-dome" into being. This constitutive speech-act takes place where the beginnings are, "where Alph, the sacred river, ran / Through caverns measureless to man" (ll. 3–4). Interjected *against* this sublime image of imperial origination is that which Bahti calls "one of poetry's most curious representations of an origin as the result of fragmentation" (*EL*, 63), the disjunctive and deictic ejaculation that opens the second strophe: "But oh! that deep romantic chasm," that "savage place!" (ll. 12, 14). The second strophe not only introduces this void or rift in the poem's landscape but declares it as another and contrary mode of origination:

> And from this chasm, with ceaseless turmoil seething,
> As if this earth in fast thick pants were breathing
> A mighty fountain momently was forced:
> Amid whose swift half-intermitted burst
> Huge fragments vaulted like rebounding hail,
> Or chaffy grain beneath the thresher's flail:
> And 'mid these dancing rocks at once and ever
> It flung up momently the sacred river. (ll. 17–25)

The passage not only claims for itself a form of origin that differs dramatically—or, better yet, differs "romantically"—from Khan's fiat, but it also claims for itself a status more originary. This is the case not merely because "the sacred river," "Alph," is "flung up" from "a mighty fountain" that "was forced" from "this romantic chasm"; but also, it is because both fountain and river are, as the poem insists, forced and flung "*momently.*" As an adverb that activates each temporal dimension of the "moment," *momently* can mean anything from "moment to moment" or "at any moment" to "instantly" or "for a single moment;" and the "momently" in these lines seems to conjure them all "at once and ever," which is perhaps the best way to express the temporal dislocation at work in the perpetually present experience of a permanent origin.

And all the while, "'mid this tumult Kubla heard" those "ancestral voices prophesying war" (l. 30). This is a poem of absolute beginnings and apocalyptic ends, but so many of both arise from or refer back to "'mids" and "midsts" and "midways": "The shadow of the dome of pleasure," for instance, "floated *midway* on the waves" (ll. 31–32, emphasis added); and the "huge fragments vaulted" "*Amid*" the "*half-intermitted*" bursts of the originary "fountain." And yet if everything in the middle strophe tends to be drawn backward or forward to these "mingled" midways, it does so without ever diminishing the sense of urgency that issues from beginnings and attaches to ends. Indeed, as hard as we might work as readers to sort out the wild swings between origins, middles, and ends in the poem, and as earnestly as might respond to the poem's imperatives to behold beginnings and to reckon with outcomes, the poem's own swirling music—a "mingled measure" that is "heard" from both "fountains" and "caves" (ll. 33, 34)—is the result of a "ceaseless" oscillation that suspends this wild to and fro "momently," "at once and ever." As readers, we may learn to identify and understand the rhetorical processes that produce these effects, but this is something that the poem "knows" in advance of us, acknowledging that the "pleasure-dome" is "miracle of rare *device*" (l. 35) without canceling any of the auratic or even sacred quality of the poem's tremulous affect.

In its sustained temporal loopings and its auratic music, "Kubla Khan" presents us with the image of a miraculating agency; and of all the "devices" of language both "rare" and common, this is an agency that appears to be the exclusive property of the image. Jean-Luc Nancy reminds us that "the German word for the image, *bild*—which designates the image in its form of fabrication—comes from a root (*bil-*) that designates a prodigious force or a miraculating sign."[19] And though we might explain and comprehend these effects with recourse to rhetoric or biography, history or form, "Kubla Khan" compels us to feel as if it had touched the very image of images, the sacred place from which the image as such issues miraculously into the world. While I cannot imagine that Nancy had "Kubla Khan" in mind during his meditations on the "ground of the image," I also cannot imagine a more precise account of the image in Coleridge's poem than this: "the prodigious force-sign of an improbable presence irrupting from the heart of a restlessness on which nothing can be built" (*GI*, 23). It is in this sense that the auratic image in "Kubla Khan" operates on "the order of the monster; the *monstrum*," as Nancy puts it, "is a prodigious sign, which warns (*moneo, monstrum*) of a divine threat" (*GI*, 23), the kind of threat about which "all *should* cry, Beware! Beware!" (l. 49, emphasis added).[20]

If "Kubla Khan" presents its readers with the scene and consequences of the miraculous origination of the image, by the third strophe it places its speaker at the mercy of the image itself. Many readers have noted how the speaker's vision is a condensed and displaced refiguring of the principal figures of the preceding strophes: from "Alph, the sacred river" to "Mount Abora," from "that deep romantic chasm," as deeply gendered as it is "enchanted," to "an Abyssinian maid" playing "on her dulcimer," from the successful performative production of Khan's "decree" of the "pleasure-dome" to what one might call the speaker's reflexive performance of the conditional, one that longs for the reiteration of that decreed dome:

> Could I revive within me
> Her symphony and song,
> To such a deep delight 'twould win me,
> That with music loud and long
> I would build that dome in air,
> That sunny dome! those caves of ice! (ll. 42–47)

Bahti's reading of the poem as "fragmentation and reflection between beginning and end" develops in lucid detail the temporal and rhetorical relationships among the pieces of this fragmented whole. Bahti demonstrates how the poem's concluding lines move from the parade of conditionals to a series of imperatives and, in the process, eliminate the present: "it cannot rightly be said that anything is present, for there is no present without the indicative or the gerund, unless it be the performance of the 'I''s wishful projections . . . [T]he poem from line 42 onward is no longer narratable but only performable. The last thirteen lines are a matter of a *possible project* of writing and reading" (*EL*, 69).

As another of de Man's brilliant students, Bahti has learned—and has learned to teach us—the difficult and necessary lessons of reading. And as my discussion of "Kubla Khan" demonstrates, he has taught me how to read a poem I thought I knew well. And yet I would argue that to come to terms with the demands made in and by the closing lines of the poem, one must understand them as something other than "a *possible project of writing and reading*." What the speaker declares to be his urgent project is to bring a "symphony and song"—which originated as an image in a vision—back into existence, to "revive" or "reoriginate" them. This is something more, or less, than "writing and reading"; and it is not something that can be accomplished with such common linguistic "devices" as metaphor. Only the miraculating power of imaging can *conjure* "at once and ever" that "dome in air, / That sunny dome! those caves of ice!" Indeed, when Bahti describes the speaker's desire "to remember, and to revive and repeat, the image of an Abyssinian maid singing of Abora," he correctly shows us how this is the desire "to construct a double continuity between origin and image" (*EL,* 67). But though this may be the *speaker's* desire at this point in the poem, he can voice it as such only because the image (not only the image of the maid but the image as such) has already revealed its own intentions by demonstrating the powers of origination. This should tell us why readers are right to ignore Wimsatt and Beardley's injunction and to read the poem's prefatory note not as an alibi but as an allegory. Bahti, in his impeccable reading, describes the note as an "allegory of figuration": "if a poem originates and begins from metaphoricity, it and its readers are already in a fragmented allegory of figuration" (*EL,* 73). Perhaps one must be the under the spell of the poem to do this, but I find myself taking Coleridge at his word in the note and therefore regard it as an allegory of a different sort: I think it matters—in the note and to the poem—that the origin is the image, that the image is understood as possessing its own powers of origination. I would argue that this is the only way we can take full measure of the "deep delight" the speaker would "win" from "reviving" the original image of the Abyssinian maid; and this is the only way to feel the genuine and urgent regard the speaker has for those who should behold the images he would build "with music loud and long." Only the reader who feels that the poem is indeed addressing the intentional structure of the Romantic image will register the urgency of these last lines and take heed of the poem's closing imperative: "close your eyes with holy dread" (l. 52). But to do so, of course, puts an end to the reading.

But if it puts an end to the reading, it does not yet define the term posed by de Man's essay and revisited by my own: what is an "intentional structure"? Since de Man is attributing this structure to the image itself, we might assume that he is not attributing to the image what we might commonly call an intentional structure: subjectivity. And yet his account of the "movement of the image" in Yeats demonstrates how "by means of a verbal transfer," the object is *made* into something like a subject, "into the perceiver" (*RR,* 154). De Man does not, however, classify perception among the "main faculties of the conscious mind": in "Intentional Structure of the Romantic Image" those faculties are limited to "will" and "imagination." But it is the definition of *intentional* as an adjective that remains intriguing in this context. The columns of definitions provided by the *OED* are saturated with notions of purposeful activity. And *intentional* often does mean what we perhaps most often take it to mean, something "done on purpose," the result of intentions, as in "intentional manslaughter." However, *intentional* also harbors operative as well as obsolete definitions that mean quite the contrary: something that is intentional can also be that which *exists solely in intentions*. This meaning of intentional, of which there are prominent examples cited well into the nineteenth century, derives from the now obsolete noun form of an *intentional* as an "appearance or phenomenon which has no substantial or concrete existence"—as, in other words, an *image*. The example cited by the *OED* is from the late seventeenth-century treatise by the Dutch logician Francis Burgersdicious, who opposes a "true being" to "appearances, or as they commonly say, *intentionals* . . . species and specters of the sense and understanding, and other things whose essence only consists in their apparition." Or, as Coleridge might call them, "miracles of rare device." This is something more than the happy accident of etymology: not only does the wild oscillation inscribed in the meaning of this word show us how one structure of the intentional *is* the image; it "revives" or reiterates the oscillations that are constitutive of the image, Romantic and otherwise.

3. Oscillations: Oblivion and Das wahre Bild der Vergangenheit

One of the tasks that Wordsworth prescribed for the poet was the task of discriminating the "living images" of imagination from mere idolatry, those dead idols "whose truth is not a motion or a shape / Instinct with vital functions, but a waxen image which yourselves have made / And ye adore." If fulfilling the requirements of this somewhat puritanical charge were not always met in Wordsworth's own poems, it does pose two clearly distinct "intentional structures" to the image. However, the images that matter most to Romantic poets (Wordsworth included) and their best readers are those that seem to issue from or to beckon to something at the threshold of language, images that seem to mark the contact zone between language and phenomenality. Perhaps it is the very nature of this liminality that lends the image its aura of the sacred, even in those poets for whom the sacred was to be engaged outside inherited theological models.

This is one of the rhetorical, formal, and even political challenges that continues to be posed by Percy Shelley's images of a poetic agency, a nontheological force or power that does not originate in the subject but seems capable of making a subject its instrument. We certainly need some structure to help us understand how the non-human forces that animate Shelley's poetry and criticism, such as the "Wild Spirit" addressed in the "Ode

to the West Wind," might be transformed into images of *human* intentionality. How else are we to assess what is at stake in that poem's most
extravagant of apostrophic demands: "Make me thy lyre, even as the forest
is: / . . . Be thou, Spirit fierce, / My spirit! Be thou me, impetuous one!" (ll.
57, 61–62). Given the rhetorical force of these imperatives, they can feel as
if they are parts of a single demand. But there are decisive differences in the
effects among this series of imperatives as the speaker escalates the demand
from *instrumentality* ("Make me thy lyre") to *animation* ("Be thou . . . My
spirit") and, finally, to *identification* ("Be thou me"). There are distinctive
poetic and historical potentialities figured in these lines. But each imperative only reaffirms the paradoxical quality of the poem's intentional structure: while the purposeful nature of the speaker's intentions in each of these
demands is lucid and unambiguous, the "intentional structure" that would
result from the wind's willingness to oblige would bear little likeness to any
conventional image of the subject we might know.

There is nothing in Shelley's poem or his poetics that promises that such
an "impetuous spirit" would accommodate the speaker's hopes, would offer
itself to this desire for a radical identification. And the speaker seems to acknowledge this in the subsequent and closing series of imperatives: "Drive
my dead thoughts over the universe / Like withered leaves to quicken a
new birth! / And, by the incantation of this verse, // Scatter, as from an
unextinguished hearth / Ashes and sparks, my words among mankind!" (ll.
64–68). If the tenor of this passage is remote indeed from the closing lines
of Coleridge's visionary fragment, the series of urgent demands performed
in an exclamatory tone is much more proximate. And given the extensive
catalogue of tropes activated in these lines, it is certainly the case that Shelley's ode is as much an "allegory of figuration"—and as much an allegory
of *poetics*—as "Kubla Khan." The intentional structure of these lines is very
much the Romantic image of the poet repeatedly and unabashedly apos-
trophizing a mute but mighty force; and in its many unanswered efforts to
make its addressee "hear," it points deictically and as if in supplication *right
here*, to the time and place of its own address, the present tense of its "incantation." Of course, the speaker recognizes that these are hopes and demands
that cannot be realized in the present; and thus the poem refers its addressee
and its readers proleptically to an always open future since the work of the
wind is never complete.

The formal and rhetorical daring of these closing lines offers us a series
of radical figures of revolutionary potentiality. But the rush and torrent of

the images and tropes that we see and hear in the poem also point us *back* through these swirling temporal effects, this dizzying to and fro, to its origin and addressee, to an "unseen presence" (l. 2). Shelley is a poet who could commit himself at one moment to a "pictured poesy" of "hues outshining heaven" (*The Witch of Atlas*) and at another moment have one of his most sympathetic dramatic characters proclaim that "the deep truth is image-less" (*Prometheus Unbound*). In Shelley in general and in "Ode to the West Wind" in particular, what de Man calls the "oscillation in the status of the image" is the oscillation between everything and nothing, between revolutionary historical redemption and the *bildlos* presence of the wind. This latter is not merely that which Shelley in "Mont Blanc" would refer to as "some unsculptured image" (l. 27), but a non-phenomenal, non-subjective, originating intentional structure. In the string of catachreses to which the speaker must resort, this "unseen presence" will be given lots of names, among them "Wild Spirit," "Uncontrollable," "Destroyer and Preserver," and, of course, "West Wind" (ll. 13, 47, 14, 1). By yet another catachresis, we can call it history. And we can call it the "intentional structure" of Shelley's "Romantic images," especially if we understand those images to be *intentionals*.

I have argued elsewhere that Shelley's poetics of history is illuminated—*redeemed* even—by Benjamin's theses "On the Concept of History": the ashes and cinders of the poetic word, remainders of a previous burning, await futurity's rekindling where they might "flash up" at "the moment" of their "recognizability."[21] This elective affinity between British Romantic poet and German Romanticist critic reveals itself most compellingly in Benjamin's fifth thesis, which proposes nothing less than a theory of the image: "The true image of the past [*Das wahre Bild der Vergangenheit*] flits by. The past can be seized only as an image that flashes up at the moment of its recognizability, and is never seen again. . . . For it is an irretrievable image of the past which threatens to disappear in any present that does not recognize itself as intended in that image."[22] The genuine mode of historical comprehension, according to Benjamin, occurs by way of the apprehension of images sent like "ashes and sparks" from the past. It is the structure of history itself that offers up these images; and these images *intend* us, single us out "momently" with the great gift of their revival. But this process is both precious and urgent: the image of the past "appears unexpectedly" "at a moment of danger" (*SW IV*, 392); but if the opportunity to "seize" it is missed, it "threatens to disappear" *at once and ever* into oblivion. For Benjamin, in other words, history itself is inscribed and produced in the oscillations by which the image is bound to oblivion.

No reader of Shelley's last great poem, *The Triumph of Life*, can fail to apprehend its own sense of historical urgency, signaled in no small part by the cultural politics implicit in its principal constellations of figures. This includes the poem's structural and formal allusion to Dante and Virgil, but more immediately by what Benjamin might call its "redemption" of the figure of Rousseau as the speaker's guide and interlocutor. I want to conclude this essay by revisiting a passage from the poem in which the figure of Rousseau beholds an image that "flashes up" and threatens everything in the poem with oblivion. Rousseau, or "what was once Rousseau," recounts to the speaker of Shelley's poem the origin of his implication in the "parade of wickedness" that has unfolded before the speaker (and the reader) and that the poem offers as the structure of history. Rousseau poses the story explicitly as a cautionary tale: he succumbed as a result of the spells and enchantments of aesthetic incantation. Rousseau didn't intend to be there; but he found himself in a "place // . . . filled with many sounds woven into one / Oblivious melody, confusing sense" (ll. 339–341). If *you* were to hear this music, he tells his interlocutor, *you*, too, would be seduced; "so sweet and deep is the oblivious spell" cast by this music that "thou wouldst forget" all ethical obligations, commitments, and intentions should "thou" hear it (ll. 331, 327). And that is when it happens:

> "And as I looked the bright omnipresence
> Of morning through the orient cavern flowed,
> And the Sun's image radiantly intense
>
> "Burned on the waters of the well that glowed
> Like gold, and threaded all the forest maze
> With winding paths of emerald fire—there stood
>
> "Amid the sun, as he amid the blaze
> Of his own glory, on the vibrating
> Floor of the fountain, paved with flashing rays,
>
> "A shape all light . . . (ll. 343–352)

By definition, "a shape all light" is not representable as such; and, in fact, it "stands there" before Rousseau as a sensory impossibility. But *as poetry*, the effects the shape has on the senses and on cognition are extensive and obliterating. In the first instance, it effaces the reflection of that most "radiantly intense" and illuminating of images, the "Sun's image," what one might have called the image of images before the appearance of "a shape all light" rendered it irrelevant. The "feet" and "sweet tune" that accompany the "shape all light" demonstrate the capacity of the shape "to blot / The thoughts of him who gazed" at it, such that "all that was seemed as if it had been not— / As if the gazer's mind was strewn beneath / Her feet like embers, and she, thought by thought, / Trampled its fires into the dust of death . . . " (ll. 382–388).

To declare that there are genuine matters at stake in the fleeting appearance of a poetic image in an unfinished text of a poet long dead runs the risk of hyperbole to the point of caricature. But to the degree that we take Shelley's poetry and poetics seriously—to the degree that we believe his *project* continues to pose a set of radical possibilities for the relationship between poetry and history—the stakes of this image are indeed considerable, for the poem's representations of Rousseau's story, of course, but also for the poem's account of the structure of history. For if *The Triumph of Life* reads history by "brushing it against the grain" in a genuine Benjaminian fashion by revealing the violence inscribed in the triumphal narratives of history, the appearance of "a shape all light" changes everything. "A shape all light" is posited here as a permanent possibility; and it produces no historical illumination. Indeed, one can say it appears *in order* to "blot the thoughts of him who gazed" on it: that is the form of its intentionality. If "a shape all light" "flashed up" to Rousseau at his own "moment of danger," it offers no "index" of "redemption" (*SW IV*, 390). We might call it an *event*, but only if we understand by event that which undoes the possibility of historical reckoning. If this is a visual image, there is nothing "pictorial" about it, since its appearance supersaturates the visual field to the point of white-out. Indeed, "a shape all light" seems to ironize to the point of oblivion Kermode's own definition of the Romantic image: "a radiant truth out of space and time," which, "standing free of intention" and "affective considerations," "provides its own vigour" (*RI*, 4, 57).

In an earlier attempt to come to terms with the nature and effects of this "shape all light," I called it a catachresis.[23] I thought that I could resist the seductions of this Romantic image by reading it as de Man taught us. But even if we have learned enough from his work to identify "a shape all light" as a catachresis, a worldly impossibility that originates from language's most originary power to posit, to arise from nothing, the instant we look back at the poem and *gaze* upon this "image," "all that was seemed as if it had been not" (l. 385): in other words, the intentional structure of the Romantic image as positing and effacement. Now I would choose the obsolete noun form of *intentional* to name this image-event partly because the definition seems rescued from oblivion, but primarily because the definition of an *intentional* as "an appearance or phenomenon which has no substantial or concrete existence"—as a "spectre of the sense and understanding," "whose essence only consists in their apparition"—conveys more accurately the poetic modes of existence and appearance of "a shape all light."

One casualty of the obliterating effects of "a shape all light" is hope, if by hope we mean the kind of expectation that is marked by desire or promise. Hope is a feature—even a principle—of Shelley's poetry in each of his major undertakings: its images flash like "glorious phantoms" through poem after poem until *The Triumph of Life*. Indeed, this last poem would seem to confirm de Man's assessment of Yeats's radically "emblematic" poetry: "those who look to Yeats for reassurance from the anxieties of our own post-romantic predicament," he writes, "will not find it in his conception of the emblem. He cautions instead against the danger of unwarranted hopeful solutions, and thus accomplishes all that the highest forms of language can for the moment accomplish" (*RR*, 238). It feels as if one could substitute the name Shelley for Yeats and "shape all light" for "emblem" and do de Man justice. And yet the appearance of "a shape all light" is not a caution but a lure, and no amount of reading and the negative knowledge it generates can undo the intentional force of an image that invites poetic oblivion.

The final sentence of "Intentional Structure of the Romantic Image"— the sentence that serves as the epigraph to this essay—was written around the same time de Man offers his assessment of Yeats, and it appears to restore to the poetic image the possibility of hope: "we are only beginning to understand how this oscillation in the status of the image is linked to the crisis that leaves the poetry of today under steady threat of extinction, although, on the other hand, it remains the depository of hopes that no other activity of mind seems able to offer" (*RR*, 17). I think it is possible to regard this closing sentence as the last remnant of a vanishing belief in the positive capacity of literature, a belief already extinguished in the dissertation chapter on Yeats. But *depository* is a curious word to describe this function of poetry: as a depository, poetry would be the place where hopes are kept, but out of circulation. "On the other hand," asserts de Man, poetry's own status as "the depository of hopes" is inseparable from its own "steady threat of extinction," its very promise, in other words, oscillating with its tendency to oblivion. If we continue to be moved by the poems enough to seek the images of hope in the texts of Romanticism, we may have to learn how to see them as the Romantic image of an *intentional*.

TEN

Ur-ability

Force and Image from Kant to Benjamin

KEVIN MCLAUGHLIN

Walter Benjamin's "dialectical image" (*dialektisches Bild*) first appeared in print in Theodor Adorno's 1933 *Habilitationsschrift* on Søren Kierkegaard.[1] In the construction of Kierkegaardian interiority, Adorno remarks at one point, myth and dialectic come together to produce what "may be called dialectical images, to use Benjamin's expression" (80; 54). Thus Adorno unveils Benjamin's discovery before it can be displayed in the latter's own published work. This did not occur until a half century later when the German edition of *The Arcades Project* appeared.[2] Adorno was aware of the "dialectical image" from the early sketches of the Paris project from which Benjamin had read while on a visit to Frankfurt and Königstein in the fall of 1929. Just beginning to work on his study of Kierkegaard at this time, Adorno appears to have seized upon Benjamin's image. Six years later Adorno famously took Benjamin to task for mishandling the dialectical image in the 1935 "Exposé" to what would become *The Arcades Project*, arguing that the image of the early notes had been drained of "objective" force through association with the dream. In the letter detailing his objections, Adorno insistently describes the loss in terms of force. Benjamin's image is said to lack its "original force" (*Ursprungsgewalt*), "objective key force" (*objective Schlüsselgewalt*), and "dialectical power" (*dialektische Macht*) (*GS* 5. 2, 1128).[3] Adorno's verdict, which has guided the influential Frankfurt School interpretation of Benjamin's dialectical image and the Paris project as a whole, fails to register the singular force of Benjamin's arresting image. In this sense, from the moment of its appearance in print, the power of the dialectical image has been resisted by some of those who have been most responsible for its transmission, beginning with Adorno and continuing with Rolf Tiedemann, the German editor of Benjamin's Paris project, who finds the dialectical image wanting in "terminological consistency."[4]

The key to the dialectical image lies precisely in the critical stress on a virtualizing force that can be found throughout Benjamin's work. In a remarkable recent study outlining the structure and extent of this fundamental tendency in Benjamin's writing, Samuel Weber makes some highly illuminating remarks on the dialectical image in this context:

"Image" for Benjamin is something very different from the familiar conception; indeed, it is something unheard-of. Image, as used here, signifies not the illustrative depiction of an external object. Rather, as something to be read rather than merely seen, the image is construed by Benjamin as both disjunctive and medial in its structure—which is to say, as both actual and virtual at the same time. Such images become a point of convergence, which Benjamin here designates as "now." This *now* coexists with the "time" from which it simultaneously sets itself apart. Time, one could say, imparts itself as now, and in a historical sense. For history signifies not a temporal continuum, nor even the continuity of an expected or sought-after meaning. Rather it contributes to the explosion of all meaning, as that "death of intention" that never ceased to fascinate Benjamin and that he here ascribes to the mode of being of the image, marking the "birth of a genuinely historical time as the time of truth." Such historical truth should not be conceived as a preserving of truth, understood as the correspondence or adequation theory, but rather as a dissolving, non-integrative dialectics of explosive convergence or coincidence.[5]

Of special note in this set of observations is what Weber characterizes as the imparting of time in Benjamin's image. According to the virtualizing logic that is the signature of Benjamin's work, the focus in this passage is on the *impartability* of time in the dialectical image. Earlier in his study Weber proposes the word *impartability* as a more accurate alternative to what is usually translated as "communicability" in Kant's *Critique of Judgment*, since the original *Mitteilbarkeit* contains the root "part" (*Teil*) that participates in a crucial nexus of philosophical terms in German, including the word for judgment itself (*Urteil*) (Weber, 13). The verb *impart* in the passage I have cited thus suggests that Benjamin's dialectical image is related to aesthetic judgment in Kant's third *Critique* and, more precisely, that the "genuinely historical time" of the dialectical image manifests itself not as a cognition that is imparted but as a capacity to impart—an impartability—that resists cognitive determination. The capacity or power connecting the dialectical image to aesthetic judgment in Kant can be found in images throughout Benjamin's writing. The image is, in this sense, the self-dividing unit of virtuality in this work.[6] What follows is an attempt to sketch the background in Kant's critique of aesthetic judgment against which the force of Benjamin's image is to be understood.

I.

An important key to the power of the image in Benjamin's criticism lies in his early essay on two versions of a poem by Friedrich Hölderlin. Throughout this interpretation the image, or what at one point is called "imageability" (*Bildhaftigkeit*), bears a decisive relation to a specific force designated by the word *Gewalt* (derived from the verb *walten*, meaning "to hold sway" or "to reign") (*GS* 2. 1, 117; *SW* 1, 29). In his political writings, Benjamin employs the word *Gewalt* in a way that draws on its capacity to signify both legitimate and illegitimate force, departing from an established tradition that seeks to define *Gewalt* in opposition to *Macht* (violence in opposition to power).[7] Benjamin's handling of this term may be understood to reach back to the Indo-German roots of *Gewalt* in the radical *val-*, which is akin to the Latin *valere*, meaning simply "to be worthy or capable" or "to have power" apart from any context in which the legitimacy of this capacity can be determined. Indeed, philological research suggests that *Gewalt* was not a technical term in Germanic law.[8] The constellation of old Germanic words from which *Gewalt* derives was understood to have the capacity to translate a wide range of Latin terms for clearly differentiated concepts in Roman law, including *imperium, sceptrum, maiestas, tyrannis, auctoritas, ius, potestas, potentia, licentia, vis, fortitudo, brachium,* and *violentia*.[9] During the medieval period *Macht* established itself as the prevalent translation of *potestas*, and *Gewalt* was consigned to *violentia*. But the substantive basis for a juridical distinction between power and violence is thrown into question by Kant's thesis in paragraph 28 of the *Critique of Judgment* (1790) that violence (*Gewalt*) can only be understood *in relation* to power (*Macht*), and vice versa. "Power [*Macht*] is a capacity that is superior to great hindrances," Kant declares. "This same capacity is called violence [*Gewalt*], when it is superior to the resistance of that which itself possesses power [*Macht*]" (*AA* 5, 260; 99).[10] Kant articulates this thesis about the relational character of power and violence in his analysis of the "dynamic sublime."[11] The idea of the sublime awakened in us by the apprehension of "power" (*Macht*) in nature demonstrates mankind's "superiority to nature" and thus reveals a mode of "self-preservation" superior to that which is threatened by nature, even while, as Kant notes, on another level—that of "physical" existence— "man must submit to the violence [*Gewalt*] of nature" (*AA* 5, 261–62; 101).

Kant's recasting of the traditional relation of power to violence in his analysis of the sublime must be understood in the context of the irreducible plurality and relationality of the mental capacities throughout and beyond his critical project. The insistence on this point is made emphatically clear by Kant's refusal, issued in the second part of the second edition of the *Critique of Pure Reason* and reiterated near the beginning of the *Critique of Judgment*, of the thesis of "a single radical, absolute fundamental power" (*B* 678; 594 and *AA* 5, 177; 16).[12] Thus cognition of an object for Kant occurs through the interaction and collaboration of mental faculties, with judgment subsuming what imagination represents under a concept provided by understanding. In an aesthetic judgment the relationality of psychic forces is highlighted in a different way. In this case the mental powers cooperate to produce, not cognition of an object, but rather a feeling that is referred to an object. This feeling, which can only be repeatedly referred to the object and never result in cognition of it, reveals an a priori principle of nature that exists only in view of the relations of our mental faculties to one another, specifically, from the perspective of the "free play" between understanding's power to conceptualize and imagination's capacity to produce representations. This singular play of the faculties is free in the sense that it is not subject to conceptual resolution. Instead of determining an object of cognition (by subsuming a particular representation under a general concept), aesthetic judgment reveals a natural principle that exists exclusively with regard to the relation among the mental powers themselves when they are freed from conceptual determination. In this way the mind discovers in its own interacting forces the communicable feeling of the "formal purposiveness" of nature that must be attributed to all similarly constituted beings—the principle that Kant himself "discovered" in the years separating

The Metaphysical Foundations of Natural Science (1786) from the *Critique of Judgment* (1790).[13]

The discovery of an a priori principle in the relation among the mental powers in aesthetic judgment not only makes possible a transcendental critique of judgment. It also allows Kant to establish the existence of a system of moving or "agitating" forces in nature and provides the basis of his effort to develop the "elementary system" of matter that would occupy the aging philosopher throughout the 1790s and into the late writings collected in the *Opus postumum* (*AA* 21, 596).[14] In this unfinished project Kant seeks the principle in the act without which the systematic character of nature would be unthinkable, namely, in the act of the subject seeking to turn itself into the object of experience—the "I exist thinking" implicit in all experience (*B* 429; 456—this quoted phrase is from the second edition of this work published in 1787). In a set of recent studies of the *Opus postumum*, Eckart Förster has argued convincingly that these late writings elaborate a doctrine of theoretical and practical self-positing on the basis of which the author of the *Critique of Pure Reason* "felt compelled to reverse the order of reason and understanding" laid out at the beginning of the critical project (and to elevate the former over the latter) (Förster, 150). In the end, Förster contends, Kant concludes that as finite rational beings we experience our own physical and moral limitation and self-constitution as a "subjective" matter that must "be regarded at the same time as given and as independent of the subject" (Förster, 171). In contrast to the various post-Kantian theories of self-positing and self-consciousness already in circulation during the later 1790s, the experience of transcendental self-affection in Kant's own later work conforms to the structure of aesthetic judgment. At this point the subject is not an object of its own experience in the cognitive sense and thus not a matter of experience according to the meaning of this concept in the first *Critique*.[15] Rather, the subject exists in transcendental self-affection with regard to two orders of moving forces that are based on principles discovered in the subjective form of a relation among its own mental capacities, which is to say, in aesthetic judgment. On the one hand, there is the theoretical principle of the natural moving forces to which we are physically subject—the formal purposiveness of nature; on the other hand, there is the practical principle of moral moving forces to which we are ethically bound—freedom.[16] These theoretical and practical principles are revealed in the act of transcendental self-affection by aesthetic judgments of the beautiful and the sublime, respectively. In both cases, Kant writes in the *Opus postumum*, "we are spectators and at the same time originators" (*Zuschauer und zugleich Urheber*) of our existence (*AA* 22, 421; 184).[17]

The distinction between power and violence is introduced by Kant in paragraph 28 of the third *Critique* in the analysis of the "dynamic sublime"—an aesthetic judgment in which the faculty of imagination, rather than engage in free play with the understanding (as in an aesthetic judgment of beauty), gets "serious about its business" and enters into a relation with practical reason and thus with freedom (*AA* 5, 245; 98). The greater force or violence to be considered in paragraph 28 is that of a mental power to overpower nature, specifically, our capacity to judge nature as a power that exercises no superior force (*Gewalt*) over us. In such a judgment natural power is "fearsome," but we are not "afraid" of it: "we can look on an object as fearsome [*furchtbar*]," Kant observes, "without being afraid *of* it" (*ohne sich vor ihm zu fürchten*) (*AA* 5, 260; 119). The ability to look on an "object" as potentially fearsome without actually being afraid of it—this capacity and nothing else—demonstrates the superiority of our mental faculties to nature's power. As soon as Kant says "can," in other words, the object of fear is potentialized by the ability to judge the dynamic sublime. The locution "we can" performs the judgment under analysis and reveals in our mental makeup a capacity to look on the moving forces of nature as potential, rather than actual, power. Yet this capacity does not establish the perspective of a detached onlooker. What we see attracts us in this case, Kant says, with a power that is proportional to the strength of the natural forces that are potentialized: "the sight [*Anblick*] of them becomes all the more attractive the more fearsome it is, provided that we are secure" (*AA* 5, 261; 120). The "sight" to which we are drawn is not detached, but it has the security provided by our power to see natural force as removed from the realm of actuality. This secure "sight" exists, therefore, at a point where our mental faculties are unaffected by the actual force of physical things in nature. Judging in this manner is a matter, Kant suggests, of "merely thinking"—in our mind's eye—of a case of physical resistance that we would want to put up against natural power in order to see that all such resistance would be in vain (*AA* 5, 260; 119–20). The ability to see natural force as having a potentiality that goes beyond all actual physical resistance thus demonstrates the greater power of our mental faculties over the power of nature. This capacity can be observed, for example, in the way a "virtuous man" (*der Tugendhafte*) looks on God: with the religious "reverence" (*Ehrfurcht*) that favors the positive "transformation of life" over the superstitious "fear" (*Furcht*) that leads to the mere currying of worldly favor, as Kant puts it later in the paragraph (*AA* 5, 264; 123).[18] The ability to look on a potential power that allows for no actual case of resistance is in this sense the basis of our moral faculty:

> so also the irresistibility of [nature's] power [*Macht*], while making us recognize our own *physical* impotence [*Ohnmacht*], considered as natural beings, yet discloses at the same time a capacity to judge ourselves independent from and superior to nature, on which is based a kind of self-preservation that is entirely different from that which can be attacked and placed in danger by the nature outside of us, such that the humanity in our person remains unbowed, even if the human being would have to submit to this violence [*Gewalt*]. In this way nature is not judged to be sublime in our aesthetic judgment insofar as it excites fear, but because it calls up our power [*Kraft*] (which is not nature) of regarding as small those things about which we care (goods, health, and life), and of regarding [nature's] power [*Macht*] (to which we are no doubt subjected with respect to these things) as nevertheless for us and our personality not such a violence [*Gewalt*] to which we must bow when it comes to our highest fundamental propositions and their assertion or abandonment. (*AA* 5, 261–62; 120–21)

Only in the feeling of the dynamic sublime, when we "recognize" the pure potentiality of nature's physical "irresistibility," can we discover the superior power of our faculty of aesthetic judgment. This capacity requires the recognition of a certain "violence" (*Gewalt*) to which the human being must and humanity must not submit. Aesthetic judgment of the dynamic sublime thus divides "humanity" from "the human being" subjected to natural force (the human person from the human thing, mankind's autonomy from mankind's autognosis). At issue, as Kant's precise use of the word *Gewalt* in this passage suggests, are two orders of violence, two kinds of relatively greater power. There is the force of the physical irresistibility of nature and the force it "calls up"—our capacity to look on fearsome natural potentiality.

The example Kant provides at this point to reassure those who may be skeptical about his analysis of the dynamic sublime is somewhat surprising, given his insistence that aesthetic judgments of this kind demonstrate an ability to "look on" potential, rather than actual, power: the greater reverence for the warrior (*der Krieger*) over the statesman "even in the most highly ethical state" (*AA* 5, 262; 121). This example seems even more "far-fetched" than the principle it is supposed to defend until we see that the power we venerate in our aesthetic judgment of the warrior consists, not of the superiority of actual physical force, but rather of the superiority *to* all such force. This power is called courage. Like the "irresistibility" of nature, the "indomitability of [the warrior's] mind" is a power against which all physical resistance would be taken in vain.[19] For us the courage of the warrior is judged to be like the force of nature—it lies beyond the field of actuality—and, therefore, our reverence for this power takes the form of an aesthetic judgment of the dynamic sublime:

> Hence whatever disputes there may be about the superiority of the respect that is to be accorded them, in the comparison of the statesman to the general, aesthetic judgment decides for the latter. War itself, if it is carried out with order and with a sacred respect for the rights of citizens, has something sublime in it, and makes the mode of thought of the people who conduct it in this manner more sublime in proportion to the many dangers to which they were exposed and on the basis of which they could declare themselves courageous. On the contrary, a long peace tends to make dominant a commercial spirit and with it low selfishness, cowardice, and softness and to debase the mode of thought of the people. (*AA* 5, 263; 122)

We may debate the relative respectability of the statesman in comparison with the field general, for instance, from the pragmatic point of view of how well each serves the state in particular or mankind in general when it comes to worldly matters of war and peace. Aesthetic judgment, however, "decides for the latter." The principle grounding this decision is courage—specifically, the power revealed, not by anything that could be carried out on an actual field of battle, but by a mental power that transcends everything that could possibly happen in such a space. The aesthetic judgment of the field general discloses the principle of courage in the relation of our mental faculties when imagination frees itself from understanding and is engaged by the supersensible realm of reason. The basis of the decision in favor of the field general, then, is *our* courage. As Kant writes earlier in this section, aesthetic judgment "gives us courage to be able to measure ourselves with the seeming omnipotence of nature" (*AA* 5, 261; 120). The aesthetic judgment of the dynamic sublime reveals courage as a communicable feeling that we must attribute to all similarly constituted beings. Or, as Kant puts it, courage enters into "the mode of thinking of the people" by way of its capacity to "look on" the power of nature with a superior power that is affected by no actual worldly force, which is to say, by way of the aesthetic judgment of the dynamic sublime.[20]

Unaffected "security" is the condition of this greater power of sight. The sight remains secure, it seems, as long as it is limited to those objects or, more precisely, those forces that resist being subsumed under a general concept—the resistance that compels the subject to fold back upon itself in search of a concept and, with respect to the dynamic sublime, to discover in its own mental faculties a force greater than that of nature. But the security gives way when the capacity for thinking that made it possible can be seen to resemble the thinking that makes possible the cognition of objects in space described by Kant at the beginning of the *Critique of Pure Reason*. We cannot represent any thing without space, Kant proposes, but "we can very well think that there are no objects to be encountered in it" (*A* 24, *B* 39; 158). The possibility of the cognition of "outer appearances" in the first *Critique*, like the possibility of the aesthetic judgment of the dynamic sublime in the third *Critique*, is secured by an act of thinking that removes worldly objects from the space in question. In both cases, thinking comes first and indeed a certain kind of "thinking" (*Denken*), namely, that which Kant distinguishes from "knowing" or "cognizing" (*Erkennen*) in the preface to the second edition of *The Critique of Pure Reason* in 1787—significantly, the same year in which he discovered the universality of aesthetic judgment in an a priori principle that was independent of cognitive knowledge (*B* xvii–xix; 16–17; 111).[21] The prior thinking in question with respect to aesthetic judgment and theoretical knowledge is distinct from the cognition of an object. Required, rather, is that we think of states of affairs that do not have to correspond to some actual, or even possible, condition: in the case of the aesthetic judgment of the dynamic sublime, we can think of an instance of powerful physical resistance bound to give way to the violence of nature; in that of the cognition of objects extended in space, we can think of space completely devoid of objects.[22] In both instances an act of simulation secures the space by virtualizing it as a field from which worldly things have been removed.

In keeping with a distinction as old as philosophy itself, such a simulated space, as distinct from the sphere of reality and truth, has traditionally been restricted to art and poetry. Kant's description of the aesthetic judgment of the sublime, including the cathartic feeling of "indirect" pleasure and the "delight" taken in images of things that would be repulsive if they were real, can be traced back through aesthetic and poetic theory to antiquity.[23] But the security of the otherworldly space that the aesthetic judgment of the sublime shares with art and poetry can become the source of insecurity when it enters into the realm of philosophical knowledge of the world and becomes the medium of what used to be understood as actual appearances. This is the possibility explored by Kant most explicitly in the *Opus postumum*.[24] Under these conditions every mental act is modified by potentiality, and experience as such is unsecured or freed from its basis in the actuality of cognitive affect. Now the sight, not only of overhanging rocks, amassing thunderclouds, volcanoes, oceans, and waterfalls, but also of every other thing in the world can call up the greater power that virtualizes moving forces while also giving us courage.

II.

Such was the greater power that Benjamin discovered in Hölderlin's poetry, specifically, in the transformation of the principle of courage that began with the poem "Poet's Courage" (*Dichtermut*) (1801). In the ultimate version of the poem, "Timidity" (*Blödigkeit*) (1803), Benjamin finds this principle reworked in a way that responds to a radicalization of the virtualizing force in Kant's discussion of the dynamic sublime. In this sense, the study of Hölderlin is linked to the analysis of the aesthetic judgment of the dynamic sublime by the principle of courage. Although Kant is never explicitly named, either in this passage or indeed anywhere else in the essay, Benjamin's comments point to the significance of Hölderlin's poem as a reinterpretation of the account of the dynamic sublime in the third *Critique*. The revisions of the poem reveal a force with the potentiality to reduce the world of things, including the human thing, to nothing—a power that at once deposes the world of objects and imposes a field of relations. This is the force of the image in Benjamin's work. Receptivity to this force calls for the courage to exist amid nothing but relations—the existence exemplified by the poet in Hölderlin's "Timidity." As Benjamin says, "the more deeply it is understood, [courage] becomes less a quality than a relation of man to world and of world to man." Courage is not a "property," but a force— "a spiritual principle" out of which life is formed (*GS* 2. 1, 123; *SW* 1, 33). Rather than provide the basis for the principle, life becomes responsive to and is formed out of the principle.

Becoming receptive to the moving force of an image that does not affect us cognitively calls for poetic courage: the courage of a poetic relation to the world that is liberated from what Benjamin characterizes as the "mythological" concept of empirical consciousness in his early essay on the "coming philosophy" (*GS* 2. 1, 162; *SW* 1, 103). Benjamin attributes this mythology, in neo-Kantian fashion, to Kant. But the discovery of the a priori principle of judgment in a virtual force that is revealed in the subject's own mental faculties exposes a dimension of experience outside the empirical intuition of inner and outer appearances covered in the first part of the *Critique of Pure Reason*. Kant's announcement of this finding in 1787 was a bold step out of the world with which the critical project had begun. Self-affection in this case is freed from the analogy to cognition that governs the subject's inner experience of itself in the first *Critique*. This is the upshot of the finding that would provide Kant, as he noted in a famous letter to Karl Reinhold, with "enough material for the rest of my life": the principle of purposiveness calls for a transcendental critique of non-cognitive self-affection (*AA* 10, 514). Such a critique addresses itself to the poetic relation to the world—or "courage"—that Benjamin discovered in Hölderlin's poetry, namely, unaffected receptivity to existence amid relations of force.[25] As with the "mode of thinking" of the people who judge the warrior superior to the statesman in Kant's analysis of the dynamic sublime, the poetic existence that Benjamin finds in Hölderlin's "Timidity" consists in a courageous attitude toward the danger affecting the entire world of physical things. In this sense, the critique of what Benjamin calls the Kantian "mythology" of "empirical consciousness" in his essay on the "coming philosophy" is outlined by Kant's critique of judgment. The force Benjamin finds in Hölderlin's poem thus has its origins in the transcendental principle of the power to judge (*Urteilskraft*) discovered by Kant.[26]

The dynamic, supercognitive field laid out by Kant's critique of the judging power is disclosed by the image in Benjamin's work. The image is the polarizing form of the virtualized world throughout his critical project. It emerges in his interpretation of Hölderlin's "Timidity" as the "more rigorous power of a world-image" (*strengere Gewalt eines Weltbildes*) (*GS* 2. 1, 118; *SW* 1, 29). The connection between this image in Hölderlin and the "dialectical image" in the Paris of the later project is indicated by the "interpenetration" (*Durchdringung*) of time in both contexts. Just as the world-image in "Timidity" is traversed by "spatiotemporal interpenetration" (*raumzeitliche Durchdringung*) in the essay on Hölderlin, so the "genuinely historical" image is stamped with "dialectical interpenetration" (*dialektische Durchdringung*) in *The Arcades Project* (*GS* 2. 1, 112; *SW* 1, 25 and *GS* 5. 2, 1027; 857). In both cases time is imparted with the force that concerns Kant in the critique of the aesthetic judgment of the dynamic sublime. In Benjamin's early essay on Hölderlin this comes out clearly from an inspection of his approach to the key revisions in the final strophes of "Timidity."

Under the conditions of "spatiotemporal interpenetration" of "the image of the world" that come to prevail in Hölderlin's poem, Benjamin proposes, "all spatial relation" inherently bears "temporal identity." The poem's "layout" (*Lage*) is thus a singular temporal space (*GS* 2. 1, 155; *SW* 1, 27).[27] Time is likewise interpenetrated by space, rather than presents itself in the mythological form of a self-consistent, independent condition of subjective experience, according to the cognitive model outlined by Kant in the first part of the first *Critique*. This is what Benjamin calls "temporal plasticity" (*GS* 2. 1, 117; 120; *SW* 1, 29, 31). We now come to the first set of revisions in last two strophes of "Timidity." At issue in these lines is a certain equality and openness that the poets share with "the god of heaven,"

> Who grants the thinking day to poor and rich,
> Who, at the turning of time, holds us, who pass away in sleep,
> Drawn upright on golden
> Leading strings, like children.
>
> Good also are, and skillfully sent to someone for something, we
> When we come, with art, and bring one
> From among the heavenly beings. Yet we ourselves
> Bring suitable hands. (Hölderlin, "Timidity," ll. 17–24)[28]

These lines were written immediately after Hölderlin's legendary "exile" in France—"a kind of caesura in his career," as one commentator suggests.[29] The gap falls, in other words, precisely between the two versions of the poem interpreted by Benjamin: "Poet's Courage" was completed in early 1801, and work on "Timidity" began in the summer of 1802 just after Hölderlin returned from his six-month stay abroad (see *Sämtliche Werke* 2. 2, 527). In a famous letter from November 1802 to Casimir Böhlendorff, Hölderlin writes of having been, "as one says of heroes, struck by Apollo" during his time in southern France (*Sämtliche Werke* 6. 1, 432; 152).[30] Back in Germany, he continues:

> The more I study it, the more powerfully [*mächtiger*] the nature of my country seizes me. The thunderstorm, not only in its highest manifestation but, precisely in this sense as power and figure [*Macht und Gestalt*] among other forms of the sky; the light in its effects, forming [*bildend*] nationally and as a principle and mode of destiny—that something is sacred to us—its force

[*Drang*] in coming and going; the characteristic element of the woods and the coinciding of various characters in nature in one area; that all sacred places of the earth are gathered around one place, and the philosophical light around my window: they are now my delight; may I remember how I have come to this point. (*StA* 6. 1, 433; *Essays and Letters*, 153)

The letter to Böhlendorff, which echoes Kant's evocation of the natural power calling forth the greater power of aesthetic judgment ("thunderclouds piling up in the sky . . . "), suggests a link between the account of the dynamic sublime in the third *Critique* and the transaction taking place in the fifth strophe of "Timidity" (*AA* 5, 261; 120).[31] Granted to the "poor and rich" of the poem, as to Hölderlin after he was "struck by Apollo," is the time of the "thinking" that Kant distinguishes from "knowing" or "cognizing" in the first *Critique*—time off from cognition. Working "nationally" (*nationell*) or originating on this day is instead a figuring or imaging (*bildende*) force.[32] This power is the source of the first alteration in strophe 5: in the earlier version the day granted was "joyful" (*fröhlich*); now it is "thinking" (*denkend*). In Kant's terms the "thinking day" is granted by a transcendental principle of judgment that lays out existence in relation to the two orders of moving forces calling for aesthetic judgment. On this day there is, in place of the cognition of objects, the aesthetic judgment of the beautiful and the sublime. In the letter to Böhlendorff just cited Hölderlin writes of the natural moving force that imparts itself in images of beauty—the gathering phenomena of natural purposiveness.[33] The lines of "Timidity" that concern us, on the other hand, offer an image of the power or violence of the dynamic sublime in the receptivity of the poets—more precisely, "the tongues of the people"—to the moral moving force of freedom that holds those "who pass away in sleep, / Drawn upright on golden / Leading strings, like children" (*die Entschlafenden / Aufgerichtet an goldnen / Gängelbanden, wie Kinder*) (ll. 18–20).[34] Significantly, the moral force of uprightness takes effect at a moment marked by the failure of cognition—the poets are "those who have fallen asleep" or, as one could also translate, "those who have passed away" (*die Entschlafenden*).[35] The bodies of the sleepwalking poets are thus suspended by a spiritual force enabling them to stand in the reason of "the thinking day."

This suspension occurs, moreover, at what is described as the "turning of time" (*Wende der Zeit*), which is the second revision in this strophe. This change also responds to the force of the transcendental principle of judgment discovered by Kant. On one level, it evokes the epochal turn or *Wende* that has been associated with the revolution in philosophy announced in the remarks on the Copernican "hypothesis" introduced, once again, in the preface to the second edition of the first *Critique* in 1787. Yet, it must be emphasized that the analogy to the Copernican revolution is not based on the replacement of one (geocentric) world-view for another (heliocentric) one. Copernicus's thought is paradigmatic for Kant, rather, as a "transformation in our way of thinking" (*Umänderung der Denkart*) according to which the cognitive relation to the world is subordinated to one dictated by freedom (*B* 22, n.; 113, n.).[36] What concerns Kant, in other words, is a standpoint that is unaffected by worldly things: freely standing—or, as Kant puts it at one point, participating—in practical reason.[37] Such a perspective cannot be oriented by a more adequate—for example, heliocentric—world-view. Hölderlin brings his poem into line with this point when he replaces the "sun god" with "heaven's god" as the source of what has become "the thinking day" in the final version. But the "turning of time" can be understood on another level as well. Instead of existing as an independent, self-consistent element in which "inner" appearances are extended, time *turns*. At this turning, in other words, time becomes versatile and figurable—in short, as Benjamin says, "plastic" (*GS* 2. 1, 120; *SW* 1, 31). By acceding to plasticity time takes on a capacity specifically denied to it in the first *Critique*, namely, the ability to turn into a figure or a layout: time, writes Kant, "belongs neither to a figure or a layout, etc." (*Gestalt, oder Lage, etc.*) (*A* 33, *B* 50; 163). This plasticity is not an analogy through which we seek to replace the figurability or turnability lacking in time and "represent the temporal sequence [by analogy] through a line progressing to infinity" (*A* 33, *B* 50; 163). Rather, a turning point exists in time in Hölderlin's poem. At this point time is no longer temporal in the sense of Kant's first *Critique*.[38]

The two alterations in lines 17–18 of "Timidity" thus bear the force of the transcendental principle of judgment in Kant. Benjamin interprets these shifts by way of a number of later philosophical developments, neo-Kantian among others.[39] For example, the interpenetration of time and space that takes effect in the final version of Hölderlin's poem is analyzed as a manifestation of Ernst Cassirer's concept of "function." Through interpenetration—at the "turning of time" and during "the thinking day"—time becomes, in Cassirer's terms, a function of space, and vice versa. This manifests itself in Benjamin's essay with the power of an image, specifically, "the more rigorous power of a world-image [*die strengere Gewalt eines Weltbildes*] . . . that turns the people [i.e., the 'poor and rich' of line 17] into a sensuous-spiritual function of the poetic life" (*GS* 2. 1, 118; *SW* 1, 29). Under the force of this image figurability is emancipated from the mythological concept of space as a self-consistent element in which objects are extended. "In the forming of this world-image," Benjamin writes, "every association with conventional mythology is ever more destroyed" (*GS* 2. 1, 120; *SW* 1, 31). After citing the example of the substitution of the "architectonic" figure of heaven for the sun in the characterization of the granting god of the poem, Benjamin invokes the liberation of figurability as another instance of the mythology-destroying force of the image: "it is clear here how the poet progressively lifts [*aufhebt*] the difference between figure and figureless" (*Gestalt und Gestaltlosem*) (*GS* 2. 1, 120; *SW* 1, 31).[40] By pressing through the boundary that separates space from time under conditions of cognition, figurability makes time impartable in the form of an image.

The poets of line 18, and by extension "the living" among whom they exist, are receptive to a projection of plasticity that breaks the space-time barrier and turns them into an "image": "Drawn erect on golden / Leading strings, like children" (*GS* 2. 1, 121; *SW* 1, 31). The greater force of the architectonic element of the last version of the poem, however, also projects figurability into the sphere of the gods and the poets "bring one / From among the heavenly beings" (ll. 22–23). Benjamin interprets this turn of events as a revolution in the relation between the god who is brought and the self-figuring power that had up to this point (i.e., in the world of the Greek gods) been his very principle. The god does not determine, but instead is determined by, "the cosmos of the poem": "Even the god must in the end serve [*dienen*] the poem to the utmost and execute [*vollstrecken*] its law, just as the people had to be the sign of its extension [*Erstreckung*]" (*GS* 2. 1, 121; *SW* 1, 32). The god becomes a part of the poem's extension—an "object" (*Gegenstand*) of its cosmos—and the poet "seizes" him (*GS* 2. 1, 121–22; *SW* 1, 32). Benjamin engages in multiple tactics to convey the "spatiotemporal interpenetration" that constitutes the dynamic sphere of this dramatic interaction. For example, time is characterized spatially in the phrase "temporal plasticity," and space is inflected temporally in the play on the etymological link in German between the words *Lage* (situation or layout) and *Gelegenheit* (opportunity or occasion). Similar effects are produced by phrases that drive time and space into one another, such as "the spatial extension of the living determines itself in the temporally inward intervention of the poet"

(*GS* 2. 1, 121; *SW* I, 32). But Benjamin also folds an image into his elucidation of the manner in which the god is handled in the last strophe of the poem:

> Figuration, the inwardly plastic principle, is so heightened that the fate [*Verhängnis*] of the dead form breaks in over the god, and—to remain within the image—plasticity is turned inside out and now the god becomes wholly an object. The temporal form is broken from the inside out as something animated. The heavenly one *is brought*. Here lies before us the highest expression of identity: the Greek god has entirely fallen prey to his own principle, the figure. (*GS* 2. 1, 121; *SW* I, 32).

The "image" to which Benjamin explicitly refers in this passage begins to take hold with the word translated as "fate"—*Verhängnis*—from the verb meaning "to drape or to veil." The phrase "the dead form" inserted into this common German expression reinforces the association of the "fate" that envelops the god with the draping of a veil or a shroud over a corpse. But there is also a twist already available in the verb of the German formulation on which Benjamin draws. I have translated the verb literally, including its prefix (*herein*), in order to indicate this: the shroud-like fate "breaks in over the god" (*über den Gott hereingebrochen ist*). The inward thrust of the verb exposes a spatial surface in the veil of fate that catches hold of the god, who is then pulled into its fold—in keeping with Benjamin's image—as figuration turns itself inside out "over the god." There is a suggestion here of a hunting figure that Benjamin will later employ to describe the bagging of images in the Paris project.[41] In the Hölderlin essay, however, the image of fate as a veil itself becomes the bag in which the poets trap the god. In this case, instead of being enfolded, the image enfolds. The reversible enveloping movement, according to which the contained (inside) can become the container (outside), and vice versa, is fundamental to the image throughout Benjamin's work.[42] In the passage that concerns us the reversibility of the image breaks out with the breaking in of temporal plasticity over the god. Thus in the image of the "fate" of the dead god the enveloping outbreak of plastic time slips into the hands that the poets "bring" in the final lines of "Timidity." In these lines the dynamic capacity of what the poets "bring" is rigorously differentiated from the "dead form" in which the god "*is brought*." This, as Benjamin notes, is the decisive point of the imposing caesura of the poem's penultimate line: "When we come, with art, and bring one / From among the heavenly beings. Yet we ourselves / Bring suitable hands" (ll.

17–24). Thus the image of the god mummified in plasticity ultimately gives way, in the penetrating pause, to the image-producing potentiality of the poets. What the poets "bring," therefore, is a capacity to impart the force of spatiotemporal interpenetration in the reversible form of the image.

In the "world-image" of Hölderlin's poem Benjamin discovers what time and space would have been in Kant if reason had taken priority over understanding and the cognitively oriented spatialization of space and time as inside and outside had been abandoned in favor of the approach suggested in the *Opus postumum*. By the same token, the spatiotemporal interpenetration of the image throughout Benjamin's work bears traces of the Kantian theory of force he found refracted in the writings of Hölderlin.[43] The "dialectical image" developed twenty years later in the Paris project lost none of this force. The critique of the "bourgeois" concept of history as progress that is fundamental to the later writings is part of Benjamin's long-standing project to distance thinking from the "mythological" model of Kant's first *Critique* according to which time along with space is regarded as an independent, self-consistent element. What needs to be stressed, however, is that the search for what Benjamin calls a time that is "not temporal but image-like" (*bildlich*) turns at once away from and toward Kant, specifically, away from the first and toward the third of Kant's *Critiques*—away from "time" and toward "force" (*GS* 5. 1, 578; 463). Thus instead of flowing continuously forward, time spaces in the dialectical image of Benjamin's studies of Paris. Even the time of Benjamin's work on this project is included in his notes as evidence of time spacing. In one anecdote from the section of *The Arcades Project* devoted to Paris streets, for example, Benjamin tells of a Sunday walk in the city when suddenly time turns itself inside out over the Place du Maroc and the "what has been" of imperial and urban expansion folds itself over the space separating the place in North Africa from the *place* in Paris that bears its name (*GS* 5. 1, 645–46; 518).[44] At such junctures time stops being "temporal" and becomes "image-like." This is the time of the dialectical image: it originates not with a time flowing but with a "time differential" (*Zeitdifferential*), as Benjamin noted when the "dialectical image" first appeared in his writing and its "image-like" time was immediately differentiated from that of Hegel's "dialectic" (*GS* 5. 2, 1037–38; 867). Instead of flowing progressively, then, time turns and is suddenly spatialized. In turning, time can then turn around and interface with "what has been." But in order to turn around, time must first space.

The image-like spacing of time is repeatedly described by Benjamin as taking place as part of a dynamic field: as a moment that "polarizes itself and becomes a force field in which the confrontation between its fore-history and after-history is played out" (GS 5. 1, 587; 470). The Paris of the late studies is in this sense the field of Benjamin's labors. Not objects or things from the past viewed from the perspective of the present, but sources with the capacity to impart "what has been" to the "now" are what concerns him. Paris in this context is a city of images and in particular dialectical images in which "what has been comes together in a flash with the now to form a constellation" (GS 5. 1, 578; 463). It is less a matter of gathering material than of bringing forth the capacity of self-dividing, polarizing units of impartability. This is the point made by Benjamin's manipulation of what seems at first to be a common agricultural figure in one of the earliest of the "epistemo-theoretical" notes to the Paris project: "All ground must at some point have been made arable by reason, must have been cleared of the undergrowth of delusion and myth" (GS 5. 1, 571; 456–57). The stress here, once again, is on "reason"—in Kant's terms "thinking" as distinct from "knowing"—and on mythology destroying force. For this reason, it is a question of arability rather than harvesting. The root of the word translated as "arable" does not share the sense of the Latin *arare* meaning "to plow." It derives instead from a cluster of words that Grimm's dictionary traces to an old verb signifying "to bring forth" (*erbern*).[45] The root of the adjective is thus rigorously in keeping with the potentializing force that Benjamin brings to the field. Yet the highly evocative syllables joined in the word that I have been withholding up to this point—*urbar*—seem to break out of the etymological container and to contain a more primal sense of potentiality that Benjamin brings to his project. The word *urbar* contains the root *ur*, which means "original" or "primal," as in those "primal phenomena" (*Urphänomene*) that fascinated Benjamin in Goethe; and the suffix *-bar*, which signifies potentiality or, as in the title of Weber's study of Benjamin, "-ability." By breaking out its two parts the word *urbar* takes on the capacity to impart primal potentiality or *Ur-ability*. The source of this capacity can be traced, as we have seen, to the primal division—*Ur-teil*—that Hölderlin discovered in Kant's critique of the transcendental power to judge (*Ur-teils-kraft*).[46]

ELEVEN

The Tongue of the Eye

What "Art History" Means

BERNARD STIEGLER

Translated by Thangam Ravindranathan,
with Bernard Geoghegan

I. The Noetic Life

We can attain *actually* [*accéder en acte*] the life that Aristotle called noetic—that is, intellectual and spiritual—only intermittently. We are constituted by the play of subsistence, existence, and consistence. Sometimes our existence raises itself toward the plane of consistence, which is that of noetic life. But most of the time our existence is dragged down to the plane of subsistence.

Ek-sistence is always between subsistence and consistence. Consistence *exceeds* existence: consistences are objects that do not exist, but which consist. It is in their difference from existence, in the *excess of their nonexistence* precisely that consistences consist, affecting existence by differentiating it precisely in this sense from subsistence. Existence is therefore that which projects a consistence that it is not, and it is thus that it distinguishes itself from subsistence. This is what happens to ek-sistence when it attains the noetic [*passe à l'acte noétique*],[1] that is to say, intermittently.

But this soul is not always noetic in actuality [*noétique en acte*]:

God alone enjoys such a privilege

wrote Aristotle, citing Simonides. Most of the time, the noetic soul is only noetic in potential, and, according to Aristotle, there are three types of souls: vegetative, sensitive, and noetic. We are the noetic souls. Yet if we are noetic only intermittently, this is because we are also and most of the time vegetative and sensitive souls. We keep to our vegetivity and our sensitivity, without at all projecting ourselves onto the noetic plane of consistence.

Most of the time, we do not project ourselves onto the plane of consistence, which tends to conceal itself, to forget itself, and to disappear. This is because we are inclined to *flee* this plane of consistence, and to regress into sensitivity and vegetivity: we tend to be noetic but in potential. We tend not to act out [*ne pas passer à l'acte*].

In effect, the soul is what is constituted by a potentiality that has the ability not to act out, and, in truth, mostly *remains* potential. What is true of the noetic soul is also true of the sensitive soul: the sensitive soul, Aristotle tells us, mostly behaves in a vegetative manner. Usually, the animal worries only about feeding itself, a function that is the sole activity of the plant (which continually coincides with its act, unlike sensitive and noetic souls). The animal acts out only when it contributes to the reproduction of its species. As for the noetic soul, it is through acting out as αλεφεια [*aletheia*] that it emerges from latency (λεφη: *lethe*) and, as Heidegger and Freud noted, truth (re)produces itself—αλεφεια [*aletheia*]. I have tried elsewhere to show why this must be understood, above all, as sign-ificance: as a sign-making that is understood as non-insignificance.[2]

Most of the time we are only potentially noetic, and actually sensitive, for example, when we behave like pigs or sheep or wolves or slugs, and, in some cases, when we remain in our unsurpassable stratum of vegetivity—in sleep, even if it is only an apparent vegetivity wherein the noetic seems to manifest itself in its nocturnal mode, as the hidden face of its waking, which is also its vigilance.

For in sleep we divide, and that which looked like our becoming-vegetal liberates our ownmost noetic capacity: imagination (φαντασια [*phantasia*]). Imagination, as Freud taught us, is a phantasmatic expression through which the noetic foundation par excellence is revealed: the unconscious, that psychic stratum in which *soma* and *psyche* are indistinguishable, and which—as a *disposition toward desire*, and a disposition that *is* desire—enables the projection of that plane of consistence that Freud describes as a capacity for sublimation, which is also to say, for idealization.

If most of the time we are only potentially noetic, there are still individual and collective practices that constitute disciplines—what the Greeks called μελετη [*melete*] and επιμελεια [*epimeleia*]—by the exercise of which the noetic soul can *train itself to attain* the noetic. The Greeks called this training γυμνασια [*gymnasia*].

Such practices thus give us access to what might be called joy, whether it be understood in a Christian, Spinozian, or Nietzschean sense. Such *therapeutic* practices, through which we take care of ourselves and of others, are the ultimate meaning of works of art and of the spirit.

II. The Industrial Exploitation of φαντασια [phantasia]

At the beginning of the twentieth century, industrial society, first developed in Western Europe and then in North America, was confronted by the problem of a diminishing rate of returns, which led to overproduction and unemployment. Marx described the ensuing crisis of capitalism as "structural," announcing that, faced with such limits, capitalism would collapse upon itself.

Various figures, including Henry Ford, fought against this diminishing rate of returns by contributing to the elaboration of a new model of industrial organization founded on consumption—an elaboration in which the much less well-known Edward Bernays also participated. Bernays, the nephew of Sigmund Freud, developed the latter's theory of libido to posit that the fight against economic crises required harnessing consumers' desire to lead them to consume things they did not need. This passage from need to desire allowed for the manipulation of desire itself, insofar as it was essentially constituted by phantasm, that is, by the activity of the φαντασια [*phantasia*], which carries within itself that deep stratum, concealed in the apparent vegetivity of sleep, which is the unconscious source of libidinal energy—that is, the sublimation whereby desire becomes desire of truth, of αλεφεια [*aletheia*], in other words, of sign-making, of significance, of meaning.

By the industrial exploitation of φαντασια [*phantasia*], Bernays advocated taking control of the libidinal economy of consumers and thereby the possibility of remote-controlling their behaviors. Like the proletarized workers, consumers would have to submit their motivity and their actions in general to automatisms. But this was less a matter of controlling bodies by the automatisms of machines (as was the case with the proletarized producers subjected to the assembly line) than steering them by stimulating the automatisms of their unconscious.

In this way Bernays recommended the production of lures capable of harnessing desire by turning it away from its immediate object and soliciting it with the objects of what would thus become consumption. In 1917 he told the American federal government—which was seeking to prevail over isolationist public opinion—that one could not persuade public opinion through the conscious layer of the psychic apparatus. It would be much more effective, he suggested, to appeal to the *phantasms* weaving through the unconscious than to the *reasons* that consciousness presents to itself.

This fabrication of lures would work for a long time, and with success. And it would generate the extraordinary power of American culture. The nexus between design, assembly lines, public relations, advertising, and marketing founded a new libidinal economy that would invent the American way of life, a lifestyle that would ultimately impose itself as an "ideal" upon the entire world (which, incidentally, was built on the Protestant foundations of American capitalism): in the United States, Ford's factories and Hollywood Studios would be built at the same time.

American capitalism is not metallurgy first and cinema second: the culture industry is at the heart of the capitalist system, and, as Adorno understood, it makes of cinema and metallurgy a system. Above all, it was a cultural model that constituted the new libidinal economy that is American capitalism, and that would soon export itself to all the capitalist countries as they developed media on the American model.

This cultural model was critiqued by Adorno and Horkheimer, the Situationists, Jean- François Lyotard, Gilles Deleuze, and many others. Yet the essential work remains to be done: we considerably underestimate, particularly within contemporary aesthetics, the importance of this new libidinal economy for the life of noetic souls—that is, those souls capable of projecting from their sensibility the plane of consistence whereby they reach their entelechy, which is to say, attain the noetic by way of their φαντασια [*phantasia*].

The point is that it was also by way of this φαντασια [*phantasia*] that Bernays took control of the economy, so that it ultimately led to what reveals itself, at its foundation, to be a regression to the level of drives that drags the noetic souls that we are toward the pig, or the sheep, or the wolf, or the slug. For the culture industries that concretize the new libidinal economy as the control of consumers' desires through phantasms stirred up by marketing and its like, progressively but irresistibly destroy libidinal economy and energy, thereby rendering objects of desire inaccessible.

These objects can attain the status of objects of desire only by projecting themselves onto the plane of consistence, which is the plane of the incalculability of that which is radically singular and as such incomparable. Marketing and its tentacles put into place computational modes of control and exploitation of desire that ruin it—desire being by its nature incompatible with computation. The object of desire is that which cannot itself be calculated, because desire constitutes itself only by encountering singularities that appear to it incomparable and, as such, infinite: desire is that which makes its object *infinite*. There is no price for a being that is loved, and this simple fact means that, for its lover, it is infinite.

The industrial harnessing of desire is, by contrast, that which makes its object *finite*. That is why this systematic exploitation of desires leads to the destruction of its objects, which is the destruction of desire itself. When desire is destroyed, however, what it *binds*, as Freud showed, remains: namely, the drives. After World War I Freud discovered that it was desire that bound contradictory and intrinsically asocial drives. This binding transformed the drives into the libidinal energy that, conversely, is the basis of social affiliation—like the φιλια [*philia*], which Aristotle made the condition of all social life.

The destruction of desire occurs all the more rapidly at the close of the twentieth century: the economic war instigated by the globalization of competition confers upon the aesthetic war waged by marketing a leading role in economic life, while the intensification in the exploitation of libidinal energy accelerates its decomposition into drives. This is how the regression that is our ordinary and unfortunate lot comes about: a drive-based television of populism, developed at the industrial level.

Finance capitalism itself becomes drive based: it wants returns on very short-term investments at an elevated rate of interest. More generally, the rule of the short term is the rule of the drive. The drive wants everything right away: it wants its immediate satisfaction. Desire, by contrast, is patient and invests by wagering on the infinite. Consider the lover's admirable patience: it is entirely opposed to the drive.

The exhaustion of libidinal energy resulting from this regression combines with the limits of industrial development, the depletion of energy supplies, the toxicity of the environment, the addictive behavior of individuals, the transformation of neurotics into psychotics, and so on—massive and worldwide phenomena that proliferate like a planetary destiny producing more anxiety day by day, for this process occurs by way of a disordering of the aesthetic.

III. The Noetic Organs

The aesthetic development [*formation*] of non-inhuman beings proceeds by means of works, which is to say through artifacts, which is also to say through technique, therein giving access to consistence, and to noetic life. So, too, it is technique that allows the noetic being to be manipulated and brought back down to the sensitive or vegetative stage by an unbinding of its drives.

Capitalism developed its techniques for the manipulation of desire to fight against what Marx identified as its limit, namely, the diminishing rate of returns. But capitalism was then confronted with its second limit: added to the diminishing returns on profits was the diminishing libidinal energy of capitalism's producers and consumers.

We live in the age of great symbolic poverty, and this signifies, moreover, that the process of trans-individuation is no longer working. The blockage of transindividuation assumes the form of a destruction of symbolic exchange, resulting in a generalized dis-individuation (that feeling of no longer being someone, which was experienced by Richard Durn when, before killing eight persons and wounding fifteen others, he wrote that he had lost the feeling that he existed), and what Marcuse already saw coming as a process of de-sublimation.

The libidinal economy having been ruined, the task of the *noetics*—artists, philosophers, scientists, lawyers, politicians, citizens endeavoring not to be reduced to the state of pigs, sheep, wolves, and slugs—is to invent a new libidinal economy. In human history, the great social transformations that brought about great civilizations have always appeared as transformations of a libidinal economy that was no longer working.

In this context, artists have a very specific responsibility: it is in the work of art that what constitutes the libido makes itself most purely visible. What is the work of an artist—say, a painter? *To produce an eye.* The eye is not simply that which is found in the eye socket in the skull. No more than the tongue is only in the mouth. The tongue [*la langue*], the organ that is in our mouth, is our tongue, not a cat's tongue [*langue de chat*[3]], only inasmuch as it also produces *language* [*la langue*]. As for our eye, it is painting, sculpture, architecture, the entire visibility of that which has been seen by those who have seen it only to the extent that they knew how to bring it to sight, that weaves it into a noetic eye—and by which it trans-individualizes itself.

Just as the tongue/language [*la langue*] is constructed, the spiritual eye that visible works give us to see is woven by the hands of artists. Therein it appears that a noetic organ always forms a system with one or several other organs that are themselves as such noetic, and that what links them passes outside the body, through a social body that is woven by a *tekhnē*: the tongue with the hand of the writer, the eye with the hand of the painter, the ear with the hand and the eye of the musician, and so on—all of which is articulated by words, papers, brushes, pianos, and other instruments.

Through this organic arrangement, which results from an organology, tongues and eyes are put outside themselves, bulging, augmented by the milieu that this organological *montage* forms, and by which means they project themselves—woven by the authors, the artists, the musicians who give us our tongue, our eye, our ear as noetic organs. Our vision frames a world of objects that it hallucinates as those of its desire. These objects, which are surfaces of projection, have a history that always passes, in some way or the other, by way of artists and their ancestors, those men from an age when there was no artist because everyone lived his or her world artistically—as with the seal hunter who sculpted the harpoon that we may now see at the ethnographic museum.

Why did Cézanne strive so ardently to paint Mont Sainte Victoire? Because it did not appear to him: what he saw, when he looked at it, was that it tended to disappear and would not appear to him as long as it *disappeared to him*, if I may dare say so, which it did ceaselessly. He was obsessed, like most modern painters (without their being necessarily aware of it) by the becoming-invisible of the visible. Cézanne, particularly in his conversation with Émile Bernard, said that things to be seen must be shown—failing which they are lost sight of. They must be painted, or if one is not a painter one must certainly go see them at the museum, and learn to look at the patterns [*motifs*] forming from that motif [*motif*] that Cézanne calls "Nature." To go to the museum is to train [*former*] the eye to see and to trans-form itself in its visions—"in nature" [*sur le motif*], as Cézanne writes. There, for him, lay modernity.

Our eye does not spontaneously see the noetic milieu it weaves when, *seeing by that noetic act that is "to see,"* for, say, a painter, it brings to sight what it has seen, making visible the very *motifs of seeing*. One finds the stages of this in the Chauvet Cave in Lascaux and in so many other places that Bataille calls miraculous (a miracle is literally an ad-miration).

Our eye can become again—and it does not cease to become again—an octopus eye. To truly see, the eye must see noetically. This seeing is that of the seal hunter who sculpts his harpoon as well as the farmer who sows only inasmuch as he worships and sacrifices in a consecrated place among statues and paintings, where he chants poems that are also prayers.

When God dies, it is with and by the artists themselves, and without gods, that the noetic eye sees by forging an aesthetic experience shorn of such practices. However, this aesthetic experience—whereby the eye opens much as the tongue loosens in the mouth when learning to speak a language that exceeds and precedes it—is today replaced by the aesthetic conditioning to which the culture industry is making us regress.

We have been destroyed and blinded—*all of us*, for what we are—by this becoming-regressive of our ever-narrowing gaze [*regard*]. We must learn to see again—that is, to *show*—the singular that is never yet seen (such is singularity: we are never finished with it, except if it loses its singular character). And this is absolutely impossible with the voyeurist gaze induced by the *buzz*, the latest find in what has become a veritable marketing of art, and a contradiction in terms.

The noetic gaze is contemplative. The gaze of the artist contemplates: it shares with other contemplators this disposition that the Greeks called *skholē* and the Romans *otium*. This contemplation is active: it is a practical activity, akin to those techniques of contemplation that interested Foucault toward the end of his life.

To paint, to write (music, literature), to perform (music, theater), to stage and to install, is to take care of oneself—and consequently of others, and of the realm of others. The practices constituting this care, and that give access to noetic organs (including the memory and brain that connect them), have been destroyed by the proletarization of the consumer subjected to the automatisms of a de-sublimated unconscious. This tends to make us return en masse—and as audiences—to the prenoetic, losing the ability to look [*savoir regarder*], trans-individuated by the ability to do [*savoir-faire*] and the ability to live [*savoir-vivre*] transmitted to us by painting and, broadly, by culture. For the culture industries and the psycho-technologies that they develop destroy the organological circuits supporting the processes of transindividuation.

IV. What Regards Us [Ce qui nous regarde]—the First Time

We who have not only an eye in our eye socket and a tongue in our mouth, but who hear and speak a language, who regard [*regardons*] and reveal an eye that regards us [*nous regarde*] in all that we see, in the works of art as much as in everyday objects, we who are technical beings, we are symbolic beings. The things that regard us [*nous regardent*] are symbols: a temple, a painting, a word, a geometric or algebraic sign, as well as a cup, a street, a urinal, a teacake [*madeleine*] in our mouth.

This regards us [*nous regarde*] because we share it: the *sumbôlon* is a shared object. In sharing, I individuate with another—and I become who I am. The symbol sees to the connection that I form with another through the symbol, and in forming this connection with the other I transform myself (falling in love with this other, becoming his enemy, or his adversary, or his counterpart, etc.). In transforming myself I transform the other, and in this way I transform the milieu in which I live with the other. Consider, for example, the milieu of language—which I attempt to transform myself, right here, with this word *transindividuation*, to have it adopted by my epoch: to trans-individuate this epoch.

There are "trans-individuators" who forge *for the first time* things or words or gestures that become symbols. What is brought to sight or to hearing in a work, painting, poetry, music, performance, and so on is this *first time* when an aspect of the thingness of things that noeticize is *sealed*. All those who share the symbols generated by transindividuation participate in the becoming of the circuits of transindividuation, for to share is to individuate oneself and individuate in turn, and to inscribe oneself within the chain of transindividuations whose first link is the work. These circuits are the circuits of social recognition, a condition of the fortune of living that the industrial world *of consumption* has destroyed—but industry does not fatally amount to such destruction.

The circuits of transindividuation are those of exclamation. Exclamation is what produces a clamor. We ex-claim when we ex-sist. And as we exclaim, we transform clamor into symbolization, into a circuit. This circuit makes others affected by that which affects me. So it was with Van Gogh, who exclaimed: "the yellow! the yellow! the yellow!" The human milieu is symbolic, which means that it is a milieu of exchange where exclamations that make signs circulate, and that it is a milieu of sign-making where each one participates in symbolic life. Such is the process of transindividuation by which we co-individuate in symbolic milieus, which are associated milieus.

However, these associated milieus have become dissociated. The industrial division of labor has meant that there are producers of symbols and consumers of symbols who do not participate in the elaboration of meaning, causing these symbols to lose their meaning: the dissociated milieus are those of desymbolization. In the continual spreading of associated milieus is that growth of the desert Nietzsche spoke of. The nihilist desert is what remains when desire and its object have been destroyed.

V. The Pre-individual Eye

Manet, facing the rejection of his painting by the academicism of the Second Empire, said one day: "Their eye will yield" [se fera]. This phrase came back to me one day when I visited the Prado Museum in Madrid—in that great collection of Western painting wherein one of its major traits is brought to view: we see Spanish painting develop between Islamic culture and what would become Flemish painting. At the Prado, we see the eye yield through space and time; we see it open, constitute itself, and deploy itself: we realize that the eye is a milieu.

We see through a milieu. Aristotle called the milieu of vision the diaphanous. But the diaphanous of the noetic eye is symbolic: over-saturated by history—by a History of the eye—it constitutes what Simondon calls a pre-individual milieu, the pre-individual foundation of vision, which is to say, of the eye that is not in the eye socket, but rather like that which constitutes the symbolic process of transindividuation giving us to see the visible as it has *never been seen*. This trans-formation of the eye—always already projected outside the eye socket just as the tongue in the mouth projects itself between the ears—is called the history of art. And this transformation occurs under organological conditions.

Symbolic milieus must be analyzed along three organological levels. What makes possible the transformation of the retinal eye into a noetic eye is the possibility for the body of the sensitive soul to organize itself and to reach noetic activity by assembling its organs (including its memory and therefore its brain) through inanimate beings such as carved flints, pigments of paint, earth, ash, which thus become organic (I have called this, elsewhere, the organized inorganic) and form the organs for the transindividuation of the eye as milieu, whose history is also that of art.

How did the men of Lascaux paint? They transformed matter that they sublimated, and this sublimation is the transindividuation of the eye as the milieu of the visible, of which the history of art is the diachronic display of sediments. Every museum gives us to see this condition of seeing, and at the same time a genealogy of the eye that regards and is regarded—like its paleontology—even while it teaches the eye to see that to which it has yet to open.

This transformation, which is the enlargening of the body by non-living organs that form a noetic and associated milieu, produces *organa*, artifices, works as well as tools and things (which are all, always, tools in some manner).[4] These artifices hold together bodies and put them in relation (the first among them is the transitional object discovered by Winnicott) and form along with them, as a linkage pervaded by the energy of the circuits of transindividuation, the symbolic milieu, the milieu wherein appear those symbols constitutive of the human that are works, traces of a passage to action in the noetic world. In this *mesotès*, which is a symbolic system— to once again appropriate and divert one of Aristotle's terms—thus appear three organological levels:

the natural organs of the body,

the organs that are artifices (materials, tools, things, works),

the social organizations that give access, by forming social rules that enable the transmission and writing of the history of psychic and collective individuation and transindividuation.

VI. From the Verdurins to the "Bobos"

Organology has a history: culture and technique change in concert, but also sometimes in a manner that dis-concerts. The technical milieus deterritorialize and vectorize very diverse milieus. Through this vectorization they destroy existing symbolic milieus and reconfigure them in depth: they re-individualize them—but they may also purely and simply dis-individualize them, that is, annihilate them. All this makes for conditions of transindividuation such that they are subjected to organological conditions that overdetermine them. And in this regard, between the nineteenth and the twentieth centuries, something very new occurs in aesthetic history with the appearance of what I have described as a machinic turn in sensibility—provoking as a consequence numerous short-circuits in the process of transindividuation.

Imagine, for example, that you are in 1870 and that you hear the music of Franz Schubert. The only possibility of that happening is were you to be playing his music. The case of classical music poses a particular problem, precisely by virtue of its status: one gains access to it only through an acculturation to musical notation, which presupposes a learning, so much so that till the end of the nineteenth century if one did not *learn* it, one could not have a connection with this music. But there was also fanfare music, village band music, practiced by a great number of people in the urban centers, at industrial sites, where there were orchestras and many who knew how to read music and play an instrument. In 1880, when the Paris Opéra produced a new work, it would send a libretto of the opera to its subscribers as well as a critical presentation of the score in the guise of a "listening guide," which allowed the bourgeois family to familiarize itself with the work, for example, through a simplified version written for piano. Rather than discover the music upon arriving at the opera, they already knew it by practicing it instrumentally at home.

To arrive at an aesthetic experience was to be inscribed within a social process of participation that engaged one in a practice: this was not a consumption, but a *sociation* that was also a *cultuality* carried through practices, an active relation, compared with which cultural consumption had no meaning. This activity could be bourgeois, religious, popular . . . until the arrival of that strange musical instrument, the phonograph, which Béla Bartók would speak of, analyze, and make great use of, which he credited with founding a real musicology. According to him, it was Edison who made possible a scientific musicology. But it is this very invention that risked leading music to its death. That is what would happen, Bartók said, if the listener were content with listening to the radio (or to the phonograph) without troubling himself to read the score: to understand the music, one had to know how to read it. And if one did not practice the music thus read, one could not understand it. This is also what Roland Barthes said about what he called *musica practica*.

In effect, the radio and the phonograph were to short-circuit transindividuation, eliminate practice, that is, participation, lead to the impasse of consumption and destroy the total aesthetic fact outside of which there is no longer any experience of the expansion of the sensible that is the encounter with a work in the noetic milieu of the ear or the eye, but an aesthetic conditioning that induces gregarious behavior—including among those whom

Arendt called "cultural philistines," subjects of that low-budget *verdurinisa-tion* that would breed the battalions of the middle-class, the "wealthiest" of whom are given that pitiful nickname "bobos" (to which I myself belong).[5]

A harmonious symbolic milieu is a milieu that rests upon long circuits of transindividuation incompatible with the symbolic poverty that has become the purported "leisure society."[6] In going to see an exhibition at the museum, in reading a novel, in watching a film in a non-consumerist manner, in opening my eye to expand my view (by means of my hands, from Lascaux to Cézanne, and after Cézanne, the hand is seized by the reproducibility set off by the fingers)—just as *my* tongue [*ma langue*] gives me access to language [*la langue*] as a process of individuation of a symbolic milieu, binding and unbinding, with my ears that heed it, with the tongue that is in my mouth—in going to see an exhibition and in reconnecting through all these paths works that I thus take care of while taking care of myself and of others, I participate in the weaving of the long circuits of transindividuation.

VII. The New Arms of Trans-individualization

Today, a great technological and industrial mutation is taking place: it is called digitalization. I founded the Centre Pompidou's Institute of Research and Innovation to participate in the reconstitution of an organology of long circuits going against the grain of the short circuits provoked by cultural consumerism—and which I fear will blow the fuses of the processes of psychic and collective individuation by which we become what we are, between beasts and gods, as the Greeks said.

This technological mutation begins an industrial mutation. I will quote Linus Torvalds, a thirty-eight-year-old Finn who has become a leading personality in the domain of information technology. This hacker perfected the Linux operating system, and has contributed decisively, following the initiatives of Richard Stallman, to the development of a new model of technological and industrial activity that constitutes the spirit of free software and *open source*.[7] He describes his collaborators' motivation—and human existence—as organized along three levels: the satisfaction of needs allowing for the simple renewal of labor, the capacity to realize one's existence through its social concretization, and the investment in that which does not exist: the projection onto the plane of that which only a noetic soul can imagine, precisely because it has an imagination, and this is the level of what is precisely called the project—imaginable by the *projector* that is, then, a noetic soul.

These three planes are quite homogenous with what at the beginning of this essay I proposed to distinguish as the planes of subsistence, existence, and consistence. What develops through digital technologies and the networks they weave are associated technical milieus that allow a true symbolic life—and it is within this milieu that free software and the Linux platform could appear: the relations of industrial work formed here are not those of the division of labor and the social roles that nineteenth-century productivism and twentieth-century consumerism had imposed: they are associative and participative. What plays out here holds major stakes for the life of arts, letters, and the spirit of our age. If it is possible for the industrial society we live in to find an escape and to re-constitute a new libidinal economy in the wake of its destruction by the Fordist model and its purportedly "post-industrial" avatars,[8] this will come to pass by mutations of this kind—and it will happen insofar as these digital technologies constitute the organological bases for a new process of transindividuation.

An artist, any artist, has to do with [*à faire*] and to deal with [*affaire*] a public. Whatever his practice, he sculpts the social, as Joseph Beuys put it, with his tongue [*langue*] in his mouth from which he makes language [*langue*] as a symbolic milieu, or with his eye endowed with hands from which he makes a visibility woven by those organs of transindividuation to which he adds clays, pigments, charcoal, paper, canvases, museums, and so on—all this contributing to the formation of what is called the public. In other words, this public is organologically overdetermined in its configuration. But today its attitudes are derived and in truth destroyed by the culture industries.

The conditions are in place, however, for reconfiguring this organology. The major political question of tomorrow is, then, that of artists, who have a very important role to play in an aesthetic war that will be carried out with new arms—those of transindividuation.

Notes

Introduction

1. Derek Jarman, *Blue* (New York: Overlook Press, 1994), 15.

2. *Blue*, dir. Derek Jarman, 1993.

3. Kaja Silverman, *World Spectators* (Stanford, Calif.: Stanford University Press, 2000).

4. See Jacques Khalip, "'The Archaeology of Sound': Derek Jarman's *Blue* and Queer Audiovisuality in the Time of AIDS," *differences* 21.2 (Summer 2010): 73–108.

5. For an influential account of the digital image as both representation and interface, see Lev Manovich, *The Language of New Media* (Cambridge, Mass.: MIT Press, 2001).

6. As Mark Hansen notes in *New Philosophy for New Media* (Cambridge, Mass.: MIT Press, 2004), the problem with Manovich's specific approach to the digital image is not only that it underestimates non-digital images, but that the concept of the "cinematic frame" that underwrites Manovich's conception of the digital image in fact makes it difficult for him to account for the ways in which "the digital image *explodes* the frame" (34).

7. Jacques Rancière, *The Future of the Image*, trans. Gregory Elliott (London: Verso, 2007), 6.

8. Marie-José Mondzain, *Image, Icon, Economy: The Byzantine Origins of the Contemporary Imaginary*, trans. Rico Franses (Stanford, Calif.: Stanford University Press, 2005).

9. Giorgio Agamben, "Judgment Day," in *Profanations*, trans. Jeff Fort (Brooklyn, N.Y.: Zone Books, 2007), 26.

10. Gottfried Boehm, *Was Ist Ein Bild?* 2nd ed. (Munich: Wilhelm Fink, 1995), 7, our translation. At the same time, complicating this history is the question of translation, for it should not be taken as a given that the English "image" is fully equivalent to the German "Bild," the French "image," or the Greek "εικξων," to name just a few of the languages in which philosophers have sought to understand images. See also W. J. T. Mitchell's "What Is an Image?" in his *Iconology: Image, Text, Ideology* (Chicago: University of Chicago Press, 1986), 7–46.

11. These critical narratives include Jonathan Crary, *Techniques of the Observer: On Vision and Modernity in the Nineteenth Century* (Cambridge, Mass.: MIT Press,

1990); and Martin Jay, *Downcast Eyes: The Denigration of Vision in Twentieth-Century French Thought* (Berkeley: University of California Press, 1993).

12. For discussions of pre-eighteenth-century theories of images and the imagination, see M. W. Bundy, "The Theory of Imagination in Classical and Medieval Thought," *University of Illinois Studies in Language and Literature* 12 (1927): 183–472; Jean Starobinski, *La Relation Critique: L'oeil Vivant II* (Paris: Gallimard, 1970), 177–89; Marie Hélène Huet, *Monstrous Imagination* (Cambridge, Mass.: Harvard University Press, 1993), 1–63; Dennis Todd, *Imagining Monsters: Miscreations of the Self in Eighteenth-Century England* (Chicago: University of Chicago Press, 1995), 52–63, 96–101.

13. David Hume, *A Treatise of Human Nature*, ed. L. A. Selby-Bigge and P. H. Nidditch (Oxford: Clarendon Press, 1978), 1; Christian von Wolff, *Vernünftige Gedancken von Gott, der Welt und der Seele des Menschen, auch allen Dingen überhaupt* (Frankfurt, 1738), 467 (§ 571), translation (slightly altered) from David Wellbery, *Lessing's Laocoon: Semiotics and Aesthetics in the Age of Reason* (Cambridge: Cambridge University Press, 1984), 10.

14. Wellbery, *Lessing's Laocoon*, 16.

15. Useful English-language discussions of Baumgarten include L. Wessel, "Alexander Baumgarten's Contribution to the Development of Aesthetics," *Journal of Aesthetics and Art Criticism* 30 (Spring 1972): 333–42; Wellbery, *Lessing's Laocoon*, 43–98; and Terry Eagleton, *The Ideology of the Aesthetic* (Cambridge, Mass.: Basil Blackwell, 1990): 13–30.

16. To render Lessing's *die bildenen Künste* as "image-arts" is admittedly contentious, as this phrase from *Laocoön* traditionally has been translated as "visual arts," and is more accurately translated as "forming arts" (*bildenden* stems from *bilden*, which means "to form"). However, as Thomas Pfau has emphasized, the concept of *Bild*—a term generally translated as "image" or "picture"—is central to late eighteenth- and early twentieth-century understandings of both *bilden* and the related concept of *Bildung* (a term often translated as "education," "development," or "culture"). In order to emphasize this particular semantic constellation of the German term *Bild*—and, at the same time, to open up more theoretical space around the English word *image* by linking it to the German *Bild*—we have thus employed the unorthodox term "image-arts" as a translation for *die bildenden Künste*. For Pfau's discussion of the relationships between *bilden*, *Bild*, and *Bildung*, see "From Mediation to Medium: Aesthetic and Anthropological Dimensions of the Image (*Bild*) and the Crisis of *Bildung* in German Modernism," in *Medium and Message in German Modernism*, ed. Thomas Pfau, a special issue of *Modernist Cultures* 1.2 (2006): 146 (http://www.js-modcult.bham.ac.uk/editor/welcome.asp).

17. Gotthold Ephraim Lessing, *Laocoön: An Essay on the Limits of Painting and Poetry*, trans. Edward Allen McCormick (Indianapolis: Bobbs-Merrill, 1962), 19.

18. So, for example, Lessing contends that Homer's description of Achilles' shield is constructed such that "images . . . rise up before our eyes [*schwellen die Bilder . . . vor unsern Augen*]" (ibid., 95, translation modified).

19. Wellbery, *Lessing's Laocoon*, esp. 99–207.

20. Lessing, *Laocoön*, 100.

21. Wolfgang Ernst, "Not Seeing the Laocoön? Lessing in the Archive of the Eighteenth Century," in *Regimes of Description: In the Archive of the Eighteenth Century*, ed. John Bender and David Wellbery (Stanford, Calif.: Stanford University Press, 2005), 134.

22. Kant distinguished between schemata (*Schemate*) and images (*Bilder*), contending that the "image is a product of the empirical faculty of the productive imagination—the schema of sensuous conceptions (of figures in space, for example) is a product, and, as it were, a monogram of the pure imagination a priori, whereby and according to which images first become possible, which, however, can be connected with the conception only mediately by means of the schema which they indicate, and are in themselves never fully adequate to it" (Immanuel Kant, *Critique of Pure Reason*, trans. Norman Kemp Smith, unabridged ed. [New York: St. Martin's Press, 1965], 183 [A 142 / B 181]).

23. Immanuel Kant, *The Critique of Judgment*, trans. James Creed Meredith (Oxford: Clarendon, 1952), 127.

24. In a different context (and one that provides a more nuanced approach to the question of the given in Kant), see Rei Terada, *Looking Away: Phenomenality and Dissatisfaction, Kant to Adorno* (Cambridge, Mass.: Harvard University Press, 2009).

25. Georg Wilhelm Friedrich Hegel, *Hegel's Philosophy of Mind: Being Part Three of the "Encyclopaedia of the Philosophical Sciences" (1830)*, trans. William Wallace, Arnold V. Miller, and Ludwig Boumann (Oxford: Clarendon Press, 1971), 203; G. W. F. Hegel, *Werke in Zwanzig Bänden, Theorie-Werkausgabe* (Frankfurt: Suhrkamp, 1970), 10: 258.

26. "Die Vorstellung oder das Bild hat aber seine Wirklichkeit an einem Anderen, als es ist" (Hegel, *Werke in Zwanzig Bänden*, 3: 336; Georg Wilhelm Friedrich Hegel, *Phenomenology of Spirit*, ed. Arnold V. Miller and J. N. Findlay [Oxford: Clarendon Press, 1977], 273).

27. G. W. F. Hegel, *Logic (Part I of the Encyclopedia of the Philosophical Sciences)*, trans. William Wallace with a foreword by J. N. Findlay (Oxford: Oxford University Press, 1975), 7, 6; Hegel, *Werke in Zwanzig Bänden*, 8: 45.

28. Hegel, *Phenomenology of Spirit*, 273; *Werke in Zwanzig Bänden*, 3: 336.

29. As Pfau notes in "From Mediation to Medium," Hegel's image functions as "the objective correlative for the historicity and 'labor of the concept' . . . the 'image' (the *Bild* in *Bildung*) must never be a random trope, a metaphor whose function within the broader history and system of *Bildung* we could not ascertain. On the contrary, as a mode of production, *Bildung* is premised on a stringent model of interpretation (what Hegel calls determinate negation)" (146).

30. For a classic account of the emergence of print culture, see Elizabeth L. Eisenstein, *The Printing Revolution in Early Modern Europe* (Cambridge: Cambridge University Press, 1983); for a more recent account, see Adrian Johns, *The Nature of the Book: Print and Knowledge in the Making* (Chicago: University of Chicago Press, 1998). In this and the following paragraphs, we are drawing heavily on the

Foucault-inspired media accounts developed by Wellbery in *Lessing's Laocoon* and by Friedrich A. Kittler in *Discourse Networks 1800/1900*, trans. Michael Metteer, with Chris Cullens, foreword by David E. Wellbery (Stanford, Calif.: Stanford University Press, 1990), and *Gramophone, Film, Typewriter*, trans. and with an introduction by Geoffrey Winthrop-Young and Michael Wut (Stanford, Calif.: Stanford University Press, 1999).

31. See especially Kittler, *Discourse Networks 1800/1900*.

32. Pioneered by nineteenth-century physiologist Hermann Ebbinghaus, "mnemometers" were primarily employed to make qualitative measurements of a subject's memory capacities. The kymograph, invented by Carl Ludwig in the 1840s, created an automatic graphical representation of changes in physiological processes, such as blood pressure or responses to experimental stimuli. The tachyscope, invented in 1889 by Ottomar Anschütz, produced the illusion of motion by illuminating still images that were mounted on a rotating disk; however, as Kittler notes, the tachyscope was also used as an experimental device that could, for example, modulate the sensory impact of a given "stimulus" (Kittler, *Discourse Networks*, 222–24, 251–56). For primary documents and images of exemplars of these experimental devices, see *The Virtual Laboratory: Essays and Resources on the Experimentalization of Life*, a website sponsored by the Max Planck Institute for the History of Science in Berlin (http://vlp.mpiwg-berlin.mpg.de/).

33. For recent discussions of the importance of indexicality for an understanding of film, see Mary Ann Doane, *The Emergence of Cinematic Time: Modernity, Contingency, the Archive* (Cambridge, Mass.: Harvard University Press, 2002), esp. 69–107; and David Norman Rodowick, *The Virtual Life of Film* (Cambridge, Mass.: Harvard University Press, 2007), esp. 110–23. For discussions of the complications of indexicality in both old and new media, see Wendy Hui Kyong Chun and Thomas Keenan, *New Media, Old Media: A History and Theory Reader* (New York: Routledge, 2006).

34. See Kittler, *Discourse Networks*, esp. 217–64.

35. Behaviorism, by contrast, developed as a method for banishing the concept of the mental image from psychology; see David Berman and William Lyons, "The First Modern Battle for Consciousness: I. B. Watson's Rejection of Mental Images," *Journal of Consciousness Studies* 14.11 (2007): 5–26.

36. Henri Bergson, *Matter and Memory*, trans. Nancy Margaret Paul and W. Scott Palmer (New York: Zone Books, 1988), 1.

37. See Gilles Deleuze, *Cinema 1: The Movement-Image*, trans. Hugh Tomlinson and Barbara Habberjam (Minneapolis: University of Minnesota Press, 1986), and *Cinema 2: The Time-Image*, trans. Hugh Tomlinson and Robert Galeta (Minneapolis: University of Minnesota Press, 1989); and Hansen, *New Philosophy for New Media*.

38. For an account of the emergence of phenomenology in the context of a more widespread philosophical attack on psychologism, see Martin Kusch, *Psychologism: A Case Study in the Sociology of Philosophical Knowledge* (London: Routledge, 1995).

39. Edmund Husserl, *Ideas: General Introduction to Pure Phenomenology*, trans.

William Ralph Boyce Gibson (New York: Collier Books, 1962), 123. Husserl's critique of mental images was extended further by Jean-Paul Sartre in *L'Imaginaire: Psychologie phenomenologique de l'imagination* (Paris: Gallimard, 1940)—translated as *The Psychology of Imagination* (New York: Philosophical Library, 1948)—in which Sartre claimed that even Husserl occasionally had fallen under the spell of seeking to explain aspects of consciousness by means of mental images.

40. Sartre, *L'Imaginaire*.

41. Renaud Barbaras provides a compelling account of the shifting significance of Husserl for Merleau-Ponty in *The Being of the Phenomenon: Merleau-Ponty's Ontology*, trans. Ted Toadvine and Leonard Lawlor (Bloomington: Indiana University Press, 2004). For Merleau-Ponty's discussions of painting and film, see especially "Cézanne's Doubt" and "The Film and the New Psychology," in Maurice Merleau-Ponty, *Sense and Non-Sense*, trans. and with an introduction by Hubert L. Dreyfus and Patricia Allen Dreyfus (Evanston, Ill.: Northwestern University Press, 1964), 9–25, 48–59, and "Eye and Mind" in Maurice Merleau-Ponty, *The Merleau-Ponty Aesthetics Reader: Philosophy and Painting*, trans. Michael B. Smith, ed. and with an introduction by Galen A. Johnson (Evanston, Ill.: Northwestern University Press, 1993), 121–49. As examples as the utility of Merleau-Ponty's approach for an understanding of film, see, for example, Vivian Carol Sobchack, *The Address of the Eye: A Phenomenology of Film Experience* (Princeton, N.J.: Princeton University Press, 1992), and *Carnal Thoughts: Embodiment and Moving Image Culture* (Berkeley: University of California Press, 2004).

42. Merleau-Ponty, "Cézanne's Doubt," 16.

43. For the importance of both Husserl and Heidegger to the neo-Hegelianism of twentieth-century French philosophy, see Vincent Descombes, *Modern French Philosophy*, trans. L. Scott-Fox and J. M. Harding (Cambridge: Cambridge University Press, 1980); and Mikkel Borch-Jacobsen, *Lacan: The Absolute Master*, trans. Douglas Brick (Stanford, Calif.: Stanford University Press, 1991), 1–20.

44. Maurice Blanchot, *The Space of Literature*, trans. Ann Smock (Lincoln: University of Nebraska Press, 1989), 254, 256.

45. For more on this aspect of the image, see both Forest Pyle's contribution to this volume and Jacques Khalip, *Anonymous Life: Romanticism and Dispossession* (Stanford, Calif.: Stanford University Press, 2009), 173–85.

46. Accounts of Benjamin's influences abound, but Miriam Hansen provides a relatively concise—and especially acute—account of many of these in "Benjamin, Cinema and Experience: The Blue Flower in the Land of Technology," *New German Critique* 40 (1987): 179–224.

47. For a brief discussion of these different uses of the term "image," see Hansen, "Benjamin, Cinema and Experience."

48. For Benjamin's critique of Bergson, see "On Some Motifs in Baudelaire," in Walter Benjamin, *Selected Writings, Volume 4, 1938–1940*, ed. Howard Eiland and Michael W. Jennings (Cambridge, Mass.: Harvard University Press, 2004), 313–55. Heideggerian phenomenology is the explicit subject of critique in Theodor W. Adorno's *The Jargon of Authenticity* (Evanston, Ill.: Northwestern

University Press, 1973), but Husserlian phenomenology also comes in for its share of criticism.

49. Sobchack, *The Address of the Eye*, 148.

50. In *The Address of the Eye*, for example, Sobchack argued that the critics must treat the film as a "body" that engages the embodied vision of the spectator by being both for the spectator but also, crucially, for-itself; the film, that is, "is not . . . merely an object for perception and expression; it is also the subject of perception and expression" (167). However, while the spectator's body is gendered (and raced, and aged, etc.), the "film's 'body' is not sexed, although it is sensible and sensual." It is precisely this difference between the spectator's gendered body and the film's ungendered body—its refusal of gender—that provides "us actual and possible modes of becoming other than we are" (162); that is, the "film's material body . . . engages us in its possibilities as a nonhuman lived-body" (163).

51. See, for example, Jean-Luc Marion, *The Idol and Distance: Five Studies*, trans. Thomas A. Carlson (New York: Fordham University Press, 2001); *The Crossing of the Visible*, trans. James K. A. Smith (Stanford, Calif.: Stanford University Press, 2004); and *The Visible and the Revealed*, trans. Christina M. Gschwandtner (New York: Fordham University Press, 2008).

52. See, for example, Mark Hansen, "The Time of Affect, or Bearing Witness to Life," *Critical Inquiry* 30 (2004): 584–626; and Carrie Noland, "Motor Intentionality: Gestural Meaning in Bill Viola and Merleau-Ponty," *Postmodern Culture* 17.3 (2007) (http://muse.jhu.edu/journals/pmc/v017/17.3noland.html). For discussion of Viola's work in the context of new media more generally, see Timothy Murray, *Digital Baroque: New Media Art and Cinematic Folds* (Minneapolis: University of Minnesota Press, 2008), 35–57.

53. W. J. T. Mitchell, *What Do Pictures Want?: The Lives and Loves of Images* (Chicago: University of Chicago Press, 2005).

54. Stephen Michael Kosslyn, *Image and Brain: The Resolution of the Imagery Debate* (Cambridge, Mass.: MIT Press, 1994). See also Michael Tye, *The Imagery Debate* (Cambridge, Mass.: MIT Press, 1991).

55. For an introduction to the project of "naturalizing phenomenology," see Jean Petitot, Francisco Varela, Bernard Pachoud, and Jean-Michel Roy, *Naturalizing Phenomenology: Issues in Contemporary Phenomenology and Cognitive Science* (Stanford, Calif.: Stanford University Press, 1999).

56. Cesare Casarino, "The Simulacrum of AIDS," *Parallax* 11.2 (2005): 60–72. For more on the spectacularization of AIDS, see Simon Watney, "The Spectacle of AIDS," in *AIDS: Cultural Analysis / Cultural Activism*, ed. Douglas Crimp (Cambridge, Mass.: MIT Press, 1988), 71–86.

57. Bernard Stiegler, *Technics and Time, I: The Fault of Epimetheus*, trans. Richard Beardsworth and George Collins (Stanford, Calif.: Stanford University Press, 1998); and *Technics and Time, 2: Disorientation*, trans. Stephen Barker (Stanford, Calif.: Stanford University Press, 2008).

58. Laura Mulvey, "Visual Pleasure and Narrative Cinema," in *Narrative, Ap-*

paratus, Ideology: A Film Theory Reader, ed. Philip Rosen (New York: Columbia University Press, 1986), 198–209.

59. For example, see the work of Sara Ahmed, Judith Butler, Mary Ann Doane, Elizabeth Grosz, Laura U. Marks, Dorothea Olkowski, Kaja Silverman, and Vivian Sobchack.

Chapter 1

1. Jacques Derrida, "The Rhetoric of Drugs: An Interview," *differences* 5.1 (1993): 25.

2. Hans Jonas, "Image-Making and the Freedom of Man," in *The Phenomenon of Life: Towards a Philosophical Biology*, trans. Lawrence Vogel (Evanston, IL: Northwestern University Press, 2001), 159.

3. On *acheiropoietoi*, see Ewa Kuryluk, *Veronica and Her Cloth: History, Symbolism, and Structure of a "True" Image* (Oxford: Basil Blackwell, 1991); and Hans Belting, *Likeness and Presence: A History of the Image Before the Era of Art*, trans. Edmund Jephcott (Chicago: University of Chicago Press, 1997), 208–24.

4. Georges Didi-Huberman, *Confronting Images: Questioning the Ends of a Certain History of Art*, trans. John Goodman (University Park: Pennsylvania State Press, 2005), 190.

5. William Henry Fox Talbot, "The New Art," *The Literary Gazette and Journal of Belles Lettres, Arts, Sciences, etc.* 1150 (2 February 1839): 73.

6. William Henry Fox Talbot, "The Pencil of Nature: A New Discovery," *The Corsair: A Gazette of Literature, Art, Dramatic Criticism, Fashion and Novelty* 1.5 (13 April 1839): 74.

7. Mary Ann Doane, *The Emergence of Cinematic Time: Modernity, Contingency, the Archive* (Cambridge, MA: Harvard University Press, 2002), 94.

8. André Bazin, "The Ontology of the Photographic Image," trans. Hugh Gray, *Film Quarterly* 13.4 (Summer 1960): 7.

9. Roland Barthes, *Camera Lucida: Reflections on Photography*, trans. Richard Howard (London: Macmillan, 1982), 87, 82. The reference in the English translation to "St. Veronica's napkin" appears to be erroneous—in the French original, Barthes refers to the Shroud of Turin. See Roland Barthes, *La chambre claire: Note sur la photographie* (Paris: Seuil, 1980), 129.

10. Walter Benjamin, "A Short History of Photography," trans. Stanley Mitchell, *Screen* 13.1 (Spring 1972): 18.

11. Rudolf Arnheim, "Die Fotografie—Sein und Aussage [Photography—Being and Expression]," in *Die Seele in der Silberschicht: Medientheoreritische Texte. Photographie—Film—Rundfunk*, ed. Helmut H. Diederichs (Frankfurt: Suhrkamp, 2004), 38.

12. Much of scientific photography relies, for example, on the partial autonomy of the apparatus, for it has to operate in realms inaccessible to the human eye. This does not amount to a claim that images produced in this manner are "objective," "self-evident," or "true." The partial autonomy of the photographic recording device

is, indeed, used precisely to bring to light something that has no clear contours. The author of such recordings plans and initiates a sequence of events, but leaves a portion of his experimental station unattended. He controls and intervenes, but remains intentionally excluded from certain processes within the experimental sequence. It is often only in retrospect that he sees what the apparatus produces under such conditions—sometimes, without being able to interpret it.

13. William Henry Fox Talbot, "Some Account of the Art of Photogenic Drawing," in *Photography in Print: Writings from 1816 to the Present*, ed. Vicki Goldberg (Albuquerque: University of New Mexico Press, 1981), 46.

14. This holds above all for sociological, semiotic, Marxist, and discourse-analytical interpretations of photography, which have, since the 1980s, taken over the field. See, for example, John Tagg, *The Burden of Representation: Essays on Photographies and Histories* (Amherst: University of Massachusetts Press, 1988); Richard Bolton, ed., *The Contest of Meaning: Critical Histories of Photography* (Cambridge, MA: MIT Press, 1989); and Victor Burgin, ed., *Thinking Photography* (London: Macmillan, 1982).

15. "Although a very faithful drawing gives far more information about the model, it would never possess the irrational power of photography to which we, despite our critical spirit, give credence" ("Die Fotografie" 37).

16. Wolfgang Kemp, "Der Sonnenhut des Heliographen: Zwei Aufnahmen—30 und 160 Jahre danach," in *Foto-Essays zur Geschichte und Theorie der Fotografie* (Munich: Schirmer/Mosel, 2006), 151.

17. Georges Didi-Huberman, *Images in Spite of All: Four Photographs from Auschwitz*, trans. Shane B. Lillis (Chicago: University of Chicago Press), 70.

18. Michel Frizot, "L'invention de l'invention," in *Les multiples inventions de la photographie*, ed. Pierre Bonhomme (Paris: Mission du Patrimoine photographique, 1989), 103.

19. Geoffrey Batchen, *Burning with Desire: The Conception of Photography* (Cambridge, MA: MIT Press, 1997), 181.

20. Georges Canguilhem, "The Object of the History of Sciences," in *Continental Philosophy of Science*, ed. Gary Gutting (Oxford: Blackwell, 2005), 198.

21. Pierre Lamy, cited in E. N. Santini, *La photographie à travers les corps opaques par les rayons électriques, cathodiques et de Röntgen avec une étude sur les photofulgurales* (Paris, 1896), 69–70.

22. Camille Flammarion, *Thunder and Lightning*, trans. Walter Mostyn (London: Chatto and Windus, 1905), 268–69, 250. On Flammarion, see also Georges Didi-Huberman, "L'empreinte du ciel," *Revue Antigone* 20 (1994): 13–64; and Philippe Dubois, "La tempête et la matière-temps, ou le sublime et le figural dans l'oeuvre de Jean Epstein," in *Jean Epstein: Cinéaste, poète, philosophe*, ed. Jacques Aumont (Paris: Cinémathèque française, 1998), 267–323.

23. *La photographie* 80.

24. Cited in Josef Maria Eder, *History of Photography*, trans. Edward Epstean (New York: Columbia University Press, 1945), 85.

25. Cited in "L'invention de l'invention" 4. The original French reads: "Du reste, tout est sensible à l'action du soleil: les rideaux des fenêtres qui passent de colour au désespoir des maitresses de maison, les robes, les étoffes, les tentures, les papiers; tout change de ton á la lumière. Le chlorure d'argent est simplement plus sensible que le reste."

26. Jacques Derrida, "A Certain Impossible Possibility of Saying the Event," trans. Gila Walker, *Critical Inquiry* 33.2 (2007): 450.

27. Hans-Jörg Rheinberger, *Toward a History of Epistemic Things: Synthesizing Proteins in the Test Tube* (Stanford, CA: Stanford University Press, 1997), 133.

28. Bruno Latour, "Do Scientific Objects Have a History? Pasteur and White-head in a Bath of Lactic Acid," *Common Knowledge* 5.1 (1996): 82.

29. Bruno Latour, "Les objets ont-ils une histoire? Rencontre de Pasteur et de Whitehead dans un bain d' acide lactique," in *L'effet Whitehead*, ed. Isabelle Stengers (Paris: Flammarion, 1994), 211.

30. Bruno Latour, *Pandora's Hope: Essays on the Reality of Science Studies* (Cambridge, MA: Harvard University Press, 1999), 182. Latour writes that "[t]his entails that we should be able to say that not only the microbes-for-us-humans changed in the 1850s, but also the microbes-for-themselves. Their encounter with Pasteur changed them as well. Pasteur, so to speak, 'happened' to them" (146).

31. Michel Foucault, "Nietzsche, Genealogy, History," in *Language, Counter-Memory, Practice: Selected Essays and Interviews*, ed. D. F. Bouchard (Ithaca, NY: Cornell University Press, 1977), 142.

32. Gaston-Henri Niewenglowski, *Chimie des manipulations photographiques* (Paris: Gauthier-Villars, 1899), 5, translation by Michael Powers.

33. Friedrich Kittler, *Optische Medien: Berliner Vorlesung 1999* (Berlin: Merve Verlag, 2002), 157.

34. See also Peter Geimer, "Picturing the Black Box: On Blanks in 19th-Century Paintings and Photographs," *Science in Context* 17 (2004): 467–501.

Chapter 2

This article was originally published in French in *Ce que Cézanne donne à penser (Actes du colloque d'Aix-en-Provence, Juillet 2006)*, edited by Denis Coutagne, © Editions Gallimard. 2008. http://www.gallimard.com.

1. Paul Cézanne, *Conversations avec Cézanne*, ed. P. M. Doran (Paris: Macula, 1978), 159, hereafter abbreviated *Conversations*; English translation, Paul Cézanne, *Conversations with Cézanne*, trans. Julie Lawrence Cochran (Berkeley: University of California Press, 2001), 158, hereafter abbreviated *CC*. When it is a matter of phrases reported by witnesses or critics, the quotations from Cézanne are drawn from this collection. I indicate the critic at the origin of the citation. Here it is Gasquet. When it is a matter of phrases drawn from the correspondence of the painter, i.e., phrases with autographic origins, it is specified as *Correspondance de Cézanne*, ed. John Rewald (Paris: Grasset, 1978), hereafter abbreviated *Correspondance*; English translation, *Paul Cézanne's Letters*, ed. John Rewald (Cambridge, MA: Da Capo

Press, 1995), hereafter abbreviated *PCL*. Whenever possible, subsequent citations from these works will appear in the body of the text. [Editors' note: Some of the translations that appear in *Paul Cézanne's Letters* and *Conversations with Cézanne* have been altered here in order to better emphasize Marion's argument.]

2. Letter to Émile Bernard, May 26, 1904, *Correspondance*, 302; *PCL*, 303. This phrase is repeated by Gasquet in *Conversations*, 118; *CC*, 119. See "the artist must avoid literature in art" (according to Larguier) (cf. *Conversations*, 14; *CC*, 16).

3. "The Assayer," in *The Discoveries and Opinions of Galileo*, ed. Stillman Drake (New York: Anchor Books, 1957), 237–238. See the *Letter F. Liceti*, January 1641: "The book of philosophy is that which stands perpetually open before our eyes, but because it is written in characters different from those of our alphabet it cannot be read by every body; and the characters of this book are triangles, squares, circles, spheres, cones, pyramids and other mathematical figures fittest for this sort of reading" (*Styles of Scientific Thinking in the European Tradition*, trans. A. Crombie [London: Duckworth, 1994], vol. 1, p. 585). See also my study *Sur la théologie blanche de Descartes* (Paris: Presses universitaires de France, 1981), 203ff., in particular 210–213.

4. Letter to Émile Bernard, May 12, 1904, *Conversations*, 28; *CC*, 30. For Gasquet's account, see 136ff; *CC*, 136.

5. "To read nature [*lire la nature*] is to see it beneath the veil of interpretation" (*Conversations*, 36; *CC*, 38). "It all comes down to this: to have sensations and to read nature" (*Conversations*, 37; *CC*, 39).

6. But meanwhile Denis rightly observes that "this is not . . . Cézanne's conception" (*Conversations*, 179; *CC*, 178).

7. Malevich obviously upheld this interpretation: "Thus Cézanne laid the outstanding and significant foundations of the Cubist trend, which has flourished in France with Braque, Picasso, Léger, Metzinger, and Gleizes, and which emerged in Russia with a new bias towards alogism" ("On New Systems in Art," in *Essays on Art: 1915–1933*, trans. Xenia Glowacki-Prus and Arnold McMillan [London: Rapp & Whiting, 1968], 95).

8. These citations refer to remarks by Cézanne as reported by Gasquet: cf. *Conversations*, 113; *CC*, 114. And at the outset of the text: "Behold what one must render. Behold what one must know. Behold the bath of science, if I may dare say so, into which one must dip his sensitive plate. In order to paint a landscape well, I must first discover the geological strata . . . The next day, a beautiful morning, the geological foundations slowly appear to me, the layers establish themselves, the majestic planes of my canvas, I mentally draw its rocky skeleton" (*Conversations*, 112–113; *CC*, 114). These texts bear witness to the influence of the works on the psychology of the earth on Cézanne (*Conversations*, 111–112; *CC*, 113) by "my friend Marion," scholar of geology and paleontology, director of the Musée d'Histoire Naturelle de Marseille (see *Conversations*, 207n15; *CC*, 250n15); and Jourdan, Vayssière, and Gastine, "Notice sur la vie et les travaux de A.-F. Marion," *Annales de la Faculté des Sciences de Marseille* 11 (1901): 1–36; or G. Reynaud and J. Beaurois, "Antoine-Fortuné Marion, 1846–1900. Initiateur de l'océanographie à Marseille," *Marseille, La Revue Culturelle de la Ville* 163 (1972): 36. His discovery of a Neolithic cave in the

Saint-Marc hill had a significant impact (see "Sur les progrès des sciences naturel-les," in *Discours prononcé le 5 décembre 1882 dans la séance solennelle des Facultés de l'Académie d'Aix* [Marseille, 1883]), as did his conference on "Premières observations sur l'ancienneté de l'homme dans les Bouches-du-Rhône," in *Extraits des séances du Congrès Scientifique de France tenu à Aix* (N.p., 1886).

9. M. Merleau-Ponty, "Le doute de Cézanne" (1945), in *Sens et Non-sens* (Paris: Nagel, 1961), 20; "Cézanne's Doubt" in *Sense and Non-sense* (Evanston, IL: North-western University Press, 1964), 15, translation altered.

10. R. M. Rilke, *Lettre à Clara Rilke*, October 9, 1907, in *Oeuvres en prose*, ed. C. David (Paris: La Pléiade, 1993), 987; *Letters on Cézanne*, trans. Joel Agee (Ann Arbor, MI: Fromm International, 1985), 34. Rilke's lexicon lacks precision here, as *object* is made equivalent to *thing*. But the distinction between the concepts none-theless remains perfectly clear.

11. P. M. Doran pertinently identifies the problem here: "An early, if not the earliest, example of the improper introduction of the cube into the literature on Cézanne," and cites—this is not an accident—Malevich: "Cézanne, the prominent and conscious individual, recognized the motive for geometrization and, in a per-fectly conscious manner, showed us the cone, *the cube*, and the sphere, considered as the characteristic varieties according to which one should *construct* nature, that is, *reduce* the object to simple geometrical expressions" ("On New Systems in Art," 94). See also: "Cézanne has called for this geometrization; he illustrated it by reduc-ing nature to the cone, *the cube*, and the sphere" (91); and once again: "Despite his formidable sense for the pictorial in the object, Cézanne has made only little progress on the plane of form; he has not been able to make a purely pictorial construction, despite his striving toward the cone, *the cube*, and the sphere" (98). Sometimes Malevich even introduces the straight line: "He [Cézanne!] said: 'I base nature on geometrical principles and reduce nature to geometrization understood not as simplification, but as the clarity of expression of the surface-plane, of the volume, of the *straight line*, of the cone, as the intersections of pictorial-plastic ex-pressions'" (91). In fact, Cézanne neither anticipates any of this, nor hesitates before any of this: he challenges the reductionism of geometrization, as well as the straight line and the cube.

12. Rivière and Schnerb, "L'atelier de Cézanne," *La Grande Revue*, December 25, 1907, in *Conversations*, 90; *CC*, 89.

13. Maurice Denis, *Journal*, cited in *Conversations*, 94; *CC*, 93.

14. Francis Jourdain, *Cézanne*, in *Conversations*, 217; *CC*, 259, emphasis added.

15. Rivière and Schnerb, "L'atelier de Cézanne," in *Conversations*, 90; *CC*, 89.

16. *Correspondance*, 304; *PCL*, 306: "I mean that in this orange which I peel, here, in an apple, a ball, a head, there is a culminating point and this point is al-ways—in spite of the terrible effect: light, shadow, sensations of color—is always the closest to our eye."

17. And also: "The eye must concentrate, encompass, the brain will formulate" (*Conversations*, 159; *CC*, 158).

18. This formulation, where *aeterne* attests to a vocative, simply amazes. If it were

a matter of a formulation improvised by Cézanne, we would have instead expected *aeternus*, nominative. The explanation of this deviation is simple: Cézanne cites here the text of the *Preface*, in the mass of the Trinity, which invokes God, evidently in the vocative: "Domine, sancte *Pater omnipotens aeterne Deus*," in *Missel quotidien des fidèles*, ed. J. Feder (Tours: Maison Mame, 1955), 810 (*Layman's Daily Missal* [Baltimore: Helicon Press, 1962], 863). Now, at the time, this *Preface* was also used every Sunday; it would occur therefore most often during the liturgical year; Cézanne cites it from memory, in assiduous fidelity to the Dominical mass.

19. Editors' note: We have altered the punctuation of the translation to make more evident Marion's point in the paragraph that follows the citation.

20. Professor of Fine Arts and member of the Institute of France (died in 1882), he published, first in literary articles in the *Gazette des Beaux-Arts* between 1860 and 1866, then in a volume in Paris in 1867, the *Grammaire des arts du dessin* (Paris: ENS-BA, 2000), hereafter abbreviated *GAD*; English translation, *The Grammar of Painting and Engraving*, trans. Kate Newell Doggett (Chicago: S. C. Griggs and Company, 1891), hereafter abbreviated *GPE*. (Whenever possible, subsequent citations from these works will appear in the body of the text.) Cézanne had surely seen it in Paris, but the work was also taught in Aix.

21. I follow chapter VIII of the *GAD*, 479; *GPE*, 48, 49.

22. H. Damisch has insisted quite rightly on this problematic, and I agree with him on this main point. But I cannot pose God as the "geometrical of every perspective," because while God would be able to see the geometrical, he is not identified with it. "La géométrie de la couleur," in *Cézanne ou la peinture en jeu* (Limoges: Critérion, 1982), 36.

23. Maurice Denis, *Théories*, in *Conversations*, 177; *CC*, 177. And additionally: "atmospheric perspective is sacrificed to the extreme" (*CC*, 177).

24. "Ingres is a pernicious classicist." See Émile Bernard, "Paul Cézanne," in *L'Occident*, February–March 1904, in *Conversations*, 36; *CC*, 38.

25. The same fate claimed David, "my great horror" (*Conversations*, 134; *CC*, 135).

26. Léo Larguier, *Le dimanche avec Paul Cézanne*, in *Conversations*, 16; *CC*, 17. See also Maurice Denis: "Thus in his truly concrete perception of objects, form is inseparable from color" (*Théories*, in *Conversations*, 176; *CC*, 176).

27. And to follow this metaphor: "If it is otherwise (if drawing does not preserve its preponderance over color), then painting hastens to its ruin: it will be undone through color as humanity was undone through Eve."

28. See also: "The fullness of color always corresponds to the fullness of drawing" (*Conversations*, 123; *CC*, 124).

29. Rivière and Schnerb, *Conversations*, 89; *CC*, 88. Émile Bernard said "*to model by coloring*" (*Conversations*, 59; *CC*, 60).

30. "Volume also finds expression in Cézanne in a scale of colors, in a series of strokes. These strokes follow one another by contrasts or by analogies by which form is interrupted or continues. This was what he liked to call 'modulation' rather than modeling" (*Conversations*, 177; *CC*, 177).

31. M.-J. Baudinet, in denoting the motif's extreme difference from the object,

goes so far as to conceive of it as a "a motorized cause of an ensemble of gestures which reconduct the image back to its constitutive conditions. The painting parts from the pure motif to give birth to the model" ("Cézanne et l'objet de la peinture," in *Cézanne et la peinture en jeu*, 138). In other words, the motif does not result from the vision of the painter, as an object, but puts into motion the modulation of form according to color in its unfolding.

32. Michel Guérin, who continues: "Moreover, purely material form, purely issued from color, suppressed worldly, anthropological, or pragmatic form, which could be called utilitarian form . . . It is with this equivalence between realization and murder, or if you prefer, with this integral substitution of the *thing* of color for the *object* of our representations, that Cézanne surpassed Impressionism" ("Humble et colossal Cézanne," in *Cézanne et la peinture en jeu*, 217). "The object of art is a *thing*, contrary to quotidian objects which we utilize and upon which our perception glides, objects beneath the empire of existing perspectives which we are" (ibid., 208).

33. The artist, "at the moment he creates, should be like a photographic plate, simply a recording device" (*Conversations*, 111–112; *CC*, 113).

34. Gasquet, *Conversations*, 120; *CC*, 121.

35. Gasquet, *Conversations*, 125; *CC*, 126.

36. See also: "I am an intellectual, if you will, but I am also a brute" (*Conversations*, 126; *CC*, 127).

37. *Conversations*, 22; *CC*, 163; Jules Borély, "Cézanne à Aix," in *L'Art Vivant* 2 (1926): 46 (English translation, 48); letter to Émile Bernard, October 23, 1905, *Correspondance*, 314, 162, 164; *PCL*, 317, 162, 163; and Émile Bernard, "Une Conversation avec Cézanne" *Mercure de France*, June 1, 1921.

38. Gasquet, *Conversations*, 121; *CC*, 122. "Monet visited him, you know, in his youth, on the Channel" (for they met each other in Deauville, through the intermediary of Boudin).

39. We return here to a note by Denis Coutagne, "Qu'est-ce qu'un Cézanne?" in *Cézanne ou la peinture en jeu*, 26n1.

40. Gasquet, *Conversations*, 122–123; *CC*, 124. How does Cézanne know Kant, if he has never read him? Perhaps precisely through Gasquet, who himself was the liaison between Cézanne and Dumesnil, who had been his professor of philosophy in Aix (he defended a thesis at the Sorbonne in 1892 on *Du rôle des concepts dans la vie intellectuelle et morale. Essai théorique d'après une vue de l'histoire*). Cézanne knew him well enough to give him two of his canvases and to mention him: "The other day, you spoke to me of Kant. I probably cannot say this clearly, but it seems to me that I'll be the subjective conscience of this landscape, just as my painting will be the objective consciousness . . . It is an interpretation. I am not an academic. I wouldn't dare talk like this in front of Dumesnil" (*Conversations*, 110; *CC*, 111).

41. Let us return once and for all to Lawrence Gowing, "Cézanne: The Logic of Organized Sensations," *CC*, 180–212.

42. Heidegger, *Being and Time* (Albany: SUNY, 1996), 25. F. Williams has rightly seen the phenomenological significance of the Cézannian enterprise, which no lon-

ger wants "mere appearance, but the appearance of something given in appearance," but wrongly returns to Merleau-Ponty (who precisely does not see it, or at least says as much in his essay, in all other respects misleadingly), when it is obviously a question of Heidegger ("Cézanne and French Phenomenology," *Journal of Aesthetics and Art Criticism* 12, no. 4 [1954]: 486); see "Cézanne, Phenomenology and Merleau-Ponty," in *The Merleau-Ponty Aesthetics Reader* (Evanston, IL: Northwestern University Press, 1993). Also see C. M. Brailsford, *Cézanne and Phenomenology* (Ann Arbor: University of Michigan Press, 1984).

43. Letter to Émile Bernard, October 23, 1905, in *Conversations*, 46; *CC*, 48.

44. Jacques Derrida thus distinguishes four possible senses of the formulation in *La vérité en peinture* (Paris: Gallimard, 1978), 9–10; *The Truth in Painting*, trans. Geoff Bennington and Ian McLeod (Chicago: University of Chicago Press, 1987), 5–7. The formulation doesn't come from a letter to Émile Mâle, but to Émile Bernard (6, with a manuscript correction).

Chapter 3

I would like to thank the many people who helped with this translation. Michael Papio and Ronald Martinez gave advice on the sections about Boccaccio and Paracelsus, and Kevin Attell kindly reviewed the entire manuscript. I cannot express my gratitude to Kevin McLaughlin enough for spending several hours discussing this text to the last syllable, for helping over many revisions, and for finding citations I thought unfindable. I also wish to warmly thank Suzanne Stewart-Steinberg for being invariably inspiring and illuminating.—Trans.

This chapter was published in Italian as *Ninfe*. Bollati Boringhieri 2007. ©Giorgio Agamben.

1. Bill Viola, *The Passions*, ed. John Walsh (Los Angeles: J. Paul Getty Museum, 2003), 199, 210.

2. Domenico da Piacenza, *Treatises and Music: Twelve Transcribed Italian Treatises and Collections in the Tradition of Domenico da Piacenza*, vol. 1, trans. A. William Smith (Stuyvesant, N.Y.: Pendragon Press, 1995), 13 [translation modified]. In Smith's translation the list of technical terms is left untranslated: *mesura, memoria, maniera cum mesura de terreno e aire*.

3. Aristotle, "On Memory and Recollection," in *Aristotle's Psychology: A Treatise on the Principle of Life (De Anima and parva naturalia)*, trans. William Alexander Hammond (New York: Macmillan, 1902), 211.

4. Albert B. Lord, *The Singer of Tales* (Cambridge, Mass.: Harvard University Press, 2000), 13.

5. Ernst Hans Gombrich, *Aby Warburg: An Intellectual Biography* (London: Warburg Institute, 1970), 108.

6. The full title of Darger's illustrated novel is *The Story of the Vivian Girls, in What Is Known as the Realms of the Unreal, of the Glandeco-Angelinnian War Storm, Caused by the Child Slave Rebellion*. Although the novel has not been published, it has been the subject of many exhibitions around the world in recent decades.

7. Walter Benjamin, *Arcades Project*, trans. Howard Eiland and Kevin McLaughlin (Cambridge, Mass.: Harvard University Press, 1999), 463.

8. Walter Benjamin, *Gesammelte Schriften*, vol. 1 (Frankfurt am Main: Surhkamp, 1974), 1229. This quotation of Henri Focillon, *The Life of Forms*, trans. George Kubler (New York: Zone Books, 1989), 55, occurs in the notes taken by Benjamin as part of his work "On the Concept of History."

9. Walter Benjamin, "On the Concept of History," *Selected Writings*, vol. 4 (Cambridge, Mass.: Harvard University Press, 2006), 396.

10. Theodor W. Adorno and Walter Benjamin, *The Complete Correspondence: 1928–1940*, trans. Henri Lonitz and Nicholas Walter (Cambridge, Mass.: Harvard University Press, 1999), 114–115.

11. Benjamin, *Arcades Project*, 466.

12. Adorno and Benjamin, *Correspondence*, 108.

13. See Enzo Melandri, *La linea e il circolo. Studio logico-filosofico sull'analogia* (Macerata, Italy: Quodlibet, 2004), 798.

14. Friedrich Theodor von Fischer, "Das Symbol," in *Altes und Neues* (Stuttgart: A. Bonz and Company, 1889), 290–342.

15. Aby Warburg, "Allgemeine Ideen," *Warburg Insitute Archive* 3, 102.1 (London, 1927), 20, 74. Cited by Georges Didi-Huberman, *L'image survivante: Histoire de l'art et temps des fantômes selon Aby Warburg* (Paris: Éditions de Minuit, 2002), 183.

16. This is the title of a 1918 essay by Warburg.

17. The allusion is to Salomon Friedländer's book *Schöpferische Indifferenz* (1918). See Walter Benjamin, "The Mendelssohns' *Der Mensch in der Handschrift*," in *Collected Writings*, vol. 2, trans. Rodney Livingstone (Cambridge, Mass.: Harvard University Press, 2005), 133.

18. Gianni Carchia, "Aby Warburg. Simbolo e tragedia," *Aut-Aut* 199–200 (1984): 100–101.

19. Warburg, "Allgemeine Ideen," 37. Cited by Didi-Huberman, *L'image survivante*, 339.

20. Didi-Huberman, *L'image survivante*, 182.

21. This quotation is from unpublished manuscripts in the Warburg Archive.

22. Gombrich, *Aby Warburg*, 255 [translation modified].

23. Paracelsus, "A Book on Nymphs, Sylphs, Pygmies, and Salamanders, and on the Other Spirits," in *Four Treatises of Theophrastus von Hohenheim*, trans. Henry E. Sigerist (Baltimore: Johns Hopkins University Press, 1941), 223–253.

24. Gombrich, *Aby Warburg*, 110.

25. Paracelsus, "A Book on Nymphs," 229.

26. Giovanni Boccaccio, *The Decameron*, vol. 1, trans. J. M. Rigg (London: A. H. Bullen, 1903), 262.

27. Giovanni Boccaccio, *The Corbaccio*, trans. Anthony K. Cassell (Urbana: University of Illinois Press, 1975), 32 [translation modified].

28. Warburg Institute Archive, General Correspondence, Aby Warburg to Karl Vossler, October 12, 1929.

29. "L'impresa di Warburg," *Aut Aut* 321–322 (2004): 97–116.

30. André Jolles, "Clio en Melpomene," *De Gids* 89.3 (1925): 400–403.

Chapter 4

1. Semir Zeki, *Inner Vision: An Exploration of Art and the Brain* (Oxford: Oxford University Press, 1999); V. S. Ramachandran, *A Brief Tour of Human Consciousness: From Imposter Poodles to Purple Numbers* (New York: Pi Press, 2004).

2. Michael Morgan, *The Space Between Our Ears: How the Brain Represents Visual Space* (London: Weidenfeld & Nicolson, 2003), 6.

3. Antonio Damasio and Hanna Damasio, "Making Images and Creating Subjectivity," in *The Mind-Brain Continuum: Sensory Processes*, ed. R. Llinas and P. S. Churchland (Cambridge, MA: MIT, 1996), 19.

4. Zeki, *Inner Vision*, 1.

5. Stephen M. Kosslyn, *Image and Brain: The Resolution of the Imagery Debate* (Cambridge, MA: MIT Press, 1994), 3.

6. J. David Lewis-Williams, *The Mind in the Cave: Consciousness and the Origins of Art* (London: Thames & Hudson, 2002), 185.

7. Semir Zeki, "A Theory of Micro-consciousness," in *The Blackwell Companion to Consciousness*, ed. M. Velmans and S. Schneide (London: Blackwell, 2007), accessed at http://www.blackwellreference.com/subscriber/uid=571/tocnode?id=g9781405120197_chunk_g9781405120197 46, 5/13/09.

8. For example, Damasio identifies the problem of synchronization as the direct result of functional specialization. Even though his work does not focus specifically on the visual brain, as does Zeki's, what he says about cross-modal synchronization reinforces the consensus I am here underscoring: "Most of our experiences are based on images of several sensory modalities occurring within the same window of time. Since the early sensory cortices for each modality are not contiguous and are not directly interconnected, it follows that our polymodal experiences must result from concurrent activity in several separate brain regions rather than in a single one. In other words, the making of images is a spatially parcellated process. But since our experiences appear integrated to our mind rather than parcellated, we must consider how integration occurs. Our idea is that timing, that is, synchronization of separate activities, plays an essential role in integration. We suspect that the neural mechanism behind synchronization requires signaling from both cortical and subcortical neuron ensembles, capable of simultaneous firing toward many separate neuron populations. Such ensembles do seem to exist and we call them convergence zones" (Damasio and Damasio, "Making Images," 21).

9. Deleuze develops the concept of transcendental sensibility in *Difference and Repetition* as a response to Kant's transcendental analysis of sensation as forms of intuition. What Deleuze is after, as he emphasized repeatedly, is not the conditions *of possibility* for experience, but the conditions *of real experience*. Rooting his theorization in the work of the post-Kantian philosophers, with a glance back at Leibniz, Deleuze positions transcendental sensibility as a transcendental domain that

lies paradoxically *with the domain of the empirical* but that is beyond the grasp of consciousness or the Kantian figures of thought (common sense and recognition). Because this domain is "invisible" to empirical consciousness, without ceasing to be empirical, we might call it "infraempirical." For a related use of the term "infraempirical," see José Gil, *Metamorphoses of the Body*, tr. S. Muecke (Minneapolis: University of Minnesota Press, 1998), Part II.

10. Zeki, "Theory." One could also add Damasio to Zeki's unenumerated list.

11. Gilles Deleuze, *Difference and Repetition*, tr. Paul Patton (New York: Columbia University Press, 1995), Chapter 3.

12. Mark B. N. Hansen, *New Philosophy for New Media* (Cambridge, MA: MIT Press, 2004).

13. Maurizio Lazzarato, "Video, Flows and Real Time," in *Art and the Moving Image: A Critical Reader*, ed. T. Leighton (London: Tate Publishing, 2007), 283–85.

14. Cited in Lazzarato, "Video, Flows and Real Time," 285–86.

15. For an account of "metapictures," see W. J. T. Mitchell, *Picture Theory: Essays on Verbal and Visual Representation* (Chicago: University of Chicago Press, 1995), Chapter 2.

16. Warren Neidich, "Blow-Up," in *Blow-Up: Photography, Cinema and the Brain* (New York: Distributed Art Publishers, 2003), 36–37, emphasis added.

17. Neidich, "The Sculpted Brain," in *Blow-Up*, 140.

18. "I am also only talking about the field of phatic signifiers at this time, although I am aware of a diametrically opposed field that exists in parallel called the field of discursive signifiers, which is a reservoir of signifiers at odds with the academic suppositions of the field of phatic signifiers. It is to this field that artistic practice can at times be tuned and from which it can extract new variables to contaminate the ongoing discourse" (Neidich, "Blow-Up," 58, note 38). In his introduction to Neidich's essays, Norman Bryson grasps the radical gambit of a neuroscientific aesthetics like Neidich's that operates precisely by vacating the signifier of cognitive force: "The radicalism of neuroscience consists in its bracketing out the signifier as the force that binds the world together: what makes the apple is not the signifier 'apple' (though this too, may play an important role in the process of reality-binding), but rather the simultaneous firing of axons and neurons within cellular and organic life. The level of the ground of being, or of the real, shifts from the signifier to the neural configuration, the orchestration of myriad plays of lightning across the ramifying branches of the brain" (Bryson, "The Neural Interface," introduction to *Blow-up*, 14).

19. The claim that selectivity is determined by efficiency is certainly the most sustained refrain of Neidich's text: indeed, his entire argument concerning the privilege of the artificial is rooted in the value of efficiency.

20. Catherine Malabou, *What Should We Do with Our Brain?* tr. S. Rand (New York: Fordham University Press, 2008). On the issue of capitalism's mimicking of cognitive networks, see Luc Boltanski and Eve Chiapello, *The New Spirit of Capitalism*, tr. G. Elliott (London: Verso, 2007), Chapter 1.

21. It is, I think, precisely with such a capitalization in mind that Malabou criticizes what she calls the "neuronal ideology," the notion that there is a determinism in the relation between brain event and qualitative experience.

22. "The findings suggest that 40-Hz oscillatory activity is not only involved in primary sensory processing per se, but forms part of a time conjunction or binding property that amalgamates sensory events occurring in perceptual time quanta into a single experience. Indeed, 40-Hz oscillator activity is prevalent in the mammalian CNS, as seen at both single-cell and multicellular levels. This oscillatory activity . . . has been viewed as a possible mechanism for the conjunction of spatially distributed visual sensory activity or multiregional cortical binding" (R. Llinas and D. Pare, "Binding by Specific-Non-Specific 40-Hz Resonant Conjunction," in *The Mind-Brain Continuum*, ed. R. Llinas and P. S. Churchland [Cambridge, MA: MIT Press, 1996], cited in Neidich, "Blow-Up," 88).

23. Neidich, "Blow-Up," 100.

24. I base my account of the work on Coupe's description, available at www.recollector.net.

25. Lazzarato, "Video, Flows and Real Time," 283, note 1.

26. Maurizio Lazzarato, "Machines to Crystallize Time," tr. A. Toscano, *Theory, Culture & Society*, 24.6 (2007): 93–122, here 93.

27. See my *New Philosophy for New Media*, introduction.

28. Following Deleuze's analysis in Chapter 3 of *Difference and Repetition*, common sense and recognition are the twin Kantian principles that render sensation a mere material for the production of *Vorstellungen*.

29. Gernot Böhme, "Atmosphäre als Grundbegriff einer neuen Ästhetik," in *Atmosphäre* (Frankfurt: Suhrkamp, 1995).

30. Bernard Stiegler, *Technics and Time, 2: Disorientation*, tr. S. Barker (Stanford, CA: Stanford University Press, 2008), Chapter 4.

31. To appreciate this point, one need only compare the relative enthusiasm for technology that Stiegler displays in the initial volume of *Technics and Time: The Fault of Epimetheus*, tr. R. Beardsworth and G. Collins (Stanford, CA: Stanford University Press, 1998) with his more pessimistic account of the cultural industrial function of cinema in *La Technique et le temps, 3: Le Temps du cinéma et la question du mal-être* (Paris: Galilée, 2001) or, for that matter, in his even more recent analyses of symbolic misery in contemporary culture (for example, *De la misère symbolique, Tome 1: L'Époque hyperindustrielle* [Paris: Galilée, 2004]).

32. The entire passage reads: "As Rehberger constructs continuities between TV light and daylight, it becomes clear to what degree his work depends on a different conception of images than the optical and metaphysical models that inform most art historical accounts. In such models, world and image tend to be posited against one another so that images are typically understood to come into being as light is *thrown* on things in the world. In contrast, Bergson's philosophy presents a model where all objects and all perceptions are themselves already light; this means that what in a more specific sense are called images are not functions of light, but of time. Images arise only as a function of the brain's ability to contract and distribute

temporal matter" (*On the Style Site: Art, Sociality, and Media Culture* [Berlin: Stern-berg Press, 2007], 104). I owe much of my appreciation for Rehberger's light works as interventions into media fluxes to Blom's excellent study of the post-video art "lamp works" created by a host of contemporary artists.

33. Margit Brehm, "Killing Time," in Tobias Rehberger, *Deaddies* (Torino: hope-fulmonster, 2002), 43.

34. Daniel Birnbaum, *Chronology* (Berlin: Sternberg Press, 2007), 150.

35. In his reading of Husserl, Stiegler adds the category of "tertiary memory" (or, as he sometimes—and in my opinion, misleadingly—calls "tertiary retention") to Husserl's two categories of "primary retention" and "recollection." "Tertiary memory" designates technically recorded and stored memory—Stiegler's examples range from scenes in movies to advertisements—and his argument is that tertiary memory has contaminated the circuits of recollection-retention-protention such that we tend to anticipate or project the future based on our memory of recorded, manufactured experiences (tertiary memories). My point here is simply that such a process, regardless of whether it happens as Stiegler describes it, would need to proceed by way of the operations of higher-order consciousness.

36. In a sense, Rehberger's work makes experientially palpable the operation of primary retention as what Jean-Michel Salanskis calls "adherent retentionality," namely, the continuity of the present that constitutes the temporal continuum (*Husserl* [Paris: Belles Lettres, 1998]). And it does so in a way that departs from the egology of Husserl's model of time-consciousness and that makes common cause with Husserl's late meditations on time in the *C-Manuscripts* (1929–34) and in par-ticular with his assistant Eugen Fink's elaboration of the concept of worldly "dep-resencing" (*Entgegenwärtigung*) (Fink describes depresencing in his dissertation, collected in *Studien zur Phänomenologie, 1930–1939* [The Hague: Nijoff, 1966]). Depresencing designates the continual going-out-of-presence of the world and, as such, is the condition of possibility for the experience of time-consciousness as the thick now (the now plus a retentional tail and a protentional antenna) that Husserl describes.

37. Mark B. N. Hansen, *Bodies in Code* (New York: Routledge, 2006).

38. This is the basic argument I advance in *Bodies in Code*.

39. See Francisco Varela, Evan Thompson, and Eleanor Rosch, *The Embodied Mind: Cognitive Science and Human Experience* (Cambridge, MA: MIT Press, 1991).

40. Gilbert Simondon, *Imagination et invention (1965–1966)*, ed. N. Simondon (Paris: Les Éditions de la Transparence, 2008), 18–19.

41. For an informative discussion of Simondon's rejection of Sartre's conception of the imagination and by implication of Husserl's analyses of the image as image consciousness (which comprise a crucial source for Sartre's treatment of the image as "imaging consciousness" [*conscience imageante*] as well as for Stiegler's introduc-tion of "tertiary memory" as a proper, third category of memory in the context of Husserl's work), see Jean-Yves Chateau's introductory *Présentation* to *Imagination et invention*, especially xiv–xxiii.

42. Francisco Varela, "The Specious Present: A Neurophenomenology of Time

Consciousness," in *Naturalizing Phenomenology: Issues in Contemporary Phenomenology and Cognitive Science*, ed. J. Petitot et al. (Stanford, CA: Stanford University Press, 1999), 266–314. Varela is by no means alone in celebrating the convergences between neuroscience and phenomenology. See, for example, Evan Thompson, *Mind in Life: Biology, Phenomenology, and the Sciences of the Mind* (Cambridge, MA: Harvard University Press, 2001), esp. Chapter 11, for an account from the philosophy side; and Benjamin Libet, *Mind-Time: The Temporal Factor in Consciousness* (Cambridge, MA: Harvard University Press, 2004), for an account from the science side.

43. In this respect, that is, precisely because he rejects the basic opposition of perception and sensation at work in Husserl and Sartre, Simondon's theory also cuts against the grain of more recent deconstructions of this opposition, notably that of Jacques Derrida in *Speech and Phenomenon* (Evanston, IL: Northwestern University Press, 1979) and of Stiegler (following Derrida) in *La Technique et le temps, 3: Le Temps du cinéma et la question du mal-être*.

44. Chateau in Simondon, *Imagination et invention*, xix.

45. Catherine Malabou, *La Plasticité au soir del'écriture* (Paris: Éditions Léo Sheer, 2005), 36, final emphasis added.

46. Gilbert Simondon, *Cours sur la perception (1964–1965)* (Paris: Les Éditions de La Transparence, 2006), 100.

47. Simondon, *Imagination et invention*, 191, emphasis added.

Chapter 5

I thank László Tarnay of the Laterna Film Academy in Pécs, Hungary, for the impetus to write this essay, first presented in 2003 at the Academy's conference, "Sound and Image: Film Theory and Practice Across Disciplines." My gratitude also goes to Ioan Allen and Karen Atherton of Dolby Labs who provided me copies of the Dolby promotional trailers before they became available on DVD, and to Elizabeth Cohen for her helpful technical knowledge and enthusiastic commentary.

This chapter was previously published as Vivian Sobchack, "When the Ear Dreams: Dolby Digital and the Imagination of Sound," *Film Quarterly*, Vol. 58, No. 4: 2–15. © 2005, The Regents of the University of California. Used by permission. All rights reserved.

1. Don Ihde, *Listening and Voice: A Phenomenology of Sound* (Athens: Ohio University Press, 1976), 4.

2. Parallel to Bachelard's "ultra-hearing," Gianluca Sergi, in "The Sonic Playground: Hollywood Cinema and Its Listeners," writes: "The Hollywood listener is bestowed with an aural experience which elevates him/her to a state which may define the super-listener—a being (not to be found in nature) able to hear sounds that in reality would not be audible or would sound substantially duller." This is cited from an online version found at http://www.filmsound.org/articles/sergei/index.htm in 1999; a more recent print version, "The Hollywood Sonic Playground: The Spectator as Listener," can be found in *Hollywood Spectatorship*, ed. Richard Maltby and Melvyn Stokes (London: BFI, 2001). Although his emphasis is different from

mine, Sergi has also recently published an extremely significant—and singular—monograph on Dolby Sound Systems and contemporary cinema: *The Dolby Era: Film Sound in Contemporary Hollywood* (Manchester, UK: Manchester University Press, 2004).

3. Gaston Bachelard, *The Poetics of Space*, trans. Maria Jolas (Boston: Beacon Press, 1964), 181.

4. Quotations taken from "Dolby News—March 1997 (ShoWest Edition)," www.dolby.com/assets/pdf/newsletter/407Dolby%20%20March%201997.pdf; and David John Farinella, "Battle of the Trailers," *Mix* (July 1, 1999), mixonline.com/mag/audio_battle_trailers.

5. Bachelard, *The Poetics of Space*, 166.

6. Obviously, the Dolby trailers promote a certain kind of sound as "good"; furthermore, as observed by my colleague Rob King, there is a commercial circularity to be found in the trailers: "good sounds are commercial sounds are the sounds of commercial cinema." Certainly, ideological critique can be leveled at the trailers, although that it is not my focus in this present essay.

7. Michel Chion, *Audio-Vision: Sound on Screen*, ed. and trans. Claudia Gorbman (New York: Columbia University Press, 1990).

8. Ihde, *Listening and Voice*, 14.

9. Maxim Gorky, "Lumière," in *Roger Ebert's Book of Film*, ed. Roger Ebert (New York: W. W. Norton & Co., 1997), 343.

10. Bachelard, *The Poetics of Space*, 178.

11. Ihde, *Listening and Voice*, 125.

12. In an extraordinary phenomenology of film sound, Steven Connor writes: "There is always something belated about auditory identification, partly because the nature of sound is to occupy a passage rather than instant of time, a duration rather than a moment. In order to hear a sound, one must have already heard it start to decay, or come to an end; one must already have started finishing hearing it." See "Sounding Out Film," an unpublished essay elaborating a paper presented at the Institute of English Studies in London in January 2000, and found online at: http://www.bbk.ac.uk/english/skc/soundingout/.

13. Bachelard, *The Poetics of Space*, 176.

14. I might add that the "ear that dreams" is not, either metaphorically or in the theater, a "point of audition." Rather, it suggests an "encompassing" ear—one that metaphorically "frames" listening and substantially "surrounds" the listener.

15. Chion, *Audio-Vision*, 63.

16. Scholar and audio engineer Elizabeth Cohen suggests that "Stomp" was produced specifically to display Dolby's latest advances in digitally encoding percussive sound, which is particularly difficult. "Stomp" illustrates the capacity of the algorithm to "faithfully" capture the sharp, impulsive, and transient signals inherent in percussive sound and also demonstrates the power of five channels to deliver full dynamic range and the subwoofer channel a percussive "feel" to the acoustic experience.

17. Bachelard, *The Poetics of Space*, 176, 178.

18. Chion, *Audio-Vision*, 109.

19. "Today's audiences don't want to *hear* sound effects, they want to *feel* them," says a spokesperson for AMC theaters. See Julie Jordan, "Bring on the Noise," *People* (July 7, 1997): 20, where it is also reported that the Motion Picture Association suggests setting for decibel levels no higher than 85: "Some digital-sound theater owners goose it to 90 decibels, sending volume peaks up to 110 decibels—the level of cutting chain saws and taxiing 747s."

20. This effect counters Chion's notion that, unlike the image, sound has no frame. Thus, I would argue with Connor's assertion in "Sounding Out Film" that," following Chion, there is "no 'framing' of sound in the metaphorical sense either: no way to put the hearing of sound into a frame and overhear it. . . . There is no ear of the mind as there is an eye of the mind." While, in particular, the Dolby trailers counter that there indeed is an ear of the mind—"the ear that dreams" and thus "frames," "overhears," and "interprets" sound—they suggest, in general, that digital theatrical sound also presents and represents itself (if in less obvious fashion) as "framed." As Sergi indicates in "The Sonic Playground," the goal of contemporary film sound is "expressiveness." "In other words, audiences are asked by the filmmakers to accept an 'interpretation' of that sound that bypasses the original features of that sound . . . in favor of narrative effectiveness."

21. The goal of THX, developed by Lucasfilm, is to theatrically re-create the sound quality digitally mastered in the mixing studio without extraneous acoustic noise; theaters must therefore meet certain stringent physical criteria to be awarded THX certification.

22. Chion, *Audio-Vision*, 150.

23. Elizabeth Cohen, in an e-mail to the author, sees Chion's critique of digital cinematic sound as "reduced" to "stereo" as historically situated. She writes: "Because of the success of personal stereo to deliver intimacy and envelop, its success has 'reverberated' into the professional theatrical market. We have now three generations of listeners who expect the immediacy and presence that a personal stereo delivers. This is an audience raised on reproduced sound."

24. Formulated in decibels, "reverberation" is customarily defined by the industry as the time sound volume relative to the area it takes to decay.

25. Sergi, in "The Sonic Playground," writes that contemporary sound is "enveloping" as "multi-channel, multi-directional sound is today organized around the auditorium, not around the image on the screen." He continues, however, with a qualification that would mark this sounding as different from—and more privatized than—that of a concert hall: although organized around the theatrical rather than filmic space, "sound is orchestrated around the *seats* to put the spectator literally 'inside' the film." That is, digital sound has enabled the enlargement of the "sweet spot"—in conventional stereo, previously that one seat equidistant from the speakers. This enlargement, however, allows each spectator to sit in an ideal yet individuated seat relative to sound, and, indeed, the architecture and morphology of multiplex seating encourages this individuation of viewing space with its high and wide seat backs and stadium seating that forestall visual contact with others. (This

is not to disallow a certain new form and sense of theatrical collectivity, but that requires another investigation.)

26. Ihde, *Listening and Voice*, 45.

27. Sean Cubitt, *Digital Aesthetics* (London: Sage Publications, 1998), 95–96.

28. Obviously, the reverberation installed in the body by amplification can move from pleasurable intensity to pain (see note 19 above). Sergi, in "The Sonic Playground," notes: "Contemporary sound systems are powerful enough to move a significant amount of air. As a consequence, the spectator can be 'hit' with sound, and thus experience the film with a far greater degree of physical involvement than ever before. This creates a situation where audiences have to deal with enough constant sound pressure to lead to physical exhaustion, if exercised over time." A witty animated THX sound system trailer takes this to its furthest extremes: using the "Simpsons" characters sitting in a movie theater, it shows eyeglasses shattering, teeth cracking, heads exploding, while deaf Grandpa yells, "Turn it up!" New digital technology allows acoustic pressure that is ten times greater than with analog sound.

29. Cubitt, *Digital Aesthetics*, 117; emphasis added.

30. Ihde, *Listening and Voice*, 88.

31. Philip Brophy, "The Animation of Sound," in *The Illusion of Life: Essays on Animation*, ed. Alan Cholodenko (Sydney: Power Publications, 1991), 82.

32. Connor, "Sounding Out Film."

33. Chion, *Audio-Vision*, 17; emphasis added.

34. Brophy, "The Animation of Sound," 74.

35. Paul Ricoeur, *The Rule of Metaphor: Multi-disciplinary Studies of the Creation of Meaning in Language*, trans. Robert Czerny et al. (Toronto: University of Toronto Press, 1975), 63. See also Connor, "Sounding Out Film," for discussion of a catachretic relation between sound being given the "substance" it lacks by other registers of perception.

36. Connor, "Sounding Out Film."

37. Brophy, "The Animation of Sound," 68; emphasis added.

Chapter 6

Unless otherwise noted, all translations from French texts are my own.

1. Paul D. Miller, "Algorithms: Erasures and the Art of Memory," in Christoph Cox and Daniel Warner, eds., *Audio Culture: Readings in Modern Music* (New York and: Continuum, 2004), 350.

2. Jean-Luc Nancy, *Listening*, trans. Charlotte Mandell (New York: Fordham University Press, 2007), 7.

3. Jean-Luc Nancy, *Au fond des images* (Paris: Galilée, 2002), 18.

4. Yves Klein, *Vers l'immatériel* (Paris: Dilecta, 2006), 125–26; 122.

5. Nancy, *Listening*, 13.

6. Francis Bacon, *The Advancement of Learning and the New Atlantis*, ed. Arthur Johnston (Oxford: Clarendon Press, 1974), 244.

7. Klein, *Vers l'immatériel*, 134.

8. Susan McClary, "Rap, Minimalism, and the Structures of Time in Late Twentieth-Century Culture," in Cox and Warner, *Audio Culture*, 293.

9. John Cage, *Silence* (Middletown, Conn.: Wesleyan University Press, 1961), 70.

10. Yehlin Lee, "Countless Count," in *2005 Yageo Sound Art* (Taipei: Et@t, 2005), 66.

11. Nancy, *Au fond des images*, 26.

12. I might add that a similar embrace of endless flow also haunts sophisticated international new media installations, whose mystical idealism I discuss in *Digital Baroque* as being particularly troubling in the works of Daniel Reeves and Bill Viola. See Timothy Murray, *Digital Baroque: New Media Art and Cinematic Folds* (Minneapolis: University of Minnesota Press, 2008), 35–57.

13. Mary Russo and Daniel Warner, "Rough Music, Futurism, and Postpunk Industrial Noise Bands," in Cox and Warner, *Audio Culture*, 53.

14. Cage, *Silence*, 63.

15. Douglas Kahn, in *Noise, Water, Meat: A History of Sound in the Arts* (Cambridge, Mass.: MIT Press, 1999), 56–67, elaborates on the impact of the noises of combat on Russolo's aesthetic approach to sound.

16. Luigi Russolo, "The Art of Noises: Futurist Manifesto," in Cox and Warner, *Audio Culture*, 13.

17. *2005 Yageo Sound Art*, 66.

18. Russolo, "The Art of Noises," 12.

19. Jun-Jieh Wang, "Alternative Frequencies: Perspectives on Sound Art," in *2005 Yageo Sound Art*, 22.

20. Cage, *Silence*, 63.

21. Jean Laplanche, *New Foundations for Psychoanalysis*, trans. David Macey (Oxford: Basil Blackwell, 1989), 45.

22. *2005 Yageo Sound Art*, 62.

23. Brandon LaBelle, *Background Noise: Perspectives on Sound Art* (New York: Continuum, 2006), 224–25.

24. Jacques Derrida, *Speech and Phenomenon and Other Essays on Husserl's Theory of Signs*, trans. David B. Allison (Evanston, Ill.: Northwestern University Press, 1973), 79.

25. Nancy, *Listening*, 7.

26. Edgard Varèse, "The Liberation of Sound," in Cox and Warner, *Audio Culture*, 18.

27. Gilles Deleuze and Félix Guattari, *A Thousand Plateaus: Capitalism and Schizophrenia*, trans. Brian Massumi (Minneapolis: University of Minnesota Press), 343–44.

28. Gilles Deleuze, *Cinema 2: The Time-Image*, trans. Hugh Tomlinson and Robert Galeta (Minneapolis: University of Minnesota Press, 1989), 272.

29. See Murray, *Digital Baroque*, 1–31.

30. Gilles Deleuze, *The Fold: Leibniz and the Baroque*, trans. Tom Conley (Minneapolis: University of Minnesota Press, 1993), 8.

31. Deleuze, *Cinema 2*, 269.

32. Yukiko Shikata, *OpenMind* (Tokyo: Mori Art Museum, 2002).

33. Ryoji Ikeda, *db*, http://www.ryojiikeda.com/formula/db/db/.

34. Kim Cascone, "The Aesthetics of Failure: 'Post-Digital' Tendencies in Contemporary Computer Music," in Cox and Warner, *Audio Culture*, 396.

35. Keichiro Shibuya, *er*, in Shikata, *OpenMind*.

36. Gilles Deleuze, *Difference and Repetition*, trans. Paul Patton (New York: Columbia University Press, 1994), 36.

Chapter 7

This essay is part of a larger project on the concept of the life-image. Over the years, many friends—far more than I can mention here—have helped me articulate this concept in a variety of ways. Here, I would like to thank in particular Morgan Adamson, Jason Christenson, Bishnupriya Ghosh, Andrea Gyenge, Eleanor Kaufman, Jacques Khalip, Kiarina Kordela, Robert Mitchell, Judith Revel, Michael Rothberg, Bhaskar Sarkar, Hans Skott-Myhre, Matthew Stoddard, Benjamin Stork, and Nicholas Thoburn, as well as an anonymous reader, for their thoughtful and encouraging comments on various versions of this essay.

1. Gilles Deleuze, *Cinema 1: The Movement-Image*, trans. Hugh Tomlinson and Barbara Habberjam (Minneapolis: University of Minnesota Press, 1986), xiv.

2. Within the copious literature on Deleuze's study of the cinema, many are the works that address specifically the questions of time, history, and periodization in this study. Among these, besides D. N. Rodowick's well-known *Gilles Deleuze's Time Machine* (Durham, NC: Duke University Press, 1997), the following works stand out as particularly insightful and especially relevant to my arguments: Richard Dienst, "Ineluctable Modalities of the Televisual," in his *Still Life in Real Time: Theory After Television* (Durham, NC: Duke University Press, 1994), 144–169 (see especially 144–145); Marie-Claire Ropars-Wuilleumier, "The Cinema, Reader of Gilles Deleuze," in *Gilles Deleuze and the Theater of Philosophy*, ed. Constantin V. Boundas and Dorothea Olkowski, trans. Dana Polan (New York: Routledge, 1994), 255–260; as well as András Bálint Kovács, "The Film History of Thought," and Angelo Restivo, "Into the Breach: Between *The Movement-Image* and *The Time-Image*," both in *The Brain Is the Screen: Deleuze and the Philosophy of the Cinema*, ed. Gregory Flaxman (Minneapolis: University of Minnesota Press, 2000), 153–170, 171–192 (especially 171–174), respectively.

3. Before his 1978–1979 lectures at the Collège de France on the birth of bio-politics, Foucault mentions the term "bio-politics" for the first time in a lecture titled "The Birth of Social Medicine," delivered in Rio de Janeiro in 1974. He returns to this term and develops it further in 1976, in that year's lectures at the Collège de France as well as in the last chapter of his *History of Sexuality, Volume 1*; Michel Foucault, "The Birth of Social Medicine," in *Essential Works of Foucault, 1954–1984: Power*, ed. James D. Faubion, trans. Robert Hurley et al. (New York: The New Press, 2000), 134–156; Michel Foucault, *"Society Must Be Defended." Lectures at the Collège de France 1975–1976*, trans. David Macey (New York: Picador, 2003), esp.

239–272; Michel Foucault, *The History of Sexuality. An Introduction, Volume 1*, trans. Robert Hurley (New York: Vintage Books, 1990), 133–159.

4. Paolo Virno, *A Grammar of the Multitude: For an Analysis of Contemporary Forms of Life*, trans. Isabella Bertoletti, James Cascaito, and Andrea Casson (New York: Semiotext(e), 2004), 83–84.

5. Karl Marx, *Capital, Volume 1*, trans. Ben Fowkes (New York: Vintage, 1977), 270.

6. Here is a more detailed version of this argument: "[T]o comprehend the rational core of the term 'bio-politics,' we should begin . . . with a much more complicated concept from a philosophical standpoint: that of *labor-power* . . . Labor-power incarnates (literally) a fundamental category of philosophical thought: specifically, the potential, the *dynamis*. And 'potential' . . . signifies that which is *not* current, that which is *not* present. Well then, something that is not present (or real) becomes, with capitalism, an exceptionally important commodity . . . [which] is at the core of the exchange between capitalist and worker. The object of the sale is not a real entity (labor services actually executed) but something that, in and of itself, does not have an autonomous spatial-temporal existence (the generic ability to work). The paradoxical characteristics of labor-power (something unreal which is, however, bought and sold as any other commodity) are the premise of bio-politics . . . [W]here something which exists only as *possibility* is sold, this something is not separable from the *living person* of the seller. The living body of the worker is the substratum of that labor-power which, in itself, has no independent existence. 'Life,' pure and simple *bios*, acquires a specific importance inasmuch as it is the tabernacle of *dynamis*, of mere potential. Capitalists are interested in the life of the worker, in the body of the worker, only for an indirect reason: this life, this body, are what contain the faculty, the potential, the *dynamis* . . . labor-power as the aggregate of the most diverse human faculties . . . Life lies at the center of politics when the prize to be won is immaterial (and in itself non-present) labor-power. For this reason, and this reason alone, it is legitimate to talk about 'bio-politics' . . . [B]io-politics is merely an effect, a reverberation, or, in fact, one articulation of that primary fact—both historical and philosophical—which consists of the commerce of potential as potential" (Virno 81–84).

7. Cesare Casarino and Antonio Negri, *In Praise of the Common: A Conversation on Philosophy and Politics* (Minneapolis: University of Minnesota Press, 2008), 148 (but see also 146–151).

8. For more detailed versions of these and related arguments by these thinkers, see especially Michael Hardt and Antonio Negri, "Biopolitical Production," in *Empire* (Cambridge, MA: Harvard University Press, 2000), 22–41, and "Metamorphoses of the Composition of Capital," in *Commonwealth* (Cambridge, MA: Harvard University Press, 2009), 131–149; as well as Judith Revel, *Michel Foucault, un'ontologia dell'attualità* (Cosenza, Italy: Rubbettino, 2003), but see also her 2008 essay "Biopolitica: Politica della vita potente," at http://www.posseweb.net/ spip.php?article229. For other very productive attempts to re-elaborate Foucault's concept of bio-politics within Marxian accounts of contemporary capitalism, see

especially Kaushik Sunder Rajan, *Biocapital: The Constitution of Postgenomic Life* (Durham, NC: Duke University Press, 2006); and Melinda Cooper, *Life as Surplus: Biotechnology & Capitalism in the Neoliberal Era* (Seattle: University of Washington Press, 2008).

9. I am well aware that the characterization of contemporary capitalism as driven dominantly by the communication of thought, language, affect, and knowledge is far from an uncontroversial one. I have discussed this and related matters elsewhere. See my "Surplus Common: A Preface," in Casarino and Negri, *In Praise of the Common*, 1–39 (especially 13–14 and 250–252n23).

10. For an alternative attempt to think this relation, see Jonathan Beller's powerful study *The Cinematic Mode of Production: Attention Economy and the Society of the Spectacle* (Lebanon, NH: Dartmouth College Press, 2006).

11. Deleuze senses and anticipates the emergence of the life-image when articulating the interference of "a cinema of the body" and "a cinema of the brain" toward the end of his study, that is, in chapter 8 of *Cinema 2*. See especially the first few pages of this chapter, in which the question of life—understood as the unthought of thought—is taken up several times. Importantly, it is also in this chapter that Deleuze writes most about 1960s and 1970s cinemas—a fact that corroborates the historical and periodizing aspect of this first thesis on the life-image. Deleuze, *Cinema 2: The Time-Image*, trans. Hugh Tomlinson and Robert Galeta (Minneapolis: University of Minnesota Press, 1989), 189–224 (see especially 189–195).

12. As is well known, Deleuze centers his seminal re-interpretation of Spinoza's entire philosophical project on the role that the term and concept of expression play in this thinker's work (Deleuze articulates this re-interpretation above all in his *Expressionism in Philosophy: Spinoza*, trans. Martin Joughin [New York: Zone Books, 1990]). I have written on expression and on its relation to representation, in Spinoza as well as in Deleuze, elsewhere: see my "Marx Before Spinoza (Notes Towards an Investigation)," in *Spinoza Now*, ed. Dimitris Vardoulakis (Minneapolis: University of Minnesota, forthcoming). Here, I will limit myself to pointing out that for Deleuze, expression constitutes the immanent condition of possibility of any form of representation: expression, in other words, is what gives life to representation. In a passage in *The Logic of Sense* (which encapsulates succinctly some of the arguments regarding the relation between expression and representation that Deleuze had articulated in a more detailed and complex manner one year earlier in *Expressionism in Philosophy*), for example, Deleuze writes: "We have encountered this difference of nature between the expression and the representation at every turn . . . By itself, representation is given up to an extrinsic relation of resemblance or similitude only. But its internal character, by which it is intrinsically 'distinct,' 'adequate,' or 'comprehensive,' comes from the manner in which it encompasses, or envelops an expression, much as it may not be able to represent it . . . For example, the perception of death as a state of affairs and as a quality, or the concept 'mortal' as a predicate of signification, remain extrinsic (deprived of sense) as long as they do not encompass the event of dying as that which is actualized in the one and expressed in the other. Representation must encompass an expression which it

does not represent, but without which it itself would not be 'comprehensive,' and would have truth only by chance or from the outside. To know that we are mortal is an apodeictic knowledge, albeit empty and abstract; effective and successive deaths do not suffice of course in fulfilling this knowledge adequately, so long as one does not come to know death as an impersonal event provided with an always open problematic structure (where and when?). In fact, two types of knowledge (*savoir*) have often been distinguished, one indifferent, remaining external to its object, and the other concrete, seeking its object wherever it is. Representation attains this topical ideal only by means of the hidden expression which it encompasses, that is, by means of the event it envelops. There is thus a 'use' of representation, without which representation would remain lifeless and senseless. Wittgenstein and his disciples are right to define meaning by means of use. But such use is not defined through a function of representation in relation to the represented, nor even through representativeness as the form of possibility. Here, as elsewhere, the functional is transcended in the direction of a topology, and use is in the relation between representation and something extra-representative, a nonrepresented and merely expressed entity. Representation envelops the event in another nature, it envelops it at its borders, it stretches until this point, and it brings about this lining or hem. This is an operation which defines living usage, to the extent that representation, when it does not reach this point, remains only a dead letter confronting that which it represents, and stupid in its representativeness" (Gilles Deleuze, *The Logic of Sense*, trans. Mark Lester with Charles Stivale, ed. Constantin V. Boundas [New York: Columbia University Press, 1990], 145–146; but see also 146–147). This implies, among other things, that for Deleuze, whereas all mimesis is a form of representation, not all forms of representation are mimetic (that is, Platonic); put differently, for Deleuze representation may either affirm and acknowledge its immanent cause in and as expression by materializing simulacra of the event, or negate and foreclose expression altogether by making recourse to mimesis and hence by materializing copies of an ideal and transcendent model (that is, by referring to its object through an "extrinsic relation of resemblance or similitude only").

13. On this concept, see Giorgio Agamben's important essay "Form-of-Life" in Agamben, *Means Without End*, trans. Vincenzo Binetti and Cesare Casarino (Minneapolis: University of Minnesota Press, 2000), 3–12 (especially 3–4, 9).

14. I am referring here to Simon Watney's pioneering work (and especially to his 1988 essay "The Spectacle of AIDS") as well as to the work of many other scholars, such as Leo Bersani, Tim Dean, Lee Edelman, Alexander García Düttmann, Donna Haraway, William Haver, Paul Morrison, Jeff Nunokawa, Cindy Patton, Suzanne Poirier, Marita Sturken, Paula Treichler, Catherine Waldby, Jeffrey Weeks, and Thomas Yingling. In particular, I have in mind Watney's pointed critique of what became rapidly the dominant paradigm for the visual representation of AIDS in the media, as articulated, for example, in the complementary dyad of, on the one hand, techno-scientific imaginaries (such as the rendition of the HIV retrovirus as a "huge technicolor asteroid" with the help of electron microscopy and computer graphics), and, on the other hand, sexual-political narratives (such as the at once

pietistic, sensationalistic, and implicitly homophobic photographs of the emaciated body or gaunt face of the dying "AIDS victim"). Thus, the story of AIDS—according to Watney—unfolded as "an exemplary and admonitory drama . . . relayed between the image of the miraculous authority of clinical medicine and the faces and bodies of individuals who clearly disclose the stigmata of their guilt" (Simon Watney, "The Spectacle of AIDS," in *AIDS: Cultural Analysis / Cultural Activism*, ed. Douglas Crimp [Cambridge, MA: MIT Press, 1988], 78).

15. Much of the first paragraph of this third thesis is partly a variation on and partly extracted from my essay "The Simulacrum of AIDS," which deals with the question of the simulacrum in Deleuze and in Hervé Guibert, and in which I discuss the relation between Debord and Deleuze as well as the relation between their critiques of representation and the AIDS pandemic in more detail than I do here (Casarino, "The Simulacrum of AIDS," *Parallax* 11.35 [2005]: 60–72).

16. On these matters, see also note 12 above.

17. *Mister Rogers' Neighborhood* is the longest-running program on PBS (it began airing in 1968 and is designed primarily for children). The first sentence of its theme song—"Won't You Be My Neighbor?"—is quoted almost verbatim by Joslin here (i.e., "It's a beautiful day in this neighborhood," as opposed to Joslin's "It's a beautiful day in the neighborhood!"). Much could be said about the sudden materialization of television as a cultural medium in general, and of this specific program in particular, in the middle of this sequence, as well as about the subtle yet intense wistfulness that echoes with childhood memories and that accompanies such a materialization. Here, I will point out simply that the reference to this television program reinforces the centrality and importance of the Silver Lake neighborhood and its vibrant life as the tacit protagonists of this sequence. In particular, the whole sequence could be understood as a complex remake of the opening credit sequence of *Mister Rogers' Neighborhood*, which consists of an aerial pan of the neighborhood, followed by Mr. Rogers' entrance into his own home shot from indoors: as opposed to the near seamlessness of the pan, and to the totalizing wholeness (and wholesomeness) of the bird's-eye view of Mr. Rogers' neighborhood that this pan affords, Joslin's sequence presents a highly fragmented, even shattered, though no less loving, audio-visual mapping of the Silver Lake neighborhood. I am grateful to Jason Christenson for having drawn my attention to the uncanny similarities and differences between these two sequences, as well as for sharing with me this most poignant fragment of his own childhood.

18. In transcribing the voice-over, I have used ellipses whenever there was hesitation in the voice—such as, for example, when pausing while searching for the right words. The text in square brackets is my own.

19. Deleuze, *Cinema 2*, 17.

20. See chapter 9 in Deleuze, *Cinema 2*, 225–261, and especially 259–261.

21. Deleuze, *Cinema 1*, 108–122, 212, as well as *Cinema 2*, 5–9.

22. Deleuze, *Cinema 2*, 215–224.

23. These arguments are articulated especially in the last chapter of *Cinema 1* and in the first chapter of *Cinema 2*. Deleuze, *Cinema 1*, 197–215, and *Cinema 2*, 1–24.

24. The argument that the power of being always involves the power of acting and the power of thinking always involves the power of knowing is a foundational argument for Deleuze and is everywhere implied in his work. It is, moreover, an argument that Deleuze attributes to and extracts from Spinoza: explicit articulations of this argument, in fact, are to be found in Deleuze's monograph on this thinker. See, for example, Deleuze, *Expressionism in Philosophy*, 120–122.

Chapter 8

1. The position developed in this essay borrows a number of formulations from my "On Producing the Concept of a Global Culture," in *Nations, Cultures, and Identities*, ed. V. Y. Mudimbe (Durham, NC: Duke University Press, 1997), 199–219.

2. Gilles Deleuze and Félix Guattari, *What Is Philosophy?* trans. Hugh Tomlinson and Graham Burchell (New York: Columbia University Press, 1994), 5–6. The quotation from Friedrich Nietzsche appears in his *The Will to Power*, trans. Walter Kaufman and R. J. Hollingdale (New York: Vintage, 1968), 409. Emphases as in original.

3. I use the term "concept" here, though to conform to the position developed later in this essay "concept" should of course be replaced by "image-concept." But since it is advisable to wait for this argument to be spelled out before introducing what seems to be a novel piece of terminology, "concept," and not "image-concept," will be used in the next few paragraphs.

4. I mention Foucault as the exemplary figure in the development of this new "theoretics" of knowledges, but Pierre Bourdieu also did significant work in this area. The most important figure for my account, however, has been Gilles Deleuze. See especially his interpretations of Foucault in *Foucault*, trans. Seán Hand (Minneapolis: University of Minnesota Press, 1986). For a more detailed treatment of the notions of concept, function, and field, see Deleuze and Guattari, *What Is Philosophy?* Deleuze has analyzed cinema as a "crystalline regime" in his two-volume work on cinema; see also his "Sur la régime crystallin," *Hors cadre* 4 (1966), 9–45. I am deeply indebted to Deleuze's texts for my account of conceptual practice.

5. A useful account of this distinction between the "rational concept" and "sensible intuition" is to be found in Levi R. Bryant's excellent *Difference and Givenness: Deleuze's Transcendental Empiricism and the Ontology of Immanence* (Evanston, IL: Northwestern University Press, 2008), 5ff. Like me, Bryant wants to argue that Deleuze's major philosophical achievement resides in the overcoming of this age-old distinction. It is impossible to do justice to Bryant's book in a note, but I think it is possible to account for the essential features of Deleuze's transcendental empiricism without pushing his thought in the direction of a "hyper-rationalism" of the kind proposed by Bryant. But there are many "Deleuzes," and Bryant's "Deleuze" is certainly among the more noteworthy of them—I am much indebted to his rigorous and thought-provoking book.

6. According to Deleuze, positioning something as a pure exteriority necessarily grants that pure exteriority an a priori ontological superiority because that exteriority then becomes the ground for any reflection on the character and function of the

empirical particular. The function of such concepts as Being, Unity, Matter, etc., is thus to order and group phenomena that would be disparate and unconnected if not placed "under" these regulative concepts. "Brute" phenomena need these regulative concepts in order to make any sense to the subject of consciousness.

7. Deleuze and Guattari, *What Is Philosophy?* 17.

8. Deleuze and Guattari, *What Is Philosophy?* 23. Deleuze derives the notion that "concepts are centers of vibrations" from Gilbert Simondon. On Simondon, see Gilles Deleuze, "Gilbert Simondon," in his collection *Desert Islands and Other Texts 1953–1974*, ed. David Lapoujade, trans. Michael Taormina (New York: Semiotext(e), 2005), 86–89. See also the essay "The Method of Dramatization" in the same volume, 94–116.

9. Gilles Deleuze, *Cinema 2: The Time-Image*, trans. Hugh Tomlinson and Robert Galeta (Minneapolis: University of Minnesota Press, 1989), 161–64. Emphases as in original. The next few quotations from Deleuze will be from this text. A lucid overview of Deleuze's philosophy of cinema is to be found in Felicity J. Colman, "Cinema: Movement-Image-Recognition-Time," in *Gilles Deleuze: Key Concepts*, ed. Charles J. Stivale (Chesham, UK: Acumen Press, 2005), 141–56.

10. The "suspension of the world" invoked here by Deleuze may appear to have affinities with the phenomenological *epoché*, in which the productions of consciousness are "bracketed" in a critical gesture that will ground these productions even more firmly in the consciousness once the "bracketing" is lifted. The key difference is that Deleuze is not making a critical gesture of the kind made by Husserl and Merleau-Ponty (say) when they employ the *epoché*, but is instead referring to a process inherent in the movement of the concept-image itself. In this strictly involuntary movement, thought or consciousness is directed to that which is unthought (and hence can never be in consciousness). The phenomenological *epoché* is a voluntary (indeed, a quite deliberate) movement of thought intended above all to safeguard the philosophy of consciousness, whereas Deleuze's primary interest is in bypassing this very philosophy by espousing the notion of an involuntary propensity constitutively situated at the very heart of thought.

11. The key metaphysical principles adverted to by Deleuze include the notion of an absolute immanence (anathema to those who believe immanence cannot be the basis of an adequate account of "the way things are"); a repudiation of the dialectic (unacceptable to those who maintain that an adequate theory of process and movement has to invoke the dialectic, even if only to do justice to its complexity); a rejection of any philosophy based on the form of God (theology) or Man (anthropology) in the name of a "monstrous" form that has not yet been tried (unacceptable to those wedded to religious and humanistic ideologies); an unrelenting empiricism (problematic for those who believe that reality cannot be accounted for if our conceptions of it are confined to the empirical domain). I am grateful to the editors of this volume for their contribution to this essay.

Chapter 9

1. Jacques Rancière, *The Politics of Aesthetics*, trans. Gabriel Rockhill (New York:

Continuum, 2004); and *The Future of the Image*, trans. Gregory Elliott (London: Verso, 2007); hereafter abbreviated *FI*. Subsequent citations from this work will appear in the body of the text. I find the direction of Rancière's critical project to be compelling (if not always convincing) and indispensable to anyone interested in thinking about the relationship between the literary and the visual image. Rancière understands the "fate of the image" to be bound to its ability to cross "the boundaries between the arts" and to *deny* "the specificity of materials" (*FI*, 42). Moreover, for Rancière this errant capacity of the image to wander among the arts is an effect of what we call Romanticism, the European moment in which "the common measurement" of the image is *abandoned* and we enter "the aesthetic regime of the image" (*FI*, 39).

2. Alain Badiou, *Theoretical Writings*, trans. Ray Brassier and Alberto Toscano (New York: Continuum, 2004), 22. Badiou's principal target is the "poeticization" of thought that can be traced back to Hegel and that persists in the wake of Heidegger. For Badiou, what we call the Romantic image is the seductive aesthetic light emitted by the poetic object that "seemingly since Nietzsche, but actually since Hegel" "grows ever brighter" (25).

3. Alain Badiou, *Infinite Thought: Truth and the Return to Philosophy*, trans. Oliver Feltham and Justin Clemens (New York: Continuum, 2003), 78.

4. Harold Bloom, ed., *Romanticism and Consciousness: Essays in Criticism* (New York: Norton, 1970), iv; hereafter abbreviated *RC*. Subsequent citations from this work will appear in the body of the text.

5. Paul de Man, *The Rhetoric of Romanticism* (New York: Columbia University Press, 1984), 151; hereafter abbreviated *RR*. Subsequent citations from this work will appear in the body of the text.

6. Frank Kermode, *Romantic Image* (London: Routledge, 1957, 2002), 4, 57; hereafter abbreviated *RI*. Subsequent citations from this work will appear in the body of the text.

7. Paul de Man, *Allegories of Reading* (New Haven, Conn.: Yale University Press, 1979), 12.

8. Ian Balfour, "History Against Historicism, Formal Matters, and the Event of the Text: De Man with Benjamin," in *Legacies of Paul de Man*, ed. Marc Redfield (New York: Fordham University Press, 2207), 54; hereafter abbreviated *LPdM*. Subsequent citations from this work will appear in the body of the text.

9. To understand how this *old* debate over the status of the image constitutes our own horizon, compare Kermode's and de Man's accounts with Rancière's recent account of Mallarmé's "self-vanishing" "art of performance": Mallarmé's poetics "proposes an art of performance, symbolized by the self-vanishing, luminous trace of fireworks or the art of a dancer who, as Mallarmé puts it, is a woman and does not dance, but simply traces the form of an idea with her 'illiterate feet'" (*FI*, 19).

10. In the only instance of which I am aware that de Man articulates what his practice of reading might entail for our understanding of the "sister arts," he asserts the necessity of supplanting seeing or listening with reading. "Literature involves the voiding, rather than the affirmation, of aesthetic categories," he writes in "The

Resistance to Theory." "One of the consequences of this is that, whereas we have traditionally been accustomed to reading literature by analogy with the plastic arts and with music, we now have to recognize the necessity of a non-perceptual, linguistic moment in painting and music, and learn how to *read* pictures rather than *imagine* meaning" (*The Resistance to Theory* [Minneapolis: University of Minnesota Press, 1986]), 10; hereafter abbreviated *RT*. Subsequent citations from this work will appear in the body of the text.

11. "Phenomenality and Materiality in Kant," in *Aesthetic Ideology* (Minneapolis: University of Minnesota Press, 1996), 79, 89, 90. For a brilliant reflection on the nature and implications of the critical relationship between seeing and reading in de Man, see Rei Terada, "Seeing Is Reading," in *Legacies of Paul de Man*, 162–177.

12. Joel Fineman argued that the performance *and* undoing of this visual loop is already completed in Shakespeare's sonnets. In Sonnet 24 ("Mine eye hath played the painter"), for example, the collision and collusion of linguisticity and visuality hinge on that poem's pivotal pun: "your true image pictur'd lies" (*Shakespeare's Perjured Eye: The Invention of Subjectivity in the Sonnets* [Berkeley: University of California Press, 1986], 135–140).

13. Earl Wasserman, *The Subtler Language* (Baltimore: Johns Hopkins University Press, 1959), 238, 237; hereafter abbreviated *SL*. Subsequent citations from this work will appear in the body of the text.

14. Citations from Shelley's poems are from *Shelley's Poetry and Prose*, ed. Donald Reiman and Neil Fraistat (New York: Norton, 2002).

15. Wasserman scrupulously avoids any reference to the sublime in his reading of "Mont Blanc"; but the poem's figure of "Power" (an atheological force that cannot be presented to the senses) produces an analogous dislocation of image and imagination to that which de Man chronicles in his reading of Kant. According to Wasserman, Shelley's "Power" is "inaccessible to sensory experience, although not completely to the imagination" (*SL*, 233).

16. Timothy Bahti, "Coleridge's 'Kubla Khan': Fragmentation and Reflection Between Beginning and End," in *Ends of the Lyric* (Baltimore: Johns Hopkins University Press, 1996), 62; hereafter abbreviated *EL*. Subsequent citations from this work will appear in the body of the text.

17. Citations of "Kubla Khan" are from *The Complete Poetical Works of Samuel Taylor Coleridge*, ed. E. H. Coleridge (London: Oxford University Press, 1912).

18. *The Verbal Icon: Studies in the Meaning of Poetry* (Lexington: University of Kentucky Press, 1954), 9; hereafter abbreviated *VI*. Subsequent citations of this work will appear in the body of the text. In the context of this volume of essays, it is worth noting that Wimsatt—author of "The Structure of Romantic Nature Imagery"—discusses the relationship between image and icon only once in his book, in a brief preliminary paragraph: "A note on the title of this book." Wimsatt identifies the icon as the term that "refers to a visual image and especially one which is a religious symbol." For Wimsatt, a genuinely *verbal* icon is "the verbal image which most fully realizes its verbal capacities," "not merely a bright picture," but "an interpretation of reality in its metaphoric and symbolic dimensions."

19. Jean-Luc Nancy, *The Ground of the Image*, trans. Jeff Fort (New York: Fordham University Press, 2005), 22; hereafter abbreviated *GI*. Subsequent citations from this work will appear in the body of the text.

20. It may only be exchanging one hyperbole for another, but one way to measure the purchase of this fear of the image is to turn to Emmanuel Levinas's still extraordinary essay "Reality and Its Shadow." For the Levinas of this post-war essay—the Levinas who is taking his leave of Sartre—the image is the fundamental constituent of the work of art, one that he opposes to the concept. "An image," writes Levinas, "marks a hold over us rather than our initiative, a fundamental passivity. Possessed, inspired, an artist, we say, harkens to a muse. An image is musical. Its passivity is directly visible in magic, song, music, and poetry. The exceptional structure of aesthetic existence invokes this singular term magic . . . " (*Collected Philosophical Papers*, ed. Alphonso Lingis [Dordrecht, The Netherlands: Martinus Nijhoff, 1987], 3).

21. Forest Pyle, "Kindling and Ash: Radical Aestheticism in Keats and Shelley," *Studies in Romanticism* 42 (Winter 2003), 427–459.

22. Walter Benjamin, "On the Concept of History," in *Selected Writings, Volume 4*, ed. Howard Eiland and Michael W. Jennings (Cambridge, MA: Harvard University Press, 2003), 391–392; hereafter abbreviated *SW IV*. Subsequent citations from this work will appear in the body of the text.

23. Forest Pyle, *The Ideology of Imagination: Subject and Society in the Discourse of Romanticism* (Stanford, CA: Stanford University Press, 1995), 117–120. If I permit myself to refer to my previous readings of *The Triumph of Life* in *The Ideology of Imagination* and "Kindling and Ash," it is in the spirit of de Man's account of Benjamin's translator: "If the text is called '*Die Aufgabe des Übersetzers*,' we have to read this title more or less as a tautology: *Aufgabe*, task, can also mean the one who has to give up . . . It is in that sense also the defeat, the giving up, of the translator" (*RT*, 80). As I understand it, my own return to this passage in *The Triumph* marks the revival of that task of reading and an acknowledgment that what I am doing here is a mode of defeat, of a "giving up" of that critical practice.

Chapter 10

1. See Rolf Tiedemann, "Dialectics at a Standstill: Approaches to the *Passagen-Werk*," in Walter Benjamin, *The Arcades Project*, trans. Howard Eiland and Kevin McLaughlin (Cambridge, Mass.: Harvard University Press, 1999), 1014–15, n. 23. The Kierkegaard book, in which the "dialectical image" first appeared, was published on the same day that Hitler became dictator of Germany (February 27, 1933), a coincidence underlined by Adorno himself many years later in his 1966 "Notiz" to the third edition (Theodor W. Adorno, *Kierkegaard. Konstruktion des Ästhetischen* [Frankfurt: Suhrkamp, 1974], 261). Adorno's retrospective observation suggests that his critique of Kierkegaard's "existential ontology," which was enjoying a revival in German intellectual circles during the 1920s (in the work, for example, of Martin Heidegger), can be seen to bear a dialectical relationship to the political development that "overshadowed" its reception (Adorno, 261). The implication is that the

critique dialectically revealed the mythological content of the "political calamity" that hung over it, only seeming to obscure its effect. Thus Adorno appears to regard in retrospect the convergence of the publication of his Kierkegaard book with the ascendency of Hitler to power in the early 1930s as a "dialectical image." The "dialectical image" in Benjamin's work, which is focused on the potentiality of a "now" interpenetrated with "what has been," is at odds with the historical perspective informing Adorno's look back on his early book. This same orientation shaped his disapproval of the drafts of Benjamin's project in 1935. Adorno views Benjamin's image through the lens of the Hegelian dialectic from which the dialectical image was abruptly distinguished the moment it appeared in Benjamin's early drafts of the project (see Walter Benjamin, *Gesammelte Schriften*, 7 vols. [Frankfurt am Main: Suhrkamp, 1972–89], vol. 5, 2, 1037–38; *The Arcades Project*, 867). Throughout this essay Benjamin's works will be cited parenthetically, with the page references first to the *Gesammelte Schriften* (hereafter *GS*), followed by the English translation. The translations published in Walter Benjamin, *Selected Writings*, 4 vols., ed. Michael W. Jennings et al. (Cambridge, Mass.: Harvard University Press, 1996–2003), will be cited as *SW* with corresponding volume and page references. Throughout this essay page references are given to the original German publications, followed by the English translation. Readers who consult the published translations will find that some adjustments have been made in the passages cited here in order to clarify particular points.

2. The outlines of the dialectical image are discernible in the "Theses on the Philosophy of History" (Über den Begriff der Geschichte), which came out in the *Neue Rundschau* in 1950. But the appearance of the phrase "dialectical image" in a published work by Benjamin had to wait until 1982 with the publication of *Das Passagen-Werk* in Germany.

3. Walter Benjamin, *The Correspondence of Walter Benjamin, 1910–1940*, ed. Gershom Scholem and Theodor W. Adorno, trans. Manfred R. Jacobson and Evelyn M. Jacobson (Chicago: University of Chicago Press, 1994), 495–96.

4. Rolf Tiedemann, "Einleitung des Herausgebers," in Benjamin, *Gesammelte Schriften*, vol. 5 (1991), 34; Tiedemann, "Dialectics at a Standstill," 942. On Adorno's critique of Benjamin, see Michael W. Jennings, *Dialectical Images: Walter Benjamin's Theory of Literary Criticism* (Ithaca, N.Y.: Cornell University Press, 1987), 30–33; Susan Buck-Morss, *The Dialectics of Seeing: Walter Benjamin and the Arcades Project* (Cambridge, Mass.: MIT Press, 1991), 66–68; and Max Pensky, *Melancholy Dialectics: Walter Benjamin and the Play of Mourning* (Amherst: University of Massachusetts Press, 1993), 225–30.

5. Samuel Weber, *Benjamin's -abilities* (Cambridge, Mass.: Harvard University Press, 2008), 49.

6. While composing the early sketches of the Paris project in which the "dialectical image" first emerged, Benjamin had, for example, just completed an essay explicating the virtual force of the image in Marcel Proust's work (see *GS* 2. 3, 1046). Benjamin's essay "On the Image of Proust" was published in three installments in the *Literarische Welt* in June and July 1929. For an illuminating explication of this

essay, see Carol Jacobs, *In the Language of Walter Benjamin* (Baltimore: Johns Hopkins University Press, 1999), especially 40–47.

7. The capacity of the German word *Gewalt* to signify legitimate and illegitimate force has often been noted in the extensive commentary on Benjamin's essay on this topic, "Toward the Critique of Violence" (Zur Kritik der Gewalt) (*GS* 2. 1, 179–203; *SW* 1, 236–52). For a clear statement on the range of significations carried by the German word *Gewalt*, see Jacques Derrida, *Force de loi. Le Fondemont mystique de l'autorité* (Paris: Galilée, 1994), 19–20. The traditional attempt to resolve the relation between *Gewalt* and *Macht*, or violence and power, into an opposition continues in the well-known essay of Hannah Arendt (see *On Violence* [New York: Harcourt, Brace and World, 1970], 4–5; see also Röttgers, "Gewalt," in *Historisches Wörterbuch der Philosophie*, ed. Joachim Ritter [Basel: Schwabe, 1978], 562–70). In Benjamin's "Toward the Critique of Violence" (1921), by contrast, violence is simply a force more powerful than any other entity seeking to hold on to power. Thus every effort of self-preservation on the part of the sovereign or the state is, Benjamin reasons, the very sign of its "perishability" (*Verderblichkeit*) (*GS* 2.1, 199; *SW* 1, 249). The relational theory of force provides the basis of Benjamin's critique of the state's attempt to appropriate or "monopolize" violence in the name of law enforcement (*GS* 2.1, 183; *SW* 1, 239). Law (in the sense of *Recht*) is power, and as such it implies greater power. The state's assertion of the absolute supremacy of its laws is an effort to hold on to power that draws on the "mythical" concept of laws that cannot be trespassed (*GS* 2.1, 198; *SW* 1, 249). But as manifestations of power, all laws are trespassable according to the thesis of relational force. This is what Benjamin calls "the supreme sovereignty of relation" (*Alleinherrschaft der Beziehung*) (*GS* 2.1, 124; *SW* 1, 34).

8. "*Vald* is interesting in various respects as a legal term. *Vald* is, as it were, an extralegal concept [*außerrechtlicher Begriff*]: it signifies a realm of personal discretion that the law limits and that the law however explicitly allows the individual within these limits. . . . The 'fundamental opposition' [*Urgegensatz*] between *Recht* and *Gewalt*, represented by the Greek poets and philosophers with the concepts of *right* and violence (for example, Pindar, fragment 169; Hesiod, *Works and Days*, verse 274) came much later to German consciousness" (Klaus von See, "Recht und Gewalt," in *Altnordische Rechtswörter. Philologische Studien zur Rechtsauffassung und Rechtsgesinnung der Germanen* [Tübingen: Max Niemeyer, 1964], 202).

9. Von See observes, "Scarcely any other Old Norse word appears more adaptable [*wandelbarer*] [to the translation of Roman legal terms] than [*vald*]" (196). On this point, see also Röttgers, "Gewalt," 562.

10. Throughout this essay, the reference to the edition of Kant's *Critique of Judgment* published in volume 5 of the *Gesammelte Schriften* is followed by references to the English translation by Werner S. Pluhar (Indianapolis: Hackett, 1987). For a succinct commentary on this passage from the *Critique of Judgment*, see Dieter Teichert, *Immanuel Kant: Kritik der Urteilskraft. Ein Einführender Kommentar* (Paderborn, Germany: Ferdinand Schöningh, 1992), 63–68.

11. Röttgers traces this thesis about violence back to Kant's 1784 *Idee zu einer*

allgemeinen Geschichte der Menschheit and cites the following statement about the legal order of civic society: "freedom under external laws can be encountered combined in the greatest possible degree with irresistible power [*Gewalt*]" (Immanuel Kant, *Gesammelte Werke* [hereafter *AA*], 29 vols. to date, ed. Königliche Preußische [later, Deutsche] Akademie der Wissenschaften [Berlin: Reimer; later, De Gruyter, 1900–], vol. 8, 22; "Idea for a Universal History with a Cosmopolitan Aim," trans. Allen. W. Wood, in *Anthropology, History, and Education* [Cambridge: Cambridge University Press, 2007], 112).

12. *A* and *B* refer to the first (1781) and substantially revised second edition (1787) of Kant's *Critique of Pure Reason*, followed by the page references to the Academy edition and the English translation by Paul Guyer and Allen W. Wood (Cambridge: Cambridge University Press, 1998). On Kant's rejection of the fundamental "unity of reason," see Dieter Henrich, *The Unity of Reason*, trans. Jeffrey Edwards, Louis Hunt, Manfred Kuehn, and Guenter Zoeller (Cambridge, Mass.: Harvard University Press, 1994), 19–27; on his refutation of the Hylozoism of Herder and others, see John H. Zammito, *The Genesis of Kant's Critique of Judgment* (Chicago: University of Chicago Press, 1992), 184–213. Henrich provides a reconstruction of the philosophical background of the eighteenth-century debate over the "unity of reason" and an illuminating overview of the complex legacy of Kant's allusion in the *Critique of Pure Reason* to the "common, but to us unknown root" in which originates "perhaps" sensibility and understanding (*A* 15, *B* 29; 152). Henrich argues that the "perhaps" in this phrase is interpreted, incorrectly from a philological point of view but productively from a philosophical perspective, from Hegel to Hermann Cohen and Heidegger, as an "allusion to still hidden but answerable questions" (47).

13. Kant communicated his discovery in a letter to Reinhold in December 1787. "Thus," writes Kant, "I am occupied now with the critique of taste which provides the opportunity [*Gelegenheit*] for the discovery of a new kind of a priori principle than existed heretofore." The discovery of this principle, Kant goes on to say, provides him "enough material for the rest of my life" (*AA* 10, 514). See Zammito, 89–90; and Eckart Förster, *Kant's Final Synthesis: An Essay on the Opus postumum* (Cambridge, Mass.: Harvard University Press, 2000), 8.

14. This "elementary system" was to lay the ground for a "transition" from Kant's *Metaphysical Foundation of Natural Science* (1786) to physics itself (see Förster, 4–13). On the distinction between Newtonian force and Lockean power, see P. M. Heimann and J. E. McGuire, "Newtonian Forces and Lockean Power: Concepts of Matter in Eighteenth-Century Thought," *Historical Studies in the Physical Sciences* 3 (1971): 233–306. For an account of Kant's critique of Newton in the *Opus postumum*, see Howard Caygill, "The Force of Kant's *Opus postumum*," *Angelaki* 10.1 (April 2005): 33–42.

15. The limitations of the theory of experience in the first *Critique* were the subject of Hermann Cohen's *Kants Theorie der Erfahrung*. In this influential book, Cohen argues that if Leibniz's approach to the question of substance as divisibility (power, *dynamis*) had been adequately understood by Kant, he would not have objected to his precursor's "dogmatism" (i.e., metaphysics). See Hermann Cohen,

Kants Theorie der Erfahrung, Werke I. I (Hildesheim, Germany: Georg Orms, 1987), 149–73. Denying the priority of understanding and sensibility over reason and thinking with regard to experience is the basis of the critique of Kant undertaken by Cohen in *Logik der reinen Erkenntnis* (Berlin: Cassirer, 1902), 32–77. On this point, see Peter Fenves, *Arresting Language: From Leibniz to Benjamin* (Stanford, CA: Stanford University Press, 2001), 188–91.

16. Förster delineates the task of analyzing practical self-affection with characteristic elegance: the question is "what endows practical reason's ideas of right with 'moving force' and makes possible their unity" (142). Förster does not consider the possible connections between this effort and the aesthetic judgment of the sublime, but instead focuses on Kant's reflection on the ontological status of God as a "moral sovereign" in the *Opus postumum*.

17. References throughout are to the English translation of the *Opus postumum* by Eckart Förster and Michael Rosen (Cambridge: Cambridge University Press, 1993).

18. Kant's qualification of the postulate of God's existence in the *Opus postumum* as meaning, practically speaking, that we must act "in such a way as if I stood under such fearsome [*furchtbaren*]—but yet, at the same time, salutary—guidance" (*AA* 22, 116; 200) is parallel to the attribute of fearsomeness to the feeling of the dynamic sublime in paragraph 28 of the third *Critique*. On the ideal of life implicit in the phrase "positive transformation of life" (*guter Lebenswandel*), see Rudolf A. Makreel, *Imagination and Interpretation in Kant: The Hermeneutic Import of the Critique of Judgment* (Chicago: University of Chicago Press, 1990), 88–107.

19. The connection between the German words *Mut* (courage) and *Gemüt* (mind) suggests that courage is a power of mind ("courage" derives from the French word for "heart"—*coeur*).

20. The aesthetic judgment of the "warrior" and of "war" in this passage is in this sense connected to Kant's reflections near the end of the third *Critique* that evoke the "war" that may lead to the establishment of "lawfulness [*Gesetzmäßigkeit*] amid the freedom of a morally grounded system of states" that would become the subject of the later essay "Toward Eternal Peace" (1795) (*AA* 5, 433; 320).

21. The discovery of the non-cognitive a priori principle of judgment in 1787 compelled Kant to revise the footnote near the beginning of the first edition of "Transcendental Aesthetic" in the *Critique of Pure Reason* (1781) in which judgments of taste are described as "merely empirical" and as such not the object of "true science" (*A* 21; 156). In the revised version of this note Kant introduces the possibility that such judgments may "share" the title of "true science" with speculative philosophy when they are considered "aesthetic . . . in the transcendental [as distinct from the psychological] sense" (*B* 36; 173). On this revision, see Förster, 8.

22. Kant makes the distinction between "thinking" and "knowing" in the preface to the second edition of the *Critique of Pure Reason* (*B* xvii–xix; 16–17).

23. See, for example, Aristotle, *Poetics* (New York: Penguin, 1996), 1448b.

24. For example, "transcendental philosophy precedes the assertion of things that are thought, as their archetype [*Urbild*], [the place] in which they must be set"

(*AA* 21, 7; 256). See also *AA* 21, 82–84; 248–50 and 99; 255. See Förster, especially 158–64.

25. "The danger exists for the courageous person," Benjamin writes, "yet he does not heed it. For he would be a coward if he heeded it; and if it did not exist for him, he would not be courageous" (*GS* 2.1, 123; *SW* 1, 33).

26. As Schulte-Sasse states it succinctly: "Hölderlin seems to have read the problems raised by Kant's first *Critique* from a viewpoint shaped by his reading of the third *Critique*" ("The Subject's Aesthetic Foundation [on Kant]," in *"The Spirit of Poesy": Essays on Jewish and German Literature and Thoughts in Honor of Géza von Molnár*, ed. Richard Block and Peter Fenves [Evanston, Ill.: Northwestern University Press, 2000], 38). Fenves traces a parallel gesture in Benjamin's early color theory: "Benjamin thus develops the concept of spirit in his *Farbenlehre* by radicalizing the 'Critique of Aesthetic Judgment' of the third *Critique* to the point where it revises the 'Transcendental Aesthetic' of the first. . . . " (*Arresting Language*, 183–84). The parallel Förster traces between Hölderlin and Kant supports this point (148–74). I expand on this point in greater detail in an explication of Kant's concept of "participation" in the writings of the 1790s in a forthcoming book, tentatively entitled "Poetic Force." A portion of this work is presented in Kevin McLaughlin, "Culture and Messianism: Disinterestedness in Arnold," *Victorian Studies* 50.4 (Summer 2008): 615–39.

27. On the way time interpenetrates the space—what Benjamin calls "the layout" (*die Lage*)—of "Timidity," see Samuel Weber, *Targets of Opportunity: On the Militarization of Thinking* (New York: Fordham University Press, 2005), 129–33.

28. Hölderlin, "Blödigkeit," in *Sämtliche Werke*, 8 vols., ed. Friedrich Beißner and Adolf Beck (Stuttgart: Cottanachfolger, 1943–85 [vols. 7–8, Stuttgart: Kohlammer]), vol. 2. 1, 66. The translation is Stanley Corngold's, published with the English version of Benjamin's Hölderlin essay (*SW* 1, 22), with the exception of the first line of the last strophe, which is offered by Weber (*Targets*, 131).

29. Richard Sieburth, Introduction to *Hymns and Fragments* by Friedrich Hölderlin (Princeton: Princeton University Press, 1984), 4.

30. The reference is to the English translation in *Essays and Letters on Theory*, trans. Thomas Pfau (Albany: State University of New York Press, 1988).

31. In October 1794—just as he was about to compose his famous critique of Fichte in "Judgment and Being" (dated to early 1795)—Hölderlin wrote to his friend Christian Ludwig Neuffer of his work on a manuscript dealing with "aesthetic ideas" that analyzed "the beautiful and the sublime" in a way that went beyond Schiller's interpretation of Kant in "Anmut und Würde" (Friedrich Hölderlin, *Sämtliche Werke*, vol. 6. 1, 137). For Kant's discussion of "aesthetic ideas" in the *Critique of Judgment*, see *AA* 5, 314; 182.

32. For Hölderlin's call for the "free use" of the word *nationell*, see the letter of December 4, 1801, to Böhlendorff (Friedrich Hölderlin, *Sämtliche Werke* [Stuttgart: W. Kohlhammer Verlag, 1954] vol. 6. 1, 425–27; *Essays and Letters on Theory*, 149–51). On this point, see Peter Szondi, *Hölderlin-Studien. Mit einem Traktat über phi-*

lologische Erkenntnis (Frankfurt am Main: Suhrkamp, 1970), 128–31, and Heidegger, *Hölderlins Hymne Der Ister*, Gesamtausgabe 53 (Frankfurt am Main: Vittorio Klostermann, 1984), 169–70; *Hölderlin's Hymn "The Ister,"* trans. William McNeill and Julia Davis (Bloomington: Indiana University Press, 1996), 135–36.

33. Martin Heidegger comments on these lines from the letter to Böhlendorff, connecting them to Hölderlin's poem "Griechenland" in "Hölderlins Erde und Himmel" (*Erläuterungen zu Hölderlins Dichtung* [Frankfurt am Main: Vittorio Klostermann, 1971], 161; *Elucidations of Hölderlin's Poetry*, trans. Keith Hoeller [Amherst, N.Y.: Humanity Books, 2000], 186).

34. These "leading strings" clearly echo Kant's characterization in the second edition of the first *Critique* of examples (*Beispiele*) that are not derived from experience but rather thought—a priori examples, as it were—as the "leading strings of the power of judgment" (*Gängelwagen der Urteilskraft*) (*Kritik der reinen Vernunft*, 2d ed. [*Akad B*], *Gesammelte Schriften*, vol. 3 [Berlin: Reimer, 1900], 173; 269). Kant employs this figure near the beginning of "An Answer to the Question: What Is Enlightenment?" (*Akad* 8, 35; *Practical Philosophy*, 17). Hannah Arendt refers to the passage from the *Critique of Pure Reason* in a highly interesting turn at the very end of her lectures on Kant (*Lectures on Kant's Political Philosophy* [Chicago: University of Chicago Press, 1992], 76). Arendt cites N. K. Smith's translation of *Gängelwagen* as "go-cart," which does not capture the sense of a device used to teach toddlers to walk: what we would call a "walker" [for the relevant passage in Smith's translation, see *Critique of Pure Reason*, 178]). In her seminar notes published along with the lectures under the title of "Imagination" Arendt—perhaps citing from memory or from a confusion with Hölderlin's poem—mistakenly points to Kant's description of examples as "the go-cart [*Gängelband*] of judgment" (84). It is noteworthy that the figure of the "leading strings" transforms Schiller's characterization of the hold of the mythological Venus over mankind in the poem "Die Götter Griechenlands" (1788).

35. Benjamin takes note of the latter possible signification by observing that these lines, like the effects to which they refer, are "most oddly strange and almost killing" (*ertötend*) (*GS* 2.1, 121; *SW* 1, 31–32).

36. Kant did not use the phrase "Copernican revolution" or "Copernican turn" (*Wende*) that has been attributed to him repeatedly throughout the history of his work's reception (see I. B. Cohen, 248–53). The association of this "Revolution" with Kant's work is, however, made in the influential work of Karl Leonard Reinhold, for example, in the 1794 essay entitled "Über das Fundament der Kritik der reinen Vernunft" (see *Beyträge zur Berichtigung bisheriger Missverständnisse der Philosophen* [Jena: Johann Michael Manke, 1790–94], vol. 2, 415–16). On the analogy drawn to Copernicus, particularly with respect to the question of perspective and standpoint in Kant's moral philosophy, see Friedrich Kaulbach, "Die Copernische Denkfigur bei Kant," *Kant-Studien* 64 (1973): 31; 34–35; 45–48; and Peter Fenves, *A Peculiar Fate: Metaphysics and World-History in Kant* (Ithaca, N.Y.: Cornell University Press, 1991), 201–4. See also Murray Miles, "Kant's 'Copernican Revolution':

Toward Rehabilitation of a Concept and Provision of a Framework for the Interpretation of the *Critique of Pure Reason*," *Kant-Studien* 97.1 (2006): 1–32.

37. On this free moral standing or participation, see Kant's handwritten notes (in the *Nachlass*) collected in *AA* 19, 163–64, in which Kant describes the transcendental process by which the moral actor "oversteps" "the participation in nature with respect to himself" in order to assume the role of the "participant of freedom with respect to others" (*Teilnehmers der Freiheit in Ansehung andrer*) (*AA* 19, 164). On this point, see Kaulbach, 44–48.

38. For a highly illuminating analysis of a similar *Wende* that appears in Hölderlin's comments on his translation of Sophocles, specifically on the *peripetia* in Oedipus, see Werner Hamacher, "Parusie, Mauer. Mittelbarkeit und Zeitlichkeit, später Hölderlin," *Hölderlin-Jahrbuch* 34 (2004–5): 121–23.

39. Peter Fenves has astutely noted the echo of Henri Bergson's concept of *durée* in Benjamin's use of the phrase "temporal plasticity" (unpublished essay).

40. On the signification of the term "architectonic" in Kant, see Giorgio Tonelli, *Kant's "Critique of Pure Reason" Within the Tradition of Modern Logic: A Commentary on Its History* (Hildesheim, Germany: George Olms Verlag, 1994), 234–36; 240–300. Tonelli offers a detailed commentary on the section of the *Critique of Pure Reason* called "The Architectonic of Pure Reason." "There is an empirical and architectonical use of reason," Tonelli notes, "only in the practical and moral fields. [Christian] Wolff enlarged our knowledge, but did not exercise the critique; his works are useful as storehouses of reason, not as architectonic of reason" (235–36). On the specific meaning and import of the term "critique" in Kant, see Giorgio Tonelli, "'Critique' and Related Terms Prior to Kant: A Historical Survey," *Kant-Studien* 69.2 (1978): 119–48. For a highly suggestive discussion of the relationship between architectonic and architecture or "housing," see Susan Bernstein, *Housing Problems: Writing and Architecture in Goethe, Walpole, Freud, and Heidegger* (Stanford, Calif.: Stanford University Press, 2008), 2–10; 12–13.

41. The allusion to hunting occurs in *The Arcades Project*: "Student and hunter. The text is a forest in which the reader is hunter. Rustling in the underbrush—the idea, skittish prey, the citation—another piece 'in the bag'" (*GS* 5. 2, 963–64; 802). The phrase "in the bag" captures the association with hunting, but not the connection of the hunt with the image, in the French word used by Benjamin—*tableau*.

42. The image-producing power is associated with hands in the essay that Benjamin composed while drawing up the early sketches to *The Arcades Project*, "On the Image of Proust" (1929). Of particular relevance to the early essay on Hölderlin, and specifically to the image Benjamin folds into his explication of the way the god is "brought" in "Timidity," is the discussion of the child's game of transforming a sock into a "bag" and then a "present" (*Mitgebrachtes*), followed by this passage on Proust's "world": "To this world belongs what happens in Proust. . . . It is never isolated, rhetorical, or visionary; carefully heralded and securely supported, it bears a fragile, precious reality: the image. It detaches itself from the structure of Proust's sentences just as that summer day at Balbec—old,

immemorial, mummified—emerged from the lace curtains under Françoise's hands" (*GS* 2. 1, 314; *SW* 2, 240).

43. It is thus certainly no accident that when the phrase "dialectical image" first appears in Benjamin's writing, he immediately distinguishes it from the Hegelian dialectic (see *GS* 5. 2, 1037–38; 867).

44. For a more detailed analysis of this passage, see Kevin McLaughlin, "Benjamin's Barbarism," *The Germanic Review* 81.1 (Winter 2006): 14–16.

45. Grimm traces the word *urbar* to the verb *erbern*, which, according to the dictionary, signifies "bringing forth" (*hervorbringen*). The noun form of the word—also *Urbar*—refers to "revenue-yielding plot of land" and by extension a "land registry" used for the purposes of taxation.

46. In his famous critique of Fichte's "absolute I" in the short text "Judgment and Being" (Urtheil und Seyn) (*Sämtliche Werke* 4, 216–17; *Essays and Letters*, 37–38), Hölderlin draws on the probably false etymological connection of the German word for "judgment"—*Ur-teil* as primal division—by breaking it down into its two syllabic parts. Hölderlin may have encountered the pseudo-etymology of *Urteil* in Reinhold (Karl Leonhard Reinhold, *Versuch einer neuen Theorie der menschlichen Vorstellungsvermögen* [Prague: Widtmann and Maukc, 1789], 435–40; see Manfred Frank, *The Philosophical Foundations of Early German Romanticism*, trans. Elizabeth Millán-Zeibart [Albany: State University of New York Press, 2004], 103) or in Fichte (see Violetta L. Waibel, *Hölderlin und Fichte 1794–1800* [Paderborn: Schöningh, 2000], 140–45).

Chapter 11

We would like to thank the French Interdisciplinary Group at Northwestern University for partially subsidizing this translation.

The title of this essay, "La langue de l'oeil: Ce que veut dire 'histoire de l'art,'" suggests several translations, each of which pertains to the broader themes of the essay. "La langue de l'oeil" could be "the tongue of the eye," "the language of the eye," or (in a more Saussurian vein) "the eye's system of language." "Ce que veut dire 'histoire de l'art'" connotes "the meaning of 'art history'" or "what 'art history' means," but translates literally as "what 'art history' wants to say." The reader should keep these different possible translations in mind, as Stiegler develops these overlapping connotations throughout the essay.—Trans.

1. In French "Passer à l'acte" often means "to act" or "to put one's threats into action." The closely related "passage à l'acte" may be translated as "taking action."

2. See *Acting Out*, trans. David Barison and Daniel Ross (Stanford, Calif.: Stanford University Press, 2008).

3. *Langue de chat* is the name given to a buttery biscuit shaped like a cat's tongue. But also, *donner sa langue au chat* (to give one's tongue to the cat) signifies declining to answer/proceed with an utterance.—Trans.

4. This is what Heidegger shows in *Being and Time* (Martin Heidegger, *Being and Time*, trans. John Macquarrie and Edward Robinson [New York: Harper & Row, 1962]).

5. "Verdurin" refers to the snobbish bourgeois couple from Proust's *À la recherche du temps perdu*. "Bobo" is short for bo-urgeois bo-hemians, and designates members of the upper-middle class who may partake in counter-cultural musical, culinary, and artistic tastes domesticated somehow for yuppie consumption.—Trans.

6. I have tried to show why in reality this is not at all a leisure society, but on the contrary a society of generalized proletarization, that is encompassing not only production but also consumption.

7. Torvalds created the Linux operating system, a freely distributed alternative to the Unix operating system. Stallman is a celebrated computer scientist and hacker who played a leading role in articulating (and implementing) the values of a "free software" movement, which likened open software to a kind of free speech. He also championed an open source alternative to Unix, which was later realized by Torvalds.—Trans.

8. Just as there is no leisure society, nor is there a post-industrial society. On this point see my book, *Mécréance et discredit* (Paris: Galilée, 2004) and also *Économie de l'hypermatériel et psychopouvoir* (Paris: Galilée, 2008).

Index